your IGNORANCE IS *our* STRENGTH

The Supreme Court
Overrules Democracy

your

IGNORANCE

IS

our

STRENGTH

Sigmund Noetzel

ℙℙ

FAULCOURT PRESS

ISBN 978-0-9975717-0-7

10 9 8 7 6 5 4 3 2 1

Published by
Faulcourt Press, LLC
10-11 50th Ave 1B
Long Island City, NY 11101

www.faulcourtpress.com

To

Chiara, Eliora, Ariah

Acknowledgement

Thanks to Mia, Debbie, Creighton and Uncle B.
Your help is apppreciated, though you may wish to
retain plausible deniiability.

CONTENTS

This work is comprised of Socratic dialogs that could and should have taken place in the wake of the 2010 *Citizens United* decision.

The named sections are somewhat arbitrary divisions: they are neither acts, scenes, nor independent chapters. Their titles are not exclusive signifiers of content.

Introduction		viii
1	Madison	1
2	Associations	11
3	Factions	27
4	Orwell	37
5	The Fallacy of Composition	45
6	The Yankees	59
7	Socrates	71
8	Corporations	81
9	The Fourteenth Amendment	95
10	The Living Constitution	107
11	Stare Decisis	113
12	Slavery	123
13	Media Corporations	143
14	Idolatry	149
	Appendix: The US Constitution	161

Your IGNORANCE IS our STRENGTH

INTRODUCTION

It is the subject matter of the dialogs that is important: the characters and the setting are rather arbitrary. However, the following physical setting is offered for those who would like to imagine it as a performance.

The Characters

MARK, a mature man. Possibly retired.

MAEVE, a woman who lives with MARK. Possibly his wife.

PAUL, a friend of MARK. A plumber.

ERICA, a member of MAEVE's book club.

NADIA, a neighbor of MARK & MAEVE.

KEVIN, a high school student. MARK's grandson.

CHARLES, a friend of MARK & MAEVE. A lawyer.

The Time

January 21, 2010. Afternoon.

The Scene.

The home of MARK & MAEVE. A living room, kitchen and dining area are all visible. The front door is on one side of the living room; on the side opposite the kitchen, there is an entrance to a hallway. The kitchen also has a hallway entrance, apparently giving access to a side door as well as the basement.

MARK is reading a newspaper in the living room. MAEVE is preparing coffee in the kitchen..

1. MADISON

MARK Why?

    (*pause*)

MAEVE Why not?

    (*short pause*)

MARK Why, why not? Why not, why?

MAEVE Why, why? Why not, why not?

MARK (*heavy sigh*) Hshsss...

    (*pause*)

MAEVE I seem to have lost the thread of the conversation here. What were we talking about?

MARK The Supreme Court ruling. The *Citizens United* case.

MAEVE Oh, that a corporation is a person.

MARK Is that the way you heard it? It's... inane.

MAEVE Well, the Supreme Court has its own way of thinking about things.

MARK But *this*? It defies all logic. *A corporation is a person*! Did you ever hear such arrant nonsense?

MAEVE I've heard a lot of nonsense. Some of it must've been arrant.

MARK Apparently our Bill of Rights now applies to a *person or association of persons*. Think about that for a minute.

    (*pause*)

MAEVE Okay. ... Was I supposed to have some sort of an epiphany?

MARK I was hoping.

MAEVE What's bothering you about it?

MARK It doesn't make sense!

MAEVE So? Where is it written that the Supreme Court has to make sense?

MARK Ah, look how cynical we've become. You'd expect better of the Supreme Court, that's all. You'd expect it to be above mutilating the Constitution for sleazy politics.

MAEVE So you're disappointed in the Supreme Court.

MARK Disappointed? That's not the half of it. But what's bothering me now is that this is *not* bothering you. How do you understand this ruling?

MAEVE Well, the Court ruled that Congress may not put any limit on the amount of money a corporation can spend on a politician's campaign.

MARK Yes, yes —the ruling was for a corporation, and to the benefit of all corporations, since it struck down a law restricting them. But to avoid the appearance of political bias, the Court had to include labor unions as well. So they said it applies to associations of persons in general.

MAEVE All associations of persons?

MARK Apparently. It doesn't seem to be restricted. Of course, they wouldn't actually say *all* either. They're keeping their options open.

MAEVE So the Supreme Court says that Congress can't limit the amount an association can spend on a political campaign.

MARK Yes. No —wait. You forgot to say '*the Constitution says*'.

MAEVE What?

MARK It's got to go like this— 'The Supreme Court says *the Constitution says…*' —like that. Because the Supreme Court can't overrule Congress or the President unless it says, *the Constitution says.*

MAEVE It's like the game Simon Says.

MARK Right. Whoever claims Simon's authority controls the game.

MAEVE But Simon's not there.

MARK Right. So no one knows what Simon *really* says.

MAEVE But we do know what the Constitution says.

MARK Exactly! That's how we know the legitimate powers of the government. It's the one thing we can rely on, to prevent any gang of despots from taking control of the government and subjecting us all to their own rules. That's why you've read it, right?

MAEVE Well of course, I've read it.

MARK So how can the Supreme Court say —reasoning from the Constitution, now— that Congress can't put any limit on political spending by an association of persons?

MAEVE Well apparently, a limit would violate the association's First Amendment right to freedom of speech.

MARK You slipped that in there nicely— *the association's* First Amendment right. And you forgot Simon.

MAEVE Okay, so legally, I think it goes like this: the Supreme Court says that *the Constitution says* that an association of persons is a *person*, and so it has the First Amendment right of freedom of speech. And the Supreme Court also says that *the Constitution says* that money is speech. So Congress may not place any limit on the amount of money any association can spend for a politician's election, because it would abridge the association's freedom of speech.

MARK Does the Constitution really say all of that?

MAEVE Of course not. The Constitution doesn't mention corporations or associations, or political contributions —*at all.*

MARK Of course not! And yet I'm reading here about the constitutional rights of a *'person or association of persons'* —as if that came from the Constitution itself!

MAEVE Sort of poetic, the way the word 'person' bookends it.

MARK It resonates with it's own self-contained logic.

MAEVE Much better than *'person or corporation.'*

MARK Or 'person or special interest group.' Or 'person or gang.' Or 'person or baby-blood-drinking satanic cult.'

MAEVE Okay, that's overboard.

MARK Where does the Court get the authority for this? It's *not* written in the Constitution, so how did the Court make the logical leap from *'person'* to *'person or association of persons'*?

MAEVE Maybe they think it's the same thing...

MARK That's what I'm afraid of! It's not a physical reality, and in logic, it's an absurdity. An association of *anything* cannot be the same thing as the *members* of the association. It's a logical impossibility!

MAEVE Well ... you know Charles is coming over, don't you?

MARK You told me. So?

MAEVE Well, he's a lawyer. Maybe he'll be able to explain it.

MARK Oh, I'm sure he will.

MAEVE Do I detect a hint of irony?

MARK Who, me, irony?

MAEVE It's coming in clearer now.

MARK We have the Constitution to guarantee our liberty, but we shouldn't try to understand it without the help of a lawyer.

MAEVE Irony.

MARK No, no irony. This is what you're telling me.

MAEVE Well, at least we'll hear his opinion.

MARK Sure. But you know what'll happen. He'll try to tell me what I believe because I'm supposed to be a conservative, but I shouldn't presume to know what liberals believe, and then he'll rant at me about an outrage that he heard from some anger-monger on the radio...

MAEVE And then everybody's accusing everybody else of hypocrisy because no one's admitting to what the other one knows he really believes.

MARK It's crazy.

MAEVE Polarized minds, you've got polarized minds. Our society is polarized because our minds are polarized.

MARK Or vice versa.

MAEVE The problem with you and Charles is like everybody else. You get drawn into a label, conserva*tism* or libera*lism*, and then you see everything through the prism of your '*ism*'. You let the label do all your thinking.

MARK *Hah!* —and you're immune to it?

MAEVE I try to see both sides.

MARK That's what's called a copout.

MAEVE Really? Now you sound like the Ancient Hippie.

MARK Who's the Ancient Hippie?

MAEVE Oh, that's Nadia's name for your friend Paul. That reminds me... (*walking to the bookshelf*) He brought over his copy of the Federalist Papers, for Kevin. (*She takes down a book.*)

MARK Why?

MAEVE Kevin told him he was studying American History, so Paul thought it was important for him to read this. Anyway, I was looking at it... (*flipping through the pages*)... He's got page corners folded down and marks in the margins... I found where James Madison analyzed today's political scene.

MARK *Today's* political scene?

MAEVE Really, you should look at this. You know the authors here —Madison, Hamilton and John Jay— studied the constitutions of all thirteen states while preparing the draft of the US Constitution. And it seems the state of Pennsylvania had authorized a commission —called the Council of Censors— to determine how well its own constitution was working out.

MARK My guess is that it wasn't.

MAEVE Yes, there were violations. But here, in Paper 50, Madison is writing about the Council itself. Well, here, read this... (she *shows Mark where to read*)

     (*Mark reads*)

MAEVE No, read it to me.

MARK (*reads*) **"Throughout the continuance of the Council, it was split into two fixed and violent parties. This fact is acknowledged and lamented by themselves. Had this not been the case, the face of their proceedings exhibits a proof equally satisfactory. In all questions, however unimportant by themselves, or unconnected with each other, the same names were invariably contrasted on the opposite columns."**

MAEVE Okay, now...

MARK So that's polarization...

MAEVE Yes, but notice Paul's underlined "**questions ... unconnected with each other**". Do we have any *questions unconnected with each other* these days?

MARK Well, we have polarized minds, and to polarized minds, everything is connected.

MAEVE Okay, so you see that, right? Take any pair of hot-button issues, like the legality of abortion and the death penalty. Ask any one person the *reasons* for her position on the legality of abortion —whatever it is— then ask about the *reasons* for her position on the death penalty.

You'll see the *reasons* will be totally different: they have to be, because the questions are unconnected. Yet she'll *believe* that her views are connected —that there's some sort of *consistency* in these positions.

MARK Well, supposedly, there's a political philosophy.

MAEVE But it's no *philosophy* at all! It's nothing more than a label. The connection is their *'ism'*. Have you ever heard anyone articulate a *philosophy* that conceptually ties abortion to execution?

Or can you even *imagine* a political philosophy that *unifies* a position on water-boarding and a position on same-sex marriage — without using the *'ism'* label? A *philosophy* that connects them? Really?

MARK Well ...

MAEVE Or ... okay, a *political philosophy* that shows how a position on the separation of church and state is consistent with a position on a corporation's freedom of speech, without using the *'ism'*?

MARK Well, you don't actually hear it articulated. Except through the word *'values'* —*underlying values*.

MAEVE A consistent emotional bias that is beyond questioning.

MARK Beyond words. Beyond articulation.

MAEVE But not beyond being aroused and manipulated by the media. Anyway, read more.

MARK (*reads*) **"In all questions, however unimportant by themselves, or unconnected with each other, the same names were invariably contrasted on the opposite columns. Every unbiased observer may infer, without danger of mistake, and at the same time without meaning to reflect on either party, or individuals of either party, that unfortunately passion, not reason must have presided over their decisions."**

MAEVE I like the decorum. He doesn't even mention the names of the sides.

MARK Maybe they didn't have names. If everybody knows who everybody else is, they don't need labels.

MAEVE Okay. And of course, by *passion* he means *emotion*. So, read more.

MARK (*reads*) **"When men exercise their reason coolly and freely on a variety of distinct questions, they inevitably fall into different opinions on some of them. When they are governed by a common passion, their opinions, if they are so to be called, will be all the same."**

MAEVE So what is that common *passion* that makes a group of people always line up on the *same side* of each of these various questions? If they all had fevered minds that would find the truth of all questions, they wouldn't all find the same truths on the different issues.

The passion is fear and anger. First, fear —that your beliefs are being threatened by opposing ideas. And the fear arouses anger at the ideas that threaten —they are wrong, *evil* ideas, that must not be respected or entertained. And there's anger at the source of those ideas —the people who propagate them.

Madison could have some perspective, because the phenomenon wasn't totally pervasive in his time.

MARK Now we've got politicized news media and political media stars that spin every story —driving everyone under their influence to line up on the same side of every issue.

MAEVE Right. Who can exercise reason *coolly* and *freely*?

MARK But … well, okay, I see your point. But for this ruling by the Supreme Court, I don't see how it's supported by any '*ism*'. I don't understand how that would work. It's simply *not* from the Constitution, and there's *no* logic that can make it so.

MAEVE You can discuss it with Charles. But coolly and freely.

MARK Yeah. I can imagine he'll say there's nothing really new here —that sort of thing has been going on forever. That's just the way things work.

MAEVE That's the *de facto* rationalization. Corruption creeps in little by little, then when somebody calls attention to it, the response is —that's the way things work, *de facto*. We don't have the power to root it out, so let's just legitimize it.

MARK But you *can't*. You can't have your whole legal system based on a logical fallacy. The Constitution says *person*: the Supreme Court says it says *person or association of persons*. It can't work. It will require reasoning through an endless miasma of contradictions.

MAEVE It'll be interesting to see what Charles says.

MARK What *is it* with you and Charles?

MAEVE Nothing. As I said, I try to see both sides.

MARK But do you really *see* both sides? You just try to compromise everything out. It's always a little bit of this and a little bit of that.

MAEVE No, not always.

MARK If one side argues that two and two are four and the other side argues that two and two are five, you'll join in to say why don't we all agree that the real answer is probably somewhere around four and a half.

MAEVE Oh, come on, that's not fair.

MARK Okay, it's a stupid example. But on real issues, with real differences of opinion, that's the sort of thing you do.

MAEVE Come on. It's not the same thing, because where there are honest differences of opinion, there isn't any one right answer.

MARK *Honest* differences of opinion? What you mean by that? A lot of political debate is based on plainly false ideas, but they're ideas that *work* to the advantage of one side or the other, so they're repeated endlessly.

MAEVE All right, so we know some people lie...

MARK No, no, you can't call it *lying*, because the people who argue these things *believe* their arguments. But you can't call it *honest*, either. The people arguing that two and two are five would believe it —after a fashion— because they would've been given a reason to believe it, *and it works in their favor.*

And if a person is given a reason to believe anything *that works in his favor*, he can't be —he *won't* be— made to examine the reason objectively. And he *won't* be capable of understanding the reasoning on the other side.

MAEVE Well, I get that. **"It is difficult to get a man to understand... when his salary depends upon his not understanding..."**

MARK That's a quote, huh?

MAEVE Of course you've heard it. It's from Upton Sinclair.

MARK But the question is, are you *trying* to *see* both sides? If you just want to placate both sides to broker a compromise, you'll be motivated to muddle the important distinctions. You don't want to see the essence of the contradiction clearly, because that makes it hard to straddle the issue.

MAEVE Oh, no, ...

MARK And ... *and*, if you're willing to compromise it out —accept a mixture of truth and absurdity— that *won't settle* the issue. It certainly won't satisfy those who believe two and two is four.

And as for those who claim that two and two is five —because it works for them— their kind of reasoning a bit looser, so it'll be tweaked to come up with the idea that two and two is really *six*.

And you know why that'll happen. They know you're going to compromise it out.

MAEVE This is a silly argument. Just give me one example.

MARK Well, ... no. No, look, I'm sorry I brought it up.

MAEVE Oh, no, no. You pointed out a character flaw, so you can't just leave it like that. You've got to give me an example.

MARK Oh, come on, don't make me rehash...

MAEVE No, no —give me an example.

MARK Okay, I remember when I first met you, when you were with what's-his-name...

MAEVE Oh, don't strain your brain.

MARK Okay, Leon. Back when Reagan was campaigning for the Republican nomination —in 1980. Leon and I got into that discussion of Reagan's economic policy. Do you remember this?

MAEVE Yeah. I remember you were so arrogant.

MARK Uh-huh. But let's remember what it was about, then. Reagan's big economic idea —*Reaganomics*— was that *reducing* tax rates would *increase* the government's revenues, and *reduce* the deficit.

MAEVE And you got upset.

MARK Well, look, it was a completely idiotic idea. George Bush, Senior, his opponent in the primaries, called it "voodoo economics."

But you see, it came with a *reason* why you should believe it: the economy was being held down by high taxes, so reducing tax rates would stimulate so much economic activity that the government would collect *more* tax *revenue*, even with the lower tax *rates*.

MAEVE And you thought Reagan was lying.

MARK No, no —I'm sure I never said *lying*. Some economic advisor gave him the idea, and it *worked for him*. He could see how it would work for his campaign, so he believed it.

MAEVE (*laughs*) Oh, yeah, I remember there was that Laffer curve.

MARK Right, that was it. A completely theoretical, pie-in-the-sky idea without a shred of data to support it. And this was supposed to be a *conservative* economic policy? Bizarre!

MAEVE I thought you two were going to get along, you were both conservatives.

MARK Conservative? Don't get me started again, Maeve. Remember, back then, integrity, responsibility, self-discipline and prudent planning for the future were conservative values. And then he comes up with this cockamamie idea that was *guaranteed* to run up deficits. But just because everybody likes tax cuts, it could get him elected. That's *responsible*?

MAEVE Okay, don't get upset...

MARK No, the *conservative* thing to do is *first* to show that you're capable of reducing expenditures, to get the federal budget out of deficit —and not the estimated budget either, but the actual income and expenditures. Then when you have a surplus, *then* you've made the case that taxes are too high, so you can think about cutting them.

MAEVE Okay, I remember the argument.

MARK Okay, but the point is, you joined in with the opinion that maybe tax cuts wouldn't actually *decrease* the deficit, but maybe they wouldn't *increase* it either. So maybe with spending cuts —which every politician promises, but gets vague about what'll get cut— he could balance the budget.

MAEVE You sounded too sure of yourself.

MARK It was an idiotic idea! But you seemed to believe that Reagan couldn't possibly be pushing bogus economic ideas, because he was a serious politician.

MAEVE He had economic advisors.

MARK Sure he did. And I'm sure they wanted to be economic advisors to a president rather than to a losing candidate.

And then Bush, senior, who had been calling him out on it in the primaries, took his vice presidential nomination and shut up about the *voodoo economics*.

MAEVE Okay, so he found out tax cuts win elections. Anyway, we don't need to talk about this.

MARK Well, I don't want to say I told you so, but... I *did inform you beforehand.* Eight years of the Reagan administration, we had tax cuts to make people happy, while the nation was being stuck with record-setting deficits, every year.

MAEVE Okay, Mark...

MARK And then... and then, to top it off, we later heard a new idea — that the massive deficits were actually a *good thing*, because they would prevent the Liberals from funding any new social programs. That was the '*starve the beast*' idea. Irresponsibility was made a virtue. A *conservative* virtue.

MAEVE Okay, look, you're right, we don't need to rehash this.

    (*pause*)

MARK Okay, so anyway, do we understand what just happened here, now? The Supreme Court said that the Constitution says that the First Amendment gives a person *or association of persons* the right of freedom of speech. Where does the authority for that come from? It's *not* in the Constitution.

MAEVE I'm not disagreeing.

MARK So if the Court said that the Constitution says that the *Second* Amendment gives a person or chimpanzee the right to bear arms, how would you respond?

MAEVE Okay, see? That's what you always do. You come up with some really silly example.

MARK Yes, but why is it silly?

MAEVE Come on, they couldn't rule that.

MARK Why not? They've already said that a *person* in the Constitution is not just a human being. But a human being is a primate as well as a person. So then a primate could be included in the definition of *person*. The chimpanzee is also a primate, and since a primate is a person, a chimpanzee is a person.

MAEVE Wait —no. That's absurd.

MARK Yes, it is absurd, and it's absurd to think the Court would ever make such a ruling — but *not* because it's *illogical*. It's no more *illogical* than the ruling they *did* make —that corporations have constitutional rights.

    But no, the Court won't make the ruling for chimps, because there's no political payoff in it. It's not in anybody's *interest* to support weapons for chimpanzees.

MAEVE Except for the chimpanzees.

MARK Right, so the difference is the difference between the political power of chimpanzees and the political power of corporations. It's *not* in the logic.

MAEVE But you're overlooking the practical aspect. Giving weapons to apes is dangerous.

MARK But, see, now you're changing the argument. Now you're saying that it's the *practical* matter of danger that should prevent that ruling. No. The *first* consideration is that it's *not* in the Constitution, so the Court doesn't have the *authority* to make the ruling.

Because when you bring up the practical aspect, it's just one illogical baby step from saying that it's *only* practical matters —whatever practical matter it sees— that the Court needs to consider. And that's just ignoring the authority of the Constitution.

And then, since the Court can't see any *danger* in giving more political power to corporations, that makes it okay to say that *the Constitution* says corporations have the rights of the Bill of Rights.

MAEVE   You know, I think that's the way it actually works.

MARK   But it's not okay! The Court's authority comes from the Constitution, which mentions only *persons* —not *chimpanzees* and not *associations of persons*. If you agree the Court couldn't interpret '*person*' as '*person or chimpanzee*,' how could it justify making the leap from '*person*' to '*person or association of persons*'?

MAEVE   Maybe they think it's the same thing.

MARK   That's exactly the *craziness* of this thinking! It's impossible! It's certainly not a physical reality, and in logic, it's absolutely false. An association of *anything* cannot be the same thing as the *members* of the association.

(*pause*)

2. ASSOCIATIONS

MAEVE I don't think that's always true. What about an association of associations?

MARK What? Oh —okay, I guess I didn't express myself clearly enough. I should have said, *in the real world*, an association can't be the *same thing* as a member of the association.

MAEVE No— *in the real world* there *are* associations of associations. They're called umbrella associations.

MARK But the members of an umbrella association are not *the same thing* as the umbrella association. If they were the *same thing*, the members would also be umbrella associations.

MAEVE Oh. Okay, all right.

MARK And *their* members would have to be umbrella associations also.

MAEVE Why?

MARK Because if the association of associations has members that are the *same thing* as it is, then *each* one of its members would have to have members that are the same thing as *it* is.

So it would have to be an association of associations of associations of associations ... and this would go on forever. An infinity of associations of associations, and *nothing physically real* in any of them.

MAEVE Hmmm.

MARK It's a theoretical idea, but it can't happen in physical reality.

(*pause*)

MAEVE Okay, I've got another example for you. An association of numbers.

MARK You mean like a vector, or a matrix?

MAEVE Nothing so fancy! I mean addition. Addition is associative, right?

MARK Well, yes, but ...

MAEVE Well, the association of three and four —in the association of addition— is seven. And that's a number. So an association of numbers is a number.

MARK Maeve, Maeve ... I appreciate you trying to give me an example from mathematics, so that I can appreciate it. And I do appreciate it. I do. But you know, there is no physical reality to mathematics. It's all conceptual. It's nothing but ideas.

MAEVE I knew you would do this, I knew it!

MARK Do what?

MAEVE Tell me my example was wrong.

MARK No, that wasn't... Wait —you knew it?

MAEVE I knew it, I knew it.

MARK How'd you know it?

MAEVE Because that's what you always do.

MARK Always? But, you don't always tell me you knew it.

MAEVE So? That's because I'm polite.

MARK Oh you are polite, no one denies that. But this time you really knew it, and it overwhelmed your politeness.

    (*pause*)

MAEVE I knew you were going to do that.

MARK What?

MAEVE Turn it around on me.

MARK Because I always do that?

MAEVE Okay, so what's wrong with my example?

MARK Well, if you want to see it clearly, you've got to look at the context. You know that there's no physical reality to anything in mathematics, right? Not even a number.

MAEVE *Hah*! Tell that to the mathematicians. They always talk about numbers *existing* and being *real*, and they sound quite sure of themselves.

MARK Yes, they use those words, but the entire mathematical domain is conceptual. In that domain, '*real*' and '*exists*' are still only ideas. When a mathematician says a number exists, he's not saying —or *she's* not saying— that the number has *physical* reality. A number is not *sensible*.

MAEVE No kidding. Some are totally irrational.

MARK No, no —I was using *sensible* in a different sense, an older sense. When I say numbers are not sensible, I mean that they can't be known through the senses. You can't see, hear, feel, smell, or taste a number. They're abstractions —just ideas.

    So when a mathematician says a number *exists*, all she's saying is that other mathematicians will agree with her, that it exists.

MAEVE Okay, you get an award from the Association of Women Mathematicians. But what makes our lady mathematician so sure that all mathematicians will agree with her?

MARK Because she has a *proof*. That's simply a text that follows all the rules of logic that mathematicians agree to, and it *compels* them to agree.

MAEVE And your point is that other mathematicians won't come up with their own *interpretations* of the proof?

MARK That wasn't exactly it. But, if a proof allows another interpretation, it's not a proof. A proof must obtain unanimous agreement that it has only one meaning.

    And you can see why. Mathematicians know that their subject matter is nothing but concepts —nothing but figments of the imagination. But imagination is wild —anything imaginable can be imagined. So to be sure everyone's imagining the same thing, imagination's got to be constrained —boxed in— by unambiguous definitions.

So all mathematical objects are created by clear, precise definitions.

MAEVE There you go, talking about *objects*. Objects are real.

MARK *Physical* objects are *physically* real. But with firm definitions, mathematical objects can be manipulated with the same confidence we have in manipulating physical objects. Yet conceptual objects —objects like *point, line, number, function, set, group*— are purely abstract.

MAEVE Purely abstract? Come on, not all of them.

MARK Yes, all. All of them.

MAEVE Look, I can show you —give me paper and pencil and I can create for you a line, a physical line —a *sensible* line.

MARK Not likely. The mathematical line is defined to have no end. It goes off to infinity in both directions.

MAEVE Well then, a finite length line —a line *segment*.

MARK A line or a line segment has zero width. So you'd have to use an infinitely fine pen point. It couldn't leave any visible trace on the paper.

MAEVE So a mathematical line is invisible.

MARK Of course. It's a *conceptual* object, not a *sensible* one. You can't see, hear, feel, smell or taste it.

MAEVE Well, I was good in geometry! And you know how I did it? By visualizing the lines. And they even give you diagrams —*sensible* pictures— in the problems and examples.

MARK The diagrams are *representations* of the mathematical objects, but the objects themselves —number, point, line, function, set, group— are just *ideas*. They're useful ideas, because they've been created to *correspond* to aspects of physical reality, but they're still just ideas.

MAEVE Well, maybe those things are just ideas —*in mathematics*. But in the language of the people, they represent real physical objects.

MARK No, not entirely. The *language of the people* is full of ambiguities. Words have multiple meanings; primary meanings, shadow meanings, connotations, metaphorical meanings, poetical meanings, ad hoc meanings derived solely from context. And ironic meanings opposite to primary meanings.

MAEVE Sure, sure —but it works, because people *want* to understand each other. And there is dialog to clear up misunderstandings.

MARK But all that breaks down when political power depends on a written text. Different parties will claim the text means *whatever works in their favor*. If they have the power, they'll change definitions to *make* it work in their favor.

And there will be *no* desire to understand each other, and *no* dialog.

MAEVE Okay, that's a special case. I'll grant that language has ambiguities, but everyday language —the language of the people— is not about mathematical abstractions. It's about physical reality.

MARK No, not entirely. And that's the problem. *Exactly* the problem. Hey, do you remember what this is all about?

MAEVE Certainly. You were pedantically *refuting* the Supreme Court's reasoning, by insisting that it was impossible for *any* association to be the *same thing* as a member of the association.

MARK And you —apparently with a passion to defend the Supreme Court— felt compelled to come up with an example to show it *was* possible.

But it was obvious to you that in *physical* reality, an association of persons — note the plural, *persons*— is *not* the same thing as —one— person. You couldn't find an example in physical reality, so you went for an example in *metaphysics*. You know what metaphysics is, right?

MAEVE Of course. *Meta* is beyond. Metaphysics is reasoning beyond the realm of physical reality.

MARK So what kind of *reality* could there be in metaphysics? An object that has no *physical* reality exists only in its *definition*. That means there must be a consensus on the definition, in order for everyone to think about it in the same way. So that we all can talk about it *as if* it were physical reality.

MAEVE You mean so we can all have the *illusion* of physical reality?

MARK So that we can all have —and be confident that we all have— the *same* illusion, whether or not it corresponds to physical reality. Physical reality has consistency; metaphysical reasoning requires its own consistency.

If, in *your* metaphysics, an association is the *same thing* as its *members*, then the members must be associations also. That's the only possible consistency.

And those member associations must be the same thing as *their* members —so their members must be associations also. For consistency, none of the associations can have members that are anything but associations. It's an idea that can exist in metaphysics, but it's not possible in physical *reality*.

MAEVE Okay, maybe, but you're being all dogmatic in your metaphysics. We were discussing a *legal* concept, and you have no expertise in the law.

MARK No, and neither do you. So when Charles spouts a bunch fancy words that makes it true in *legal* language, we'll just have to accept it. Not understand it, but accept it —as reality.

MAEVE Well, no. Reality can't just depend on language. In the words of the Bard, **"A rose by any other name would smell as sweet."**

MARK He's right. *Physical* reality doesn't depend on language. The Bard is telling us that a rose is a physical object —a *sensible* object— that we know through our sense of smell in particular. Language can't easily fool you about the properties of physical objects.

But when the poet Burns says his "...**love is like a red, red rose**," is *he* talking about physical reality?

MAEVE Well, that's poetic language. He's looking at her through rose-colored glasses.

MARK Right. She might even be the Yellow Rose of Texas. Anything is possible in poetic language. But is that the kind of language we expect of the law?

MAEVE Of course not. The law can't be that arbitrary.

MARK It *shouldn't* be. Especially for a government that claims its legitimacy is in the consent of the governed. The origins of the law must be clear to the *entire* society, not just the lawyers.

MAEVE That's obvious.

MARK But when you're being fooled, it is *not* obvious that you're being fooled. You can't easily be fooled by language that holds to physical reality, but when language ventures into metaphysics, reality depends on *consensus* in definitions. The same definition must be held by both speaker and listener, both writer and reader.

MAEVE You already made that point about mathematical language. It's metaphysics, but everything is precisely defined.

MARK Yes. But when common language stumbles into metaphysics, the metaphysical objects have *no* precise definitions, and don't appear in every mind as the same thing. That's where you can be fooled.

   And we are being fooled. Not only are we lacking consensus definitions for abstractions, but we're not even aware of the boundary between the material world and metaphysics.

MAEVE Well, I don't know about that. When people talk about a rose, I think we know whether they mean an actual flower or whether they're referring to an ideal of aesthetic perfection.

MARK So you see the difference there. But you just told me that words like *set* and *group* —precisely defined abstractions in mathematics— represent physical objects in the language of the people.

MAEVE Well, yes, they're physical realities.

MARK No. Not true at all. *Set* and *group* are abstractions in common language also. I'm sure you remember, back in grade school, when you learned that nouns represent *things*, that there were *concrete* nouns for physical things and *abstract* nouns for conceptual things.

MAEVE Sure. Concrete nouns are words for material things. Things that are physically real —*sensible*. Like, "...**shoes and ships and sealing-wax, cabbages and kings**."

MARK Umm, I'm not okay with *kings*.

MAEVE Oh. Because a king is just an idea.

MARK It is. You studied history. You know it's sometimes been a bloody business to get a consensus on the *idea* of king.

MAEVE Then we could substitute …

MARK MIRVs?

MAEVE I don't like acronyms.

MARK Then let's just say multiple-warhead independently targetable reentry vehicles.

MAEVE That doesn't scan. Also, I wouldn't want to call them *sensible.*

MARK They're sensible, even if they're not sensible. Anyway, what do we have for *abstract* nouns?

MAEVE *Abstract* nouns are words for things that are conceptual. Things you can't know through your senses. Like law, hope, interest, debt, contracts, promises.

MARK And collateralized credit default options.

MAEVE They're just ideas.

MARK Right. And among the abstract nouns are those called collective nouns. *Set* and *group* are prime examples. They must be abstract because they are used in the singular —for a single *thing*— and yet they represent *multiple* objects. We call the plural objects their *elements* or *members.*

   You remember all this, don't you?

   (*pause*)

MAEVE Umm, sure. Of course.

MARK You don't sound convinced.

MAEVE I haven't thought about it.

MARK Maeve, do we have any eggs?

MAEVE Yes, I think … (*walks to refrigerator, opens door*) Yeah, we've got a whole bunch.

MARK A *whole* bunch. That's better than I expected.

MAEVE What do you want to make?

MARK I was thinking of an omelet.

MAEVE Now? I could make an omelet.

MARK Not yet. I'm still thinking about it. But since we have a *whole bunch* of eggs, you could start by putting some of them on the counter. Then you'd have a bunch on the counter, and another bunch in the refrigerator. Two bunches.

MAEVE Sure, but they wouldn't be whole bunches.

MARK What, *half* bunches?

MAEVE There's no such thing as a half bunch.

MARK You're just making this up, aren't you?

MAEVE No, everybody knows this.

MARK So then if you took the one bunch and put it back together with the other bunch you get...

MAEVE A whole bunch.

MARK How'd you say you did in arithmetic?

MAEVE I did just fine. It doesn't work for bananas though.

MARK What?

MAEVE If you split a bunch of bananas you get two bunches. But if you put the two bunches together, you don't get one bunch.

MARK Oh, right ... still two bunches. Hmmm. And then if you split each of the bunches, you'd have a *bunch* of bunches of bananas...

MAEVE Yes...

MARK And then, and then... (*getting excited*) ... if you keep splitting those bunches till you couldn't split any more, you wouldn't have *any* bunches of bananas at all...

MAEVE Right.

MARK ... just a whole bunch of bananas.

MAEVE No, that wouldn't be a bunch.

MARK I didn't say a bunch; I said a *whole* bunch.

MAEVE Well I don't know. Maybe.

MARK I thought you knew these things.

MAEVE You have to use the word *loose* then.

MARK So when you think about it, *bunch* is a concrete noun in one sense, when it's used with bananas or grapes, but an abstract noun —a collective— when used with eggs or apples.

MAEVE That's quite perceptive of you. But do you want an omelet?

MARK Not yet. I'm trying to think of a way... to get back to your example.

MAEVE Yes, you never said what was wrong with it.

MARK Well, numbers have no physical reality...

MAEVE Yes, you said that. Not even real numbers.

MARK Right, and neither does a *bunch*, when you use it in the collective sense, like a bunch of eggs.

MAEVE So you're saying a bunch is not real?

MARK Not *physically* real. Look, for that bunch, the bunch of eggs, you could have identified it with any of the collective nouns —a set, a group, a collection, an aggregation, or an association. They're all the same.

MAEVE I wouldn't call it an association.

MARK Well of course we choose the word for its connotations, and the connotations are different, but they're all collective nouns. If I mentioned a new set of dishes, you'd assume the dishes —the *members* of the set— would all have the same style and pattern.

MAEVE A new set of dishes. Now there's a good idea.

MARK But the idea is just an example, completely hypothetical. Our set of dishes is still a *set*, even though they don't quite all match. The connotation —that the members of the set should match— is not that important.

MAEVE *You* don't think it's important.

MARK Or, for example, if I told you that I bought a new set of tires for the car, what would you assume?

MAEVE That it was completely hypothetical.

MARK Yes, yes, hypothetical, not only because it's a collective, but it's an imagined collective. But you'd assume the tires would all be the same type.

MAEVE Oh, a matched set of dishes is not important, but a matched set of tires is?

MARK It is. Or maybe it isn't —but that's not the point! I'm just saying that the *connotation* of the word *set* is that the members are matched, but that's just a nuance, a flavoring. If it were part of the definition, there'd never be a reason to talk of a *matched* set.

MAEVE A set is just a collection.

MARK Yes, but you see now, the word *collection* has a different connotation, a connotation of variety, because the members were collected from different places.

MAEVE Not necessarily. Your collection of plastic take-out soup containers is all from Hunan Valley.

MARK I don't collect them, they just happen to collect. Anyway, that would be a collection that's a matched set. See, the connotation is not the definition. So you could call that bunch of eggs a *set*, a *bunch*, a *group*, a *collection*, an *aggregation*, or an *association* of eggs.

MAEVE I still wouldn't call it an association.

MARK Maybe you wouldn't, because of a connotation. But all these words are actually synonyms. They're just different words for the same *thing*.

MAEVE The same *thing*?

MARK Yes they're all singular nouns. They all designate the same thing.

MAEVE But it's not a *thing*.

MARK Yes, it must be. A singular noun must name a single *thing*. But a collective noun names a *conceptual* thing —an abstraction— because there's no singular *physical* object there.

MAEVE The eggs are physical.

MARK But there are more than one, so we talk about *them* in the plural. We could talk about *them* as *members* of the group. But when we talk about the *group* —in the singular— what is *it*?

(*pause*)

MAEVE Hmmm.

MARK *It* can't be 'the eggs.' *Eggs* is plural.

MAEVE It's the unity … the togetherness of them.

MARK Nice abstraction, *togetherness*. How about the *association* of them?

MAEVE I guess...

MARK In your mind, they're associated. They're together.

MAEVE But the word *association* is about social beings, associating through social interaction.

MARK The word 'society' is a collective also, but for an association of social beings. But an association in general doesn't require social interaction. I myself am a member of several associations in which I socialize with no one.

MAEVE So an association can have members that are antisocial.

MARK Not antisocial. Maybe just *asocial*.

MAEVE Like eggs. Associations of eggheads.

MARK But the idea of the *group*, your idea of the *togetherness* of the members — it's an abstraction. How can you even imagine it?

MAEVE It's, um...an invisible aura that holds them all together.

MARK Your imagination is powerful enough to see the invisible?

MAEVE Mine is indeed. But if it's just a figment of imagination, how do we know that it even exists?

MARK It doesn't exist in the same way a physical object exists. But just like mathematicians can talk about conceptual objects existing, the group exists because there is a *consensus* in the definition. So if —*if!*— it appears in everyone's mind in the same way, then we can talk about it as an object.

MAEVE That could be a pretty big *if*.

MARK Yes, but our language helps us see that we have the same idea in mind. About your bunch of eggs in the refrigerator —what color is it?

MAEVE Well, the *eggs* are all white.

MARK There you go! I asked you about the color of the *group* —in the singular— and you switched back to the plural for your answer — "the *eggs* are white." Do you know why you did that?

MAEVE We don't talk about a white bunch of eggs.

MARK Yeah, it's okay to talk about a group of white eggs, but not a white group of eggs. Why is that?

MAEVE Okay, because the group —the *togetherness*— does not have a color.

MARK   Right. The group —or set, or collection, or association— is an abstraction. It has no physical reality, so no physical properties. No color.

MAEVE   Well, I don't know. If some of the eggs were white and some were brown, we could say *it* was multicolored.

MARK   Amazing! The group can't have a color, but it can be multicolored. How does that work?

MAEVE   Okay, because if the eggs are all single-colored, you couldn't notice any multi-coloring until you had more than one.

MARK   That's exactly it. Multi-coloring is a property ... well, you could also call it a *feature* or *characteristic*, but *property* is the usual term. But it's a property of the collective —the *group* or *set*— not a property of the individual eggs.

And this is an example of a general principle: *the properties of a set are not the same properties as the properties of the members of the set.*

MAEVE   Oh, come on, now. We could have multicolored eggs, too.

MARK   Like decorated Easter eggs, with each egg colored in a pattern of different colors?

MAEVE   Sure.

MARK   But then we wouldn't say the *set* was multicolored.

MAEVE   My point is that multicoloring is a property that could belong to either the set of eggs or the eggs themselves.

MARK   Yes, but they're different properties! Look, there's always a potential for confusion when one word names different *things*. But the multicolor property of the *set* is not the same as the multicolor property of an *egg*.

An egg is multicolored if different parts of its surface area have different colors. But *a set* of eggs is called multicolored if it contains *eggs* of different colors.

MAEVE   But then different parts of *its* surface area would have different colors.

MARK   No, no —*the set* doesn't have a surface area. There is no single area that encompasses the set. There are multiple surface areas, but they belong to the *eggs*.

MAEVE   But you could *add up* the surface areas of the eggs and that would be the surface area of the set.

MARK   You could, but then you're taking measurements of area, and doing arithmetic to add them up. That's a conceptualization —an abstraction. There is no *physical* surface of that size.

MAEVE   But there is. You would see it if you took all of the egg shells and flattened them out, and squished them together to make one physical surface area.

MARK   But that's still a *conceptualization*, not physical reality.

MAEVE   But *if you actually did it* —it would be a reality!

MARK   *If you actually did it*, you'd have a physical thing —a *composition* of egg shells. And that's an entirely different thing than the *conceptual* thing we are talking about —the *association* of eggs.

And if you create that physical thing —the composition of eggshells— you no longer have the conceptual thing —the association of eggs.

So the general rule is: no property of the *association* can be the same as a property of a *member* of the association.

MAEVE I don't think you can jump to a general rule, just because multi-coloring for an egg is different than multi-coloring for the set.

MARK It's not just from one example. The set is an abstraction —it's your idea of the *togetherness* of multiple objects. The properties of the set do not appear in any one object, but *emerge* when there are multiple objects.

The properties of the set are called *emergent* properties.

They can be about similarities or differences among the members of the set; you see that in words like *matched* or *mixed*, *uniform* or *diverse*. Or they can be *statistics* taken from the members. These do not describe the individual members.

MAEVE I think it's an arbitrary distinction.

MARK No, no —it's the only rule that's *not* arbitrary. Could you say that *some* of the properties of the set are the properties of the members, and some not? Then what rule would determine which are, and which are not? There is none —nothing but arbitrariness.

MAEVE Well, I don't know. It's confusing.

MARK But why should it be confusing? If you can see the property in a single egg, it's a property of the egg. If you see it only when you have a number of eggs, it's a property of the set.

MAEVE A number of eggs? Well, suppose the number is one.

MARK No, when I said a *number* of eggs, I meant a number greater than one.

MAEVE But why couldn't the number be one?

(*pause*)

MARK No, Maeve, we can't go there. A collective is a reference to *multiple* items. At least two.

MAEVE But why can't it be one? A *mathematical* set can have just one member, can't it?

MARK Yes, but we're not doing math! So when *we* use the word *set* —or group, or association— we mean a *multiplicity* of items. You don't have a *set* of anything until you have more than one.

MAEVE So why are you raving about mathematical definitions, when you're not even using them?

MARK Only because mathematics is an *example* of metaphysics that works. And it works because of precise, consistent and agreed-upon definitions. All metaphysics needs those qualities, but not necessarily the *same* vocabulary and definitions as mathematics.

MAEVE And you're saying that the common language doesn't have those qualities.

MARK It doesn't. Well, it has enough for people to understand each other —as you said, when they *want* to. And as long as the language is limited to physical things, which we know through our senses, there's not much room for deception.

But when language is intended to direct and *constrain* human behavior —as we expect of the text of a contract, law or *constitution*— and the language ventures into metaphysics, its vagueness and the lack of consensus are openings for deception. The purpose of the text can be hijacked by those who have the power to alter the definitions.

MAEVE Then perhaps you could explain this to me. Why is it that by the *precise* mathematical definition, a set can have a single member, but in ordinary language it can't?

MARK Mathematicians obviously found some advantage in their definition. Look, every collective has a property of *number* —the number of its members...

MAEVE You mean in the mathematical definition, it does.

MARK And in common language, too. It's the one property common to all collectives.

When you talk about a set or group or association, it's presumed that you know what the membership is. So the idea that it has a certain number of members is always present. How many dishes do we have in our set of dishes?

MAEVE Who knows? I haven't counted.

MARK Okay, but we agree that there *is* a number —it *exists,* as a concept —even if you don't know what it is.

MAEVE You're so pedantic— '*the property of number.*' People usually just talk about the *size* of a set.

MARK Sure. Even when we use words like *large* or *small*, we're not being precise, but we're referring to the *number*.

MAEVE Unless we're referring to the objects —the members of the set.

MARK Oh, the sizes of the members? Again, there's a possible confusion, using the same word for a property of the collective and a property of the members. But they *can't* be the same property.

The size *of the set* is an abstraction —the number of its members. And the sizes of the *members* are physical features, which can be seen, or felt, and measured in various ways. These properties are completely unrelated.

MAEVE You can have a small set of large dishes or a large set of small dishes.

MARK Or any combination. The words small and large have different meanings for the set and its members.

MAEVE Hmmm.

MARK And the Los Angeles Lakers is a small association of large people, and the Girl Scouts of America is a large association of small people.

MAEVE Yes, I've always said that.

MARK So every collective in common language has the property of *number*. Even if you don't know the number, you know it's more than one.

That's *our* consensus definition. The fact that mathematicians found it convenient to generalize their concept of a set, so its number could be one —or even zero— doesn't change that at all.

MAEVE Yes, but look —maybe the mathematicians are right! Maybe a set really *doesn't* have to have more than one member.

MARK *Really* doesn't? What kind of *really* are you talking about? A conceptual object is *created* by its definition. It has no *reality* before, or outside of, its definition.

MAEVE Okay, so … when they defined the word *set*, they just *made up* what the word defined.

MARK Exactly!

MAEVE Well, still, maybe the mathematical definition is *better*.

MARK I assume it's better for mathematicians. But that's irrelevant, because that's not what *we* mean when we talk about a set.

Anyway, how would it work, if you couldn't assume a set had multiple members? If a set of dishes could be just a single dish, would it be a set of *dish*?

MAEVE How about just a dish set?

MARK No, look, a collective cannot be the *same thing* as its members, because *its members* are plural, and the collective is singular. That's a fundamental distinction.

But if a set could have just one member, there's no longer that distinction. If you could have a dish set with just one dish, would it be the same *thing* as the dish?

MAEVE No, I think the set would still be an abstraction.

MARK But how could you hold to any distinction between the set and its one member? If the collective is *the invisible aura that holds the members together*, and there's just one member, you couldn't even see that *invisible aura*.

And the properties of a collective are those that emerge from the *plurality* of the members. But no properties emerge from a single object, so the collective would have no properties.

MAEVE Well, excuse me, but how do the mathematicians do it, then?

MARK In mathematics, *all* objects are conceptual —both the set and its single member. But the set is *defined* to be a different *thing* than its member. Each has its own *defined* properties, and they're not shared.

In mathematics, the distinction between a set of one object and the object itself is maintained in the *discipline* of holding to definitions.

MAEVE Okay, so maybe it's not such a good idea for the common language. Common language deals with the real world. The world of physical objects.

MARK But no, not entirely. It deals with abstractions, too.

MAEVE Okay, but the difference is that physical objects are not created by definitions. A dish is a dish. Once you've seen and used one, you know what it is.

MARK Sure. The definition of the word just connects it with the physical object.

MAEVE Okay, so if a single dish could constitute a *set* ... hmmm ...

(*pause*)

MAEVE Okay, then I guess the physical reality of the dish would just overwhelm the abstract idea of the set. So you wouldn't see a distinction.

MARK Sure. And suppose an association of persons could have just one member. Then it would be easy to argue that that association is the *same thing* as the member.

Then since *that* association has all the properties of a person, every association must have those properties, and so an association of persons *is* a person.

This is a specious argument. It's fallacious. It's just *wrong*.

MAEVE But —wait a minute! Isn't that the argument the Supreme Court is using to rule that an association of persons is a person?

MARK We don't know what the Court's argument is, but it's got to be a fallacy.

An association of persons must have more than one member, and all of its properties emerge from the *association* of the persons, not from the characteristics of one individual.

MAEVE So I guess that's your point, then. *An association of anything cannot be the same thing as the members of the association.*

MARK True. But why am I hearing irony, here?

MAEVE I gave you an example where it's *not true*. Addition is an association of numbers that is also a number.

MARK But ...

MAEVE Oh, but numbers have no physical reality —they're purely conceptual.

MARK Yes, good point.

MAEVE And sets, groups, associations —all collectives— are conceptual, too. Even if their members are physical objects.

MARK I'm glad we understand that.

MAEVE I don't see how that relates to my example.

MARK A little patience. We were just getting the context clear. Okay, so if the *members* of a group are physical objects, they have physical properties.

MAEVE Like size. We have ten-inch plates in our set of dishes —did you know that? But that's a number, so it's not a physical property.

MARK Not the number itself. The physical property of size is sensible —it can be seen and felt. We can obtain numbers from some physical properties —by measuring— but that doesn't change the nature of those properties.

MAEVE But then those numbers are also properties. So you're admitting that physical objects can have abstract properties.

MARK Of course they can! That's not an issue. But the reality of those properties is the reality of consensus. In the store you'll find shelves of physical objects marked with an abstract property —price.

Physical objects *can* have abstract properties. The point is that abstract objects *can't* have physical properties. And collectives are abstract, so they have no physical properties.

MAEVE Come on, none? None at all?

MARK No, none.

MAEVE Now, that's too extreme. It's like you're saying a set is not even in the physical world. Like it has no physical location.

MARK No, it doesn't.

MAEVE Oh, come on, now —our *set* of dishes is located in the cabinet.

MARK So, what are you telling me … that you emptied the dishwasher?

MAEVE Well … no, actually, I didn't. But anyway, the *bunch of eggs* is in the refrigerator. That's its *physical* location.

MARK That's where the *eggs* are. But if you put a few of them on the counter, then what's the location of the *group*?

MAEVE In the refrigerator and on the counter.

MARK That's two locations. The group is singular— if it has a location, it's got to be one location.

MAEVE It's in the kitchen, then.

MARK And if I brought a couple of them into the living room? Then the group would be…

MAEVE Then it would be in our house.

MARK And if I gave one to Nadia, next door?

MAEVE Well, then it's on this block.

MARK And if I gave one to your friend Gordon, the astronaut, and he took it with him to the orbiting space station?

MAEVE Then it's located in the solar system.

MARK Seriously? You couldn't locate the group any more precisely than the solar system?

MAEVE You're just getting weird.

MARK Look, the *eggs* are physical objects. Each one of the *eggs* has a physical location, and if it's specified with any precision, it must be different from the location of every other egg —because no two physical objects can occupy the same space. So there's no one location that's a *physical* location of the group.

MAEVE But we *talk* about its location.

MARK Yes, since the group is an idea, we could conjure another idea —*make up* some rule related to the locations of the eggs— and *call* it a location. It doesn't matter how vague it is, as long as we think we have an agreement on the rule, we could *say* the group has that location. But that would be our *invention* —an abstract property, not a physical one.

MAEVE Okay, okay. You didn't really want an omelet, did you? You just wanted to talk about eggs.

MARK No, not eggs —a set of eggs. Or a group, or bunch, or collection, or an association of eggs.

MAEVE I still wouldn't call it an association.

MARK Maeve,...

　　(*The phone, on the kitchen wall, rings. Maeve answers.*)

MAEVE Hello ... okay ... sure, *now* is good ... okay! (*She hangs up the phone.*) Paul's here. He's coming in to look at the faucet.

MARK Did you tell him I already replaced the washer?

MAEVE Yes, he knows that. But he'll take a look.

　　(*pause*)

MARK Anyway...

MAEVE Well, anyway, I think you're just playing with words, to make things seem to fit in the categories you've set up.

MARK Maeve, why did we get into this? The Supreme Court just said that a corporation is a *person*. And not only that, but it said that *the Constitution says* a corporation is a person. And, because it's a person, it has rights of the Bill of Rights.

　　And by that ruling, the Supreme Court gives *itself* the power to overrule legislatures —the representatives of the people— when they make laws regulating corporations.

　　And it was the legislatures that created corporations in the first place!

　　And you think *I'm* the one that's playing with words?

MAEVE Well, you're being very pedantic.

MARK If we can't think straight, we'll just be dupes...

3. FACTIONS

(*Paul enters through the front door.*)

PAUL Hello!

MARK Come on in, Paul.

PAUL I was in the neighborhood. I thought I'd check out the faucet.

MARK I put in a new washer.

PAUL Yeah. (*Paul inspects faucet in kitchen sink, turns the faucet handles on and off.*) All right. We might have to replace the fixture. (*He opens the cabinet under the sink and crouches to look inside, then gets down on his knees and his head disappears into the cabinet. After a minute, he pulls himself out.*)

The valve is frozen. Do you have some lubricant? WD-40?

MARK I think so. Let me look...

(*Leaving, through the side entrance.*) In case you need them, there's a bunch of tools under the sink, on the left side.

(*Mark leaves.*)

MAEVE Well, I just won the argument.

PAUL Good for you. (*Standing up.*) What was the argument?

MAEVE It was silly. He was arguing that a collective noun, like *bunch*, is an abstraction, so it doesn't have *any* physical properties. Not even a location. And then he walks out saying there's a bunch of tools under the sink.

PAUL He wants to impose his definitions to get the upper hand in the argument.

MAEVE Just one of his pedantic quirks.

PAUL Hey, *The Federalist*'s still here. (*He picks up the book on the counter.*) You didn't give it to the kid... Kevin?

MAEVE He hasn't shown up for a couple of days.

PAUL He said he was studying American History.

MAEVE I don't think it's his highest priority.

PAUL I was remembering my High School history teacher, Mr. Halpern, made us read some of the Federalist Papers.

MAEVE I noticed how your book was all marked up.

PAUL Yeah, but I got the book a lot later. In high school he just gave us some of the papers. I couldn't say how much I got out of them, but I remember Halpern talking about *factions*. He hated factions. I got the idea they were gangs of mean-spirited, evil men.

MAEVE They're just political parties.

PAUL Oh, Maeve, no. That's just wrong. A political party is a broad coalition, hopefully broad enough to win elections. A faction is a smaller group, with *particular* interests. It wants influence in the government, in order to protect and serve *its* interests. *Special interest* —that's the modern name for a faction.

Just think about it. A faction doesn't have enough votes on its own to elect the politicians that will serve its interests, and it certainly can't attract votes by *publicizing* its interests. So it joins in alliance with other factions —that's where the political parties come from.

MAEVE So the parties are coalitions of factions.

PAUL Sure. And the parties will use whatever works —*whatever works!*— to attract votes. But, they can *not* attract votes by revealing what the special interests are, and what they really want.

MAEVE So you're saying there's deception at the heart of democracy.

PAUL Come on Maeve, I'm sure that's not news to you. The authors of the Federalist Papers were trying to win support for the ratification of the Constitution. They admitted that there are and always will be factions. But they tried to make the case that the Constitution offers the means to control them —at least, to prevent any one faction from taking control of the government, and then using the law to solidify its power, for permanent control.

MAEVE And you learned that in high school?

PAUL I don't know how much I learned in high school. All I *cared* about was baseball... and girls ... and cars.

MAEVE And smoking pot.

PAUL No, no, Maeve. I don't know what stories Nadia told you, but not in high school. Anyway, he seemed interested.

MAEVE You mean Kevin?

PAUL Yeah. I don't know what they learn in high school these days. You *taught* history didn't you?

MAEVE Only to the seventh grade.

PAUL Did you read the Federalist papers?

MAEVE Not to seventh graders.

PAUL I mean yourself.

MAEVE Some, in college ...

PAUL Here... (*he thumbs through pages of the book*)... this is Madison, explaining it in Paper Ten. (*reads*) "**The latent causes of faction are thus sown in the nature of man; and we see them everywhere brought into different degrees of activity, according to the different circumstances of civil society. A zeal for different opinions concerning religion, concerning government, and many other points, as well of speculation as of practice;...**"

... I wasn't exactly sure what he meant there, "as well of speculation as of practice..."

MAEVE Speculation is just theory —ideas, ideology. He's saying opinions based on ideas alone can be as strong as opinions grounded in practical experience.

PAUL That's for sure. (*reads*) "... **an attachment to different leaders ambitiously contending for preeminence and power**..."

MAEVE Politicians.

PAUL (*reads*) "... **or to persons of other descriptions whose fortunes have been interesting to the human passions...**"

MAEVE Movie stars, athletes, singers, obsessive narcissists…

PAUL And bodybuilders, wrestlers, preachers, comedians turned politician. Okay, (*reads*) "... **, have, in turn, divided mankind into parties, inflamed them with mutual animosity, and rendered them much more disposed to vex and oppress each other than to co-operate for their common good.**"

MAEVE Really, is there such a thing as the common good?

PAUL I think his point is it gets lost if your ideology demands that you oppose every issue that the other party supports.

Anyway, (*reads*) "**So strong is this propensity of mankind to fall into mutual animosities that where no substantial occasion presents itself the most frivolous and fanciful distinctions have been sufficient to kindle their unfriendly passions and excite their most violent conflicts.**"

MAEVE *Frivolous and fanciful* distinctions. I wonder if they had flag pins.

PAUL Flag pins, family values, loyalty oaths, pledges —*whatever works*. (*reads*) "**But the most common and durable source of factions has been the verious and unequal distribution of property. Those who hold and those who are without property have ever formed distinct interests in society. Those who are creditors, and those who are debtors, fall under a like discrimination.**"

MAEVE Some things don't change.

PAUL Yeah. Maeve, do you remember back in 2005, the great popular uprising against injustice? I mean, the injustice of people escaping their debts by declaring bankruptcy?

MAEVE What? No, I don't remember that.

PAUL Well, do you remember politicians making bold campaign promises to end the free ride people were getting through bankruptcy?

MAEVE I don't remember that, either.

PAUL No, you don't, because none of that happened. Yet with zero interest by the public, and no campaigning on the issue, just about three quarters of our Congress thought it was important to pass the *Bankruptcy Abuse Prevention and Consumer Protection Act.*

It was the only significant legislation passed in that Congress. It made declaring personal bankruptcy a lot harder, and made its terms a lot harsher.

MAEVE Well, Consumer Protection is part of the act, too, right?

PAUL Do you know of anything in that law that actually protects consumers?

MAEVE Well, I haven't looked into it.

PAUL So you're okay with believing the title.

MAEVE No...

PAUL You actually *want* to be fooled, don't you?

MAEVE That's not fair.

PAUL Yes, because you desperately want to believe our democracy's working.

MAEVE No...

PAUL When they make it illegal to criticize the government, they'll call it the '*Defense of Freedom of Speech Act*,' and that'll make it okay with you.

MAEVE Look, I know it was the *banks* that pushed for the bankruptcy law, but it was apparently not *opposed* by the public either.

PAUL Mostly because they didn't know about it. It didn't get a lot of publicity before it was passed.

MAEVE Actually, *I* heard about it. The opinion in the media was that it was good for everybody, because if banks could cut their losses from bankruptcies, they could offer higher interest on savings accounts and also reduce their fees.

PAUL You remember that happening?

MAEVE No, I remember the opposite. Savings rates went down, and bank fees went up.

PAUL You know what else went up? Bank profits. And not just because of the bankruptcy law and the fees. The banks began packaging low-quality mortgages and selling them as high-quality investments, and the investment rating agencies went along with the scam.

Then, in 2008, it was the *banks* that all went bankrupt. No, wait —let me make this clear. They all *should* have gone bankrupt, under the law, because they had *all* overextended themselves borrowing and making loans, and didn't have the cash reserves to repay their creditors when the loans defaulted.

MAEVE That's irony, huh? The bankruptcy law didn't apply to the banks.

PAUL Of course not. The banks wanted a law that made bankruptcy tougher on *people*, not *banks*! Only one, Lehman Brothers, went bankrupt. All the others got government bailouts.

MAEVE The banks were too big to fail.

PAUL And the financial meltdown resulted in bank mergers. Now the banks are *way* too big to fail.

MAEVE So, you think Madison foresaw all this?

PAUL Foresaw? Come on, give the man a break. Nobody can see the future. At the time, Madison couldn't even have foreseen... electricity... or, for that matter, railroads, or cars, telephones, radio, television, photography, movies, airplanes, satellites, space vehicles, relativity, atomic energy, nuclear weapons, quantum mechanics, microorganisms, evolution, the genetic code, computers, the Internet, or collateralized credit default options.

But, given all that, he knew human nature. He knew *factions*.

MAEVE Human nature doesn't change.

PAUL Okay, here's more. (*reads*) "**A landed interest, a manufacturing interest, a mercantile interest, a moneyed interest, with many lesser interests, grow up of necessity in civilized nations, and divide them into different classes, actuated by different sentiments and views.**"

MAEVE Now, *that* seems much of an eighteenth-century view.

PAUL Why?

MAEVE He couldn't have foreseen corporations either.

PAUL I think they had corporations then.

MAEVE Oh, but they were not at all the same as today's corporations. Back then, corporations were occasional things, chartered individually by the government, to achieve some end that the *government* considered to be in the public's interest. The chance of making profits was offered to attract investment, but the *purpose* of the charter was the benefit to society.

PAUL And so?

MAEVE So back then, businesses were owned individually, or in partnership. The owner managed the business. And his interests —his lifelong interests— were those of his particular *kind* of business. That's why Madison can talk of the manufacturing interest, the mercantile interest, and such. They were separate interests —separate factions— in competition with each other.

PAUL You don't think that's true now?

MAEVE It's a lot less true now. Owners of corporations are not managers. Corporations, and shares of corporations, are commodities, bought and sold. Owners have interests in businesses in all types. Even individual corporations are in different types of business. So factions associated with particular *types* of business have become relatively weaker.

PAUL Yeah, maybe. But the *moneyed interest* sure hasn't become weaker.

MAEVE Well, no, that's the one faction that's gotten a lot stronger. Now finance is not just for operating a business, but for buying and selling companies. And speculating on shares, commodities, *futures*, in all markets. Finance is the lifeblood of the economy.

PAUL And the moneyed interest has its fingers on the jugular.

MAEVE Okay, so... you made your point. And you think Kevin should know this?

PAUL Well, I asked him what he knows about the Constitution. He tells me the Constitution describes the form of our government. So what is the form of our government? He knows there are three branches —Congress, the Presidency, and the Supreme Court. And there are these *checks and balances* that guarantee that no one branch will take over the others.

MAEVE Good. He knows about the checks and balances.

PAUL Wait —not that much. So what are those checks and balances? He knows the President can check Congress by vetoing a bill that Congress passed, and that Congress can check the President by overriding the veto with a two-thirds majority.

MAEVE Okay.

PAUL But there are *three* branches. Are the checks and balances *only* between the President and Congress? And he doesn't have any answer.

MAEVE Well, you can understand that, can't you?

PAUL Can I, really? I don't know. Look, I'm not being critical. I don't know *what* I knew in high school. But is that all a high school student should know?

MAEVE I think the main lesson here is respect for the Constitution.

PAUL Respect? What exactly do you mean by that?

MAEVE Well, to be aware of its importance in guaranteeing our freedom...

PAUL But it's a document! You can praise the language and rave about it's history —uniting the people to create the nation— is that what you mean by respecting it?

MAEVE Not exactly... .

PAUL Or you can take a pilgrimage to Washington and stand in awe of the sacred relic in its glass case. Maybe to *demonstrate* your respect, you could bow before it, or genuflect. Is that what you're talking about?

MAEVE Of course that's not what I mean.

PAUL Of course not. That kind of respect —that's just *awe* at its magnificence— is useless. It's just worship —a retreat into an emotional state of submissiveness. Like an infant.

MAEVE Ah, I see Nadia's influence, here. Now you're getting into child psychology.

PAUL No, don't bring Nadia into it. And so what if it's her influence? Sure, she'd say political motivations are emotional, but Madison wrote about that, too — about political *passions*. And now we have *professionals* —from the institutes, foundations and think tanks— whose *job it is* to shape political beliefs. You can bet they know all about your psychology, about how to manipulate your passions. And they don't want *you* to know how they do it.

MAEVE Well, come on —that infantile state of *submissiveness* can hardly be called *passion*.

PAUL No, it's not. And it's also not a dignified state for an adult. Except if it's submission to an abstraction —to some great principle or ideal whose truth and power are unassailable— *that's* a form of submission you can take *pride* in.

MAEVE But is that *passion*?

PAUL It's *power*. When you submit to that great abstraction, you *identify* with it. Its power and glory become your own. You can defend it and promote it. It becomes a *cause.*

MAEVE So you're saying *submissiveness* to an abstraction is *power.*

PAUL Right, right. That's how it works. Look, if you're taught to *respect* and *submit* to the Constitution, and you don't know what it says, you're just ripe for the despots to tell you the Constitution says *this*, the Constitution says *that*, the sacred Constitution is the answer to all our social and political problems. You must submit to it —*everybody* must submit to it.

But that doesn't happen. Then when people don't revere the Constitution like you do, you can get angry. You *should* get angry —it's righteous anger. Those people are *evil.*

And your political outlook is aligned with what you've been *told* the Constitution says.

MAEVE Yes, okay, okay. In that sense, it can be misused. But when you learn about the Constitution in school, you should be taught what it actually says, not what some people *say* it says.

PAUL Is that what's really happening? I don't think so.

Look, when Kevin tells me the Constitution describes our government, he's already wrong. It doesn't describe our government. It describes what our government *ought to be.*

MAEVE Well, hopefully, that's the same thing.

PAUL *Hopefully.* But if you can't see the difference between what we the people agreed that our government should be, and what it's actually become under the pressure of special interests —always seeking more influence, more power and control— then the Constitution is *useless.*

MAEVE Yes, but it's not the sort of thing you can easily teach in high school.

PAUL But you've got to! If you just teach *respect* for the Constitution, if you try to make people good citizens by telling them they must *obey* the Constitution, and they don't know what it says, you're just setting them up as *patsies* for the despots who'll take control of the Constitution — tell them it's too sacred and awesome for them to understand, but they must obey what *they* say it says!

MAEVE Okay, take it easy, Paul. It's not so simple...

PAUL No, it's not simple. That's why I thought he should read the Federalist papers. They were written as advocacy for the ratification of the Constitution, so they explained all the features of the proposed government, and the reasons for them.

MAEVE A lot of books do that.

PAUL Yeah, and they *idolize* it. What sells is the sort of mythical —*worshipful*— view of the Founders as all-knowing patriotic deities that had all the answers to all the problems of self-government for all time.

MAEVE I think the Civil War showed that they didn't.

PAUL Of course. Look, they were mortals —*politicians*— struggling with the idea of government by the people, while struggling against each other to protect their own interests. They didn't have any exalted view of human nature. And they didn't have any exalted view of government, either. They thought of it in practical terms —as units with different functions— that should be able to contain the pressures of factions.

MAEVE They agreed that concentrated power was the precondition for tyranny.

PAUL Right. They knew monarchy wasn't the answer. They had enough examples of the arbitrary and capricious rule of kings. And *any* head of government, no matter how he's chosen, could become a dictator, if he were allowed to gain enough power to make his rule permanent.

MAEVE Well, they were also afraid of too much power in the legislature. They had the example —which was recent for them— of the British Parliament that took over, raised an army, executed King Charles, and established its own despotic rule.

PAUL Right, so the fundamental principle was that *power must not be concentrated*. No one person or group, neither the *executive* nor the *legislature*, should be allowed unlimited, unchecked power.

MAEVE That's why they wrote in the checks and balances.

PAUL Yes, and they *hoped* they were enough to keep the government from being taken over by any faction.

MAEVE Well, sure, they defined and limited the powers of each branch of the government, but how does that restrain the *factions*?

PAUL I think the assumption was, that if a faction succeeded in gaining control of one branch of the government —using it, of course, to serve its own interests— that branch would find opposition rather than cooperation from the other branches.

MAEVE Then we'd have a dysfunctional government.

PAUL That's one symptom of the rising power of a faction. But also, the faction could succeed with its agenda only if the branch it controlled *usurped* the powers of the other branches.

But the *attempt* by one branch to take power not authorized by the Constitution should be *a big red flag* —and the people must unite to oppose it.

Because—think about it— what is the purpose of a constitution to begin with?

MAEVE It's the agreement on the legitimate powers of each of the government branches.

PAUL Sure, an *agreement*. Who's going to hold them to the agreement?

MAEVE All government officers take an oath to uphold the Constitution.

PAUL An *oath*. Who's going to hold them to their oath?

MAEVE That's traditionally been the function of the Supreme Court.

PAUL Oh, *traditionally*. But the *Constitution* doesn't say that's their function.

MAEVE That's true, ... but someone has to...

PAUL And if a branch of the government takes that power —not authorized by the

Constitution— who's going to hold *it* to its legitimate powers?

MAEVE The checks and balances don't give any branch the power to permanently overrule the other branches. That would violate the principle of not allowing concentrations of power.

PAUL Right. The fundamental purpose of the Constitution is *visibility* —to allow everyone, in and out of government, to know how the government *ought* to be working.

So when the people see a usurpation of power —when they see one branch seeking to dominate the other branches, and take over their functions— the *people* must defend the Constitution. That's where the ultimate power must be.

MAEVE The problem is, Paul, usurpations always come with reasons — justifications. They'll say exceptional conditions, unforeseen by the founders, pose grave dangers to the nation.

PAUL There have always been and always will be exceptional conditions, dangers, crises. And crises' can be created by determined groups in and out of the government.

But whatever justification is offered, usurpation is a clear signal that one branch considers that expanding its own power is more important than the limitations imposed by the Constitution.

And if that justification is accepted, and the usurpation succeeds, the faction controlling that branch will gain power, confidence, and legitimacy. And further power-grabs will be inevitable, because it will no longer be possible to oppose them.

And it will continue until the other branches are entirely subdued. Power seeking is relentless and inexorable.

MAEVE Well, I don't know. That's such an extreme view.

PAUL Maeve, any group —any faction, any organization or unit of government— that has power will seek to preserve its power, and expand it. It will not limit itself. If there are to be any limits, they must be imposed from the outside.

MAEVE Yes, but what if a faction could gain control of all branches simultaneously? There's no guarantee that couldn't happen.

PAUL Absolutely there's no guarantee! The Framers were well aware that their theory of constitutional government just theory —an ideal— unsupported by evidence. More *speculation than practice*.

What examples did they have from history, of people ruling themselves?

MAEVE There were the ancient Greek and Roman democracies.

PAUL Yeah, and they ended in tyrannies.

MAEVE Then there were a few attempts at democracy in later European states. But they didn't last long.

PAUL Right, the Framers knew the odds were against it lasting. They called it an *experiment*.

But they thought it was a chance that had to be taken, since all other forms of government even more quickly turned into tyrannies.

But the constitutional form requires a politically educated public that knows its Constitution, knows about the pressure of factions seeking influence, power and control, and vigilantly guards against usurpations.

MAEVE That's certainly the ideal.

PAUL I hope you don't mean by *ideal* that it can't become reality. It's a *necessity*.

MAEVE I don't think high school students can understand all the nuances of a constitutional form of government.

PAUL But they've got to! If high school students don't learn it, fully and clearly, the Constitution is *worthless*.

MAEVE High school students will take it literally.

PAUL And they ought to!

MAEVE But then they see what's happening. They hear about the Supreme Court striking down laws, and they'll ask, where is that in the Constitution?

PAUL And they ought to!

MAEVE Then the teacher has got to get into the nuances…

PAUL The hypocrisy.

MAEVE Well, yeah, what teacher wants to be accused of hypocrisy?

PAUL Uh-huh.

MAEVE So the teacher has to walk a fine line, explain that even though the Supreme Court's power to overrule the President and Congress is *not* in the Constitution, it's been *accepted*.

PAUL And the students will ask, who came up with the idea, and who accepted it, and why?

And if one branch of the government *actually* has unlimited power to overrule the other branches, in spite of all that ballyhoo about checks and balances, and that power is *not even mentioned* in the Constitution, then what good is the Constitution?

MAEVE That's a lot to explain. And if you don't pull it off, you're just creating cynicism.

4. ORWELL

(*Erica enters the kitchen from the hallway. She is carrying a grocery bag.*)

ERICA No, no, you don't want *cynicism*. The teacher's got to be good at doublethink —good enough to teach it.

MAEVE Oh, hi, Erica.

ERICA Hi. Hi, Paul. 'Scuse me, I got your groceries here. (*She leaves the bag on the counter.*) I'll be back later with the snacks for the book club meeting.

MAEVE Thanks, Erica. But, *doublethink*? We talked about that.

ERICA Yeah, when we discussed *1984*.

MAEVE *1984* ?

PAUL She means Orwell's novel *1984*. She wanted the book club to read it.

ERICA And I still think we should.

MAEVE Oh. Well, the club was not into sci-fi…

ERICA It's not *sci-fi*! Orwell was a sharp political observer.

MAEVE Well, what we heard about it was so far-fetched. I mean, a government with the slogan SLAVERY IS FREEDOM? Who could believe that?

ERICA Nobody! And nobody believed it. Believing it was not the point. The Inner Party controlled all the mass media, and saturated the society with its ideological world-view. The slogans, like WAR IS PEACE, and IGNORANCE IS STRENGTH, were everywhere, but you can't even talk of whether they were *believed*, because they were not *understood*. They were there to be *accepted*, that's all.

MAEVE But they're just contradictory.

ERICA And it's not that nobody noticed. Many people were aware of it, but they couldn't make a coherent argument against them, because their words —words they thought they knew— didn't work for them any more. The definitions had changed. The Inner Party controlled the definitions of words.

And when words don't hold on to their meanings, reasoning is impossible, and arguments can't gain any traction. So the Inner Party's propositions were true *by definition*. You can't argue against a proposition that's true by definition.

Orwell wrote about the politicization of language. A totalitarian regime can allow freedom of speech, as long as it can effectively deny freedom of *thought*.

MAEVE Is that what's meant by doublethink?

ERICA Not exactly. The corruption of the language was to keep the general population confused, divided and unable to form opposition.

Doublethink was for the Party members —the lackeys and true believers— privileged to be a social class above the common people. It was their function to propagate the ideology used to subdue the people. They had to be trained for it.

It's the skill of believing two contradictory ideas, using whichever one the situation requires, and reflexively self-censoring —that is, *fearing, and immediately interrupting*— any thought that might expose the contradiction.

MAEVE I don't think History teachers have been trained for it.

ERICA Bu now we all get a chance to play this role. The media, controlled by the interest that controls the media, trains us

We're taught to accept ideals —exalted principles— and to hold them as high values. We're expected to revere these ideals. Any hint of skepticism or suspicion about them is taboo, socially unacceptable.

But in reality —well, we have the demands of reality. We must accept other ideas —very practical ones— because they are simply *necessary*.

Is there a contradiction?

MAEVE I don't know. I mean ... you're talking such in *generalities*.

ERICA Of course. If you don't see a contradiction, there's *doublethink*.

Anyway, I gotta run. I'll be back for the meeting.

MAEVE Oh, okay.

(*Erica leaves.*)

MAEVE Now we'll have to read the book.

PAUL Don't worry. She won't give up on it.

But anyway, here's my idea of what they teach the kids in school. The Constitution is our guarantee of freedom, because everyone can read it and see how our government *ought* to work. And no faction will ever be able to take over the government, because *everyone* must respect and *obey* the Constitution.

But as a practical matter, the Constitution has a lot of implications, so it's necessary for the Supreme Court to decide what it really means —what *they say* it says, even if it doesn't say it. And the Supreme Court has absolute power —so everyone must *obey*, and there's no appeal.

MAEVE Well, that's a rather ... *radical* way of putting it.

PAUL Oh, it's just too radical to say how things really work?

(*Mark returns.*)

MARK I'm sorry, I thought I had some, but, no.

PAUL No lubricant? All right, *whatever*. There's not much we can do about this right now.

MARK So, what's happening?

PAUL So I'll get a replacement for the fixture, and be back in a while. I got another stop to make anyway.

MARK Okay. I might not be here, but Maeve will.

PAUL Don't forget, Maeve —you won the argument.

MAEVE What?

PAUL Remember? Mark told you where his bunch of tools was.

MAEVE Oh, right, under the sink. He admitted that a *bunch* has a location.

MARK Admitted? Maeve, I didn't admit…

PAUL She's got you, Mark.

MARK No, no, it's a matter of definition…

PAUL Yeah, sure —you're trying to control the definitions.

MARK Not *control*, no. We just need a consensus.

PAUL Yeah, a consensus on *your* definition.

MARK No, not necessarily. Look, a consensus is a common understanding —but that means an *understanding*. That's all I'm proposing.

PAUL Yeah, sure.

MARK Seriously. If you think we can have a consensus on a different idea, I'll try to understand it. But you can't argue effectively against an idea you don't understand.

MAEVE A neat theory. But, *it is difficult to get a man to understand... when his salary depends upon his not understanding.*

MARK That's in reference to whom?

MAEVE Oh, no one. It was just a thought.

MARK Well, I'm presuming Paul doesn't have a dog in this race.

PAUL Really, I got better things to worry about.

MARK So, Maeve, tell him what it was about.

MAEVE I don't think he's interested.

PAUL No, tell me.

MAEVE All right, then. Mark says that collective nouns —words like *bunch* or *set* or *group*...

MARK Or association.

MAEVE … okay, or *association* —they're all abstract nouns. Which means they represent concepts, with no physical reality —no physical properties.

   (*Mark opens the cabinet below the sink.*)

MARK Not even a location. (*He reaches into the cabinet and grabs tools in each hand. He puts a few on the kitchen counter and goes to the dining area.*)

MAEVE Not even a location. A bunch doesn't have a location.

   (*Mark leaves several tools on the table and returns.*)

PAUL But then you said the bunch of tools was located under the sink.

MARK Yeah, I used an idiom. But if you believe the bunch of tools has a location, what is that location now?

PAUL Well, …

MAEVE No, no —*wait*! What *bunch* of tools are you referring to, Mark?

MARK The bunch ... comprised of the tools that were under the sink.

MAEVE Oh, come on! Who talks like that— "*bunch comprised of...*"? Why don't you just say, "The bunch that was under the sink"?

MARK Normally I would. Loosely speaking, ... well, that's how I speak when I don't expect my meaning to be questioned. Or distorted.

MAEVE Your meaning was quite clear.

MARK Yes, it was casual speech, idiomatic. Good enough for the intended purpose. But if you think it proves the *bunch* has a location, then tell me, what is its location now?

PAUL Okay, so now it doesn't have a location, but you know why? The tools are not in a bunch. That bunch doesn't exist anymore.

MARK Doesn't exist anymore! You mean it just went out of existence? *Poof*? Not even a *poof*, not even a puff of smoke? Physical things can't just vanish like that.

So I think you're proving my point. The bunch doesn't have any *physical* existence at all.

(*pause*)

But as far as existing, it still *exists* in our minds, as an idea. Which is the only existence it ever had.

PAUL Yeah, but people don't think about it that way. You're just splitting hairs.

MARK No, no —actually, the opposite is true. Distinctions are necessary. We can't communicate —or even think— without them. But for the benefit of *consensus*, we should make our distinctions along fault lines that can be universally recognized. There's no need to split hairs.

PAUL But that's what *you're* doing —splitting hairs. Making a big deal about a difference between the bunch and the things in the bunch.

MARK A big deal? It's the distinction between an idea and physical reality. It's the biggest deal I can think of. *Sanity* depends on it.

And all it needs is this simple, uniform rule: a conceptual object has no physical properties. Understanding that shouldn't be a big deal.

PAUL No, but you're wrong. Look, you go to the store and buy a bunch of apples. You know how you pay for it? By its *weight*. You put the bunch on a scale and you weigh it. So a bunch has a weight: a physical weight.

MARK Okay, I gave you a simple rule, but you want a more complicated one. You want to say a bunch has a physical property. So if it has one, why not others? Now you have a problem.

PAUL *I* don't have a problem.

(*Maeve has taken a bag of apples from the shopping bag on the counter, and is about to put it the refrigerator.*)

MARK Wait —just a minute! Would you give me the apples, Maeve?

(He takes the bag from her and dumps the contents —four green apples— onto the counter.)

MAEVE What are you doing?

MARK I want to determine the height —the *physical height* of this bunch of apples.

PAUL No, it's not the same thing.

MARK Why not? We'll just make a stack of the bunch, then use a ruler to get a height measurement.

PAUL No. Height is not a physical property of the bunch.

MARK Why not?

PAUL Because it's arbitrary. It changes whenever you rearrange the bunch. It's not a *persistent* feature.

MARK Okay, so the bunch doesn't have a physical height, but you still believe it has a physical weight. So let's weigh it and see.

MAEVE I don't think we can. The only scale we have goes up to only eight ounces.

MARK So we'll have to weigh each apple individually, and then add up the weights. Now, Paul, is that what you meant by the physical weight of the bunch?

Because I'd call that a conceptual weight. It's the *sum* of the weights of the *apples*.

PAUL But at the store, you put the whole bunch on the scale, so you get the weight —the *physical* weight— of the *bunch*.

MARK Yes, but if you put the apples on the scale one at a time you would see the scale reading increase by the weight of each apple you add. So the scale is *adding* up the weights of the *apples*.

PAUL But the weight that the scale is showing represents an actual *physical force* that's exerted on the scale, so it's the physical weight —of the *bunch*.

MARK But that physical force exists only when the apples are in the same place. That's not a persistent property of the bunch.

PAUL Sure it is. The bunch has exactly the same weight no matter where you take it.

MARK Each *apple* exerts its weight as a physical force, no matter where you take it. But forces that are not exerted at the same place do not make one physical force.

You can add them up and *call* it the weight of the bunch, but it's just an idea —a *statistic*, derived from the weights of the individual apples. It should be called the *total weight* of the bunch.

And there are other statistics, other conceptual weights. The bunch has an average weight, a minimum weight, a maximum weight, a median—

PAUL Okay, okay. So there are different ways of looking at it, but what's the point? Why do you need to insist that a bunch has no physical properties, when they're actually very useful concepts?

MARK But *physical properties* are not *concepts*. Physical reality is what we know through our senses, and what we assume others know similarly through their senses, because it's what we assume exists in the material world, whether or not any person is observing or thinking about it.

And my point was simply to recognize that *collectives* are conceptual, so all of their properties are conceptual, not physical.

PAUL It seems to me to be splitting hairs.

MARK If you don't care about the distinction between the members of a group and the group itself, you're losing the distinction between physical reality and ideology.

PAUL I can see the distinction. You don't have to split hairs.

MARK Then it wouldn't bother you to be told that this bunch of Granny Smith apples is a *green* bunch of apples?

PAUL It wouldn't bother me. That's just using words loosely. What's the big deal?

MARK So then you're okay with the bunch being green because the apples are green? Then by the same thinking, the Girl Scouts of America wears a green uniform.

PAUL What the hell do Girl Scouts have to do with it?

MARK The Girl Scouts of America is an association of girls. And it wears a green uniform.

PAUL No, the *Girl Scouts* wear green uniforms. Not the association.

MARK So now you see a difference. But maybe the association can't get into the uniform because it's overweight. How much do you think it weighs?

PAUL How much *it* weighs? How much the *Girl Scouts of America* weighs?

MARK Yeah. Just a ballpark guess.

PAUL That's a stupid question.

MARK Why? If bunch of apples has a weight, why not a bunch of girls?

PAUL The Girl Scouts of America is not just a bunch of girls. It's an organization. An organization doesn't have a weight.

MARK Oh, this is a distinction I didn't know about. If it's an organization, it doesn't have a weight. So if the bunch of apples got organized, it would lose its weight?

PAUL Oh, that's cute. Have you ever seen a bunch of apples get organized?

MARK No, but I can't imagine why that would cause it to lose its weight.

PAUL Well, we just don't think about an organization in terms of its physical properties.

MARK Right —because it doesn't have any.

PAUL Actually, it does, it's just not useful to think about it. You don't buy Girl Scouts by the pound.

MARK So The Girl Scouts of America actually has a physical weight? But suppose the organization disbanded —went out of business. Where would all that weight go?

    (*pause*)

PAUL All right. Look, I'll tell you what. You guys can go on and argue this forever, but I got things to do.

MARK Okay, so... what's happening?

PAUL I'll be back. With a new faucet, and my own bunch of tools ... which, incidentally, is located in my van.

MARK You mean the *tools* of the bunch are.

PAUL Yeah, whatever. See you in a while. (*Paul leaves.*)

5. THE FALLACY OF COMPOSITION

MAEVE How do you always get into an augment with Paul?

MARK What argument? There was no argument.

MAEVE He was getting a bit testy.

MARK That's just Paul. He thought *we* were having an argument.

MAEVE *We* weren't having an argument.

MARK Not at all, not at all. You just had this idea that an association of persons could be the *same thing* as a person.

MAEVE Hey, the Supreme Court said so.

MARK Yeah, but it's impossible for an association of *anything* to be the *same thing* as the members of the association.

MAEVE But an association is just an idea, so it's a matter of opinion. Yours against the Supreme Court's.

MARK But there can't be any consistency to that idea. It will *inevitably* lead to contradictions.

MAEVE Well, I told you an association of numbers could be a number, and you never showed that it leads to any contradiction.

MARK You said *addition*! But addition is *not* an association —not a collective, like bunch, set, or group. It's a *composition* of numbers.

In the composition of addition, the elements three and four produce a *composite* —seven— that's nothing but a number. But you can't tell from the composite what elements went into it. You don't know whether the *seven* was obtained from the composition of three and four, or from six and one, or from some other pair of numbers.

The elements of a composition lose their identity —they're *absorbed* into the composition.

That's what makes it different from an association. The elements of an association *keep their identity* in the association.

Addition is a *composition*, not an association.

MAEVE Well, then, excuse me! I mistook a composition for an association.

MARK But still, it was an imaginative example.

MAEVE Well, of course it was *imaginative* —because it was purely abstract. And you could have told me right away that that was the problem.

MARK No —let's be clear, abstraction itself wasn't the problem. The *real* problem is the muddling of the distinction between an association —which is always abstract— and a composition —which can be either physical or abstract.

Look, in the refrigerator, we have an association of eggs. It is not the same thing as a *composition* of eggs.

MAEVE How could we have a *composition* of eggs?

MARK How do you make an omelet?

MAEVE *Oh*! You can't make an omelet without cracking some eggs.

MARK Right. You start with an association, then combine the members so they lose their individual identities.

MAEVE You break the yolks and mix them all together. And put in a bit of Tabasco sauce.

MARK Sure, but the point is, you now have a *composition* of eggs — *and no longer have an association.*

MAEVE *Aha.*

MARK A composition doesn't even need the *one* property that every association has —the property of *number*. If you have an omelet, you don't even know how many eggs went into it.

MAEVE You could look at the recipe.

MARK You don't follow a recipe.

MAEVE Well, I don't, but you could count the eggshells.

MARK But you throw them into the disposal right away.

MAEVE Funny, I give you an example from mathematics, and you turn it into a cooking lesson.

MARK No, this is not about cooking —although actually, you might ease up on the Tabasco sauce. You know, I've got this acid reflux.

MAEVE I could substitute arsenic.

MARK Okay, but before you do that, listen. I was just trying to give your example from mathematics the respect it deserves. It was imaginative.

MAEVE But it's wrong. Addition is a composition, not an association.

MARK So you understand the difference.

MAEVE It's the difference between a bunch of eggs and an omelet. I should make an omelet anyway, before the eggs get rotten.

MARK And then we'd have a rotten bunch of eggs?

MAEVE No, no —just a bunch of rotten eggs. Properties of the members are not properties of the collective. And also, no omelet.

MARK Why not?

MAEVE I wouldn't make an omelet with putrid eggs. You'd get a putrid omelet.

MARK Right. Putrid eggs do not make a putrid association, but they will make a putrid composition.

A property of the elements of a composition *can* become a property of the *composite.*

MAEVE Not always. White eggs don't make a white omelet.

MARK Of course. Things can combine in many different ways, and their properties can either vanish, be transformed or become properties of the composite.

The point is that it's *not* possible for an association. The members retain all of their properties, and they don't become properties of the association.

MAEVE I think you made your point, now.

MARK And yet, thinking of an association as some sort of composition is a common error. They have a name for it — *the fallacy of composition.*

MAEVE *Who* has a name for it?

MARK Logicians. It's taught in logic. You *have heard* of the fallacy of composition, haven't you?

MAEVE Um … I'm offended that you would even ask me such a question.

MARK I'll take that for a negative. It doesn't matter. The point is to *recognize* the fallacy.

MAEVE *The fallacy of composition* is saying a bunch of green apples is a green bunch of apples.

MARK Good. And the *fallacy of composition* is saying the Girl Scouts of America wears a green uniform.

MAEVE Shame that Paul's missing this lesson on *the fallacy of composition.*

MARK I think he got it with the Girl Scouts fallacy.

MAEVE I don't believe anyone's ever made *that* particular mistake.

MARK But it happens all the time, in casual language. Like saying the Los Angeles Lakers is a tall basketball team.

MAEVE That's the fallacy … No, wait. Wait. I assume the *players* are tall, and of course height is of some importance in basketball. So I get what you mean when you say the Lakers is a tall team. I don't know if it's true, but what you *mean* is that it's tall *compared to other teams*.

So it seems to me that height is a useful concept for comparing basketball teams.

MARK Yes, that's just it, a *concept*, not a physical height. And as concept, it depends on a *consensus* —we must agree on how that team height is computed. Is it the average height of all the players? Or the median height? Or is it the average, or of median, of the starting five? Or some statistic taken from the centers and forwards? Or some average weighted by playing time?

MAEVE Picky, picky.

MARK Look, if you're inclined to agree with the assertion, there's no need for a consensus on how to determine that conceptual height.

Maybe you just want to pass the time arguing about it. So then, okay.

But if your livelihood and entire fortune depended on a *legal* determination about a team's height, you ought to get picky, because the *fallacy of composition* is fertile ground for deception.

MAEVE Okay, the *players* on the team may be tall, but the *team* is an abstraction — it doesn't have any physical height.

MARK Right. And the *fallacy of composition* is saying that the Mormon Tabernacle Choir is a Mormon.

(*pause*)

MAEVE No, wait. Now that's *really* different. Now you've taken it too far.

MARK Why?

MAEVE Because religion is not a *physical* property. It's ideology —it's totally abstract.

I mean, if you ask *me* if the Mormon Tabernacle Choir is a Mormon, I'd say, no —*in my opinion.* But I'm not qualified to make that judgment. Only the Elders of the Church of Jesus Christ of Latter-day Saints have the authority to say what a Mormon is.

MARK No, no. The Elders may be able to say *who* is a Mormon, but it's a universal —a societal consensus— that only a *person* can have a religion.

MAEVE The Elders might disagree with you. There may be some esoteric theological reasoning that's unknown to you.

MARK But whatever that reasoning might be, it would still depend on a trick of words —applying the same label to entirely different *things.* A person that's a Mormon is *not the same thing* as an association that's a Mormon, even if it's decreed that the label Mormon must apply to both.

And there's no religious bias here. The Southern Baptist Convention is not a Baptist. The College of Cardinals is not a Cardinal —nor is it a Catholic.

And if the Pope were to issue an encyclical that said it was a Catholic, he'd simply be changing the definition of the *noun* Catholic —a *person* of the Catholic faith— by including non-human entities.

MAEVE Well, maybe. But the Supreme Court seems to assume that an association of persons *is* a person.

MARK It's nothing but the *fallacy of composition.*

(*pause*)

MAEVE I'll tell you what your problem is, Mark. You live in this world of metaphysics and you think you can apply it to the real world.

MARK You're not going to claim mathematics has no relation to the real world?

MAEVE Of course it does, but it doesn't go far enough. If putting numbers together just makes *compositions,* you don't have any associations.

MARK No, no, there *are* associations of numbers. I just said *addition* wasn't one of them.

If they're in an association, the numbers don't lose their identities. That's done through the *discipline* of mathematics.

MAEVE Oh, by some mathematical hocus-pocus.

MARK No, it's not magic. I could show an example. Think of the numbers as lengths of line segments that have different orientations.

Suppose this… (*he extends an index finger*)… is a line segment of a certain length. And this… (*he extends his other index finger*)… is another.

Now if the two line segments have the same orientation… (*he points both fingers in the same direction*) … and you put them end to end … (*keeping them pointed the same way, he puts the tip of one finger at the knuckle of the other*) …

… then you could have a single line segment with a length that's the sum of the two lengths.

MAEVE Umm, that would seem to be a *composition* of line segments.

MARK Yes. Yes, it is. But if they have different orientations… (*pointing off in various directions*) … the line lengths will not add, so they'll maintain their identity in an association of line segments.

MAEVE Oh, but you were telling me about an association of *numbers*.

MARK Yes, that would be the set of numbers representing the *lengths* of the segments. But, because the segments are not oriented the same way, it makes no sense to add their lengths. The numbers keep their identity. There's no composition.

MAEVE Umm, so what's an association of line segments?

MARK Any random line segments you want to consider as a set. Or, more usefully, you could select them to meet certain conditions.

Here, suppose you have three line segments, in different orientations. One… (*he extends the index finger of his left hand*)… two … (*he extends the thumb of his left hand*) … three (*he extends the index finger of his right hand*).

Now, as long as the length of each line segment is less than the sum of the lengths of the other two, we can put the endpoint of each segment at the same place as the endpoint of one other segment … (*he brings the tips of both index fingers together, and the tip of the left thumb to the knuckle of the right index finger.*)

… and you have an association of line segments.

MAEVE Aha. A triangle.

MARK Yes. And what are its properties? It is *two-dimensional*. It has *corners*. It has *angles*. It has *sides*. It has an *area*.

These are *not* the properties of a line segment.

MAEVE They must be your *emergent* properties.

MARK Of course. They *emerge* in the association. And, the properties of a line segment —one length, two end points— are *not* the properties of a triangle.

Could you imagine anyone claiming that this association of line segments —a triangle— *is* a line segment?

MAEVE Well, that would *seem* to be an extreme case of the fallacy of composition.

MARK Of course!

MAEVE But, since everything here depends on definitions, it could be true *by definition*.

MARK No! The contradictions you'd get would be overwhelming. For example, if two line segments with different orientations intersect, they can intersect at only one point. That's not true, and you can't make it true, for triangles.

An association of line segments is a completely different *thing* than a line segment.

MAEVE Okay, but what I'm saying is that since the only reality of an abstraction is *consensus* on a definition, if there were a Supreme Court of Mathematics, it could simply *rule* that by definition, a triangle *is* a line segment.

Then the consensus would have to follow, because of the Court's power to make it true *by definition*.

MARK Well, yeah, but then real mathematicians would leave the field, because they couldn't handle all the contradictions.

Of course, as long as there's money and status in the field, they'd be replaced by hacks and charlatans, who would advance their careers by reinventing mathematics as the discipline of guessing what will please the Supreme Court.

(*pause*)

MAEVE But your academic examples are too simple.

MARK No, no. The simple examples demonstrate the *fundamental* principles, clearly.

MAEVE But you can't apply that to everything in the real world! In the real world, things are more complex.

MARK Yes, there are a lot of details that distract and maybe confuse you. That's why the simple example is important.

MAEVE But if you consider an association of living beings, it's fundamentally different.

MARK It is different, but not fundamentally. What's fundamental is what you have after stripping away the details. That's what I demonstrated. An association has emergent properties, and they are not the properties of the members. And the members' properties are not properties of the association.

MAEVE But living creatures interact with each other. That makes things dynamic, more complex. You don't see emergent properties...

(*A knock on the front door. Mark goes to the door and opens it. No one is there.*)

NADIA (*from outside*) Come look!

(*Mark goes out the door. The honking of geese is heard. Maeve goes to the door. Mark enters, followed by Nadia, who is carrying a laundry bag.*)

MAEVE What were you looking at?

NADIA A skein of Canada geese, right overhead —in a perfect Vee.

MAEVE Canadian geese?

NADIA Canada geese. From a distance, a skein always seems to have quite an acute angle. But from right below, you can see the angle's wider, maybe more than 45 degrees.

MAEVE Oh, you mean the angle the flock makes.

NADIA Well, I call it a skein.

MAEVE The angle?

NADIA No, the flock. It's the archaic word for the collective being. From times when people were more sensitive to nature.

MAEVE So we call it a flock. Is that insensitive?

NADIA I don't think the skein is offended. But if both sheep and pigeons can form a flock, it seems to me a generic term for a shapeless blob. Nothing like that elegant V-shaped being formed by Canada geese.

MARK Nadia, you came to do laundry?

NADIA Yes. Oh, I'm sorry, I told Maeve...

MAEVE Her washer's still out...

MARK Yeah, okay, but at the moment I've got a load in our machine.

NADIA So I'll come back later...

MARK No —it'll just be a few minutes.

MAEVE Stay. I've got some fresh coffee.

NADIA Okay, thanks. Coffee sounds good.

MAEVE I'm wondering why you call the skein a *being*.

NADIA I just mean that it's alive. It's a life form. Now don't ask me what life is.

MAEVE But it's the *geese* that are alive. Why do you call the *skein* a being?

NADIA A *being* is a rather general idea: a life form that exhibits a seemingly intentional behavior. Human beings and animals are physical beings. Also, perhaps, the extraterrestrials that may or may not have visited us.

There are supernatural beings, as angels or devils. And there are fictional beings —dragons, unicorns, Godzilla and Dr. Frankenstein's monster.

And there are also abstract beings —groups of various kinds. Herds, flocks — collectives under different names.

MAEVE I don't see what they all have in common.

NADIA It's a broad generality. If there's anything you don't want to include, just leave it out.

MAEVE Umm ...

NADIA   Then if anything's left at all, that's what I'm talking about.

MAEVE   But, umm … okay, you said an *animal* is a being. Also, an association of animals is a being. But then, because animals are beings, the association of animals would be an association of beings.

So then you're saying that an association of beings is a being.

And Mark should be getting upset about that, because *he* claims that's impossible.

MARK   It may *sound* like it, but that wasn't my point.

MAEVE   Oh, I should have known. He always does this.

MARK   Well, look, I'm sure you'd agree that an apple is a fruit. But I don't suppose you'd agree if I said that an apple is *the same thing* as a fruit.

MAEVE   No, then the bananas and peaches would feel left out.

MARK   Right. It's easily understood with physical things. But in metaphysics, things exist only in their definitions.

So anyone can create —through definition— weird and unnatural metaphysical objects.

NADIA   A strange use of the word *unnatural* — for metaphysical objects.

MARK   Right, right. They're all *unnatural*. What I meant was the bizarre business of uniting physical and abstract objects in a single definition, through the use of the word '*or*'.

For example —and I'm not sure Nadia said this, exactly, but— suppose she had defined a *being* to be *either* an animal —*or*— an association of beings.

With that definition, it would be correct to say that an association of beings *is* a being —just like an apple *is* a fruit.

But it would not be right to say that an association of beings is *the same thing as* a being —any more than an apple is *the same thing as* a fruit.

MAEVE   But that's completely obvious.

MARK   So that's all I was saying! An association of *anything* cannot be *the same thing* as the members of the association.

MAEVE   But that's *obvious*. If you didn't use the word '*or*' to include an animal as part of the definition, you'd be defining a *being* to be an *association* of beings.

And that would be a totally circular definition. Meaningless.

MARK   Right! That's what I was telling you before.

MAEVE   That much is obvious. But … even so, there's a problem. Even if an association of beings is just one *alternative* in your definition —as one *kind* of being— what's the justification for it?

MARK   There is none. It's the power of definition. I could define, uh, a *queetfloop* to be, uh, … a left-handed pipe wrench —*or*— a purple sunset.

MAEVE   What's a queetfloop?

MARK A left-handed pipe wrench or a purple sunset.

MAEVE That's crazy. Where is the commonality?

MARK There doesn't have to be any. They're united only in the definition.

MAEVE I can't even get my head around what you might be talking about if you were to use that word.

NADIA No, Mark. What you've actually done there, is to give one word two different definitions. That is, it has two different *senses.* In use, one or the other will be chosen, from context.

MAEVE That's right. Like a *ball* can be thrown to get a runner out, or a *ball* can be thrown to honor the debutants. The word *ball* has different definitions.

NADIA And so does *throw.* But the context easily shows which definition is being used.

MARK Sure, sure —that's the way language *usually* works. But if I'm the legal authority, I can deliver an *edict*: "All queetfloops are equal."

NADIA But then, that too would depend on context. If the edict were given in the context of a plumbing job, you'd be saying all left-handed pipe wrenches are equal, and if—

MARK No, *no*! If I'm the legal authority with *absolute power*, I can insist that my edict means "*All* queetfloops are equal, *regardless of kind.*"

MAEVE But that's *crazy*! Declaring that wrenches and sunsets are equal? You can't make things that are fundamentally different equal just by declaring that they are!

NADIA Words can't change reality.

MARK You should tell that to the Supreme Court. They just ruled that a human being and a business organization are *equal*, because they're *persons.*

MAEVE Oh, come on, now you're back to that again?

MARK Maeve, what do you think this is about? If you accept a definition, you accept the nonsense that's built into it.

MAEVE Maybe, but … okay, wait. Wait. I want to understand this. If Nadia's defined a *being* to be either an animal or an association of beings, then you could say an association of beings *is* a being. Not just that it's *like* a being, or *similar to* a being, but that it *is* a being. That means it has *all* of the properties of a being— whatever they might be.

Like an apple is a fruit, because it has all of the properties of a fruit. And so does a banana. And if you wanted to know whether a tomato's a fruit, you'd ask whether it has *all* the properties of a fruit. If it does, it is; if it doesn't, it isn't.

So by her definition, we get that an association of beings *is* a being, and that's saying that an association of beings has *all* the properties of a being. And isn't that just the fallacy of composition?

MARK It would be, if it weren't for the '*or.*' In her definition, an association of beings *doesn't* have to have *all* of the properties that define a being, just all of one set of properties, out of two sets.

By that definition, a being must have *either* all the properties that define an animal, *or* all the properties that define an association of beings.

MAEVE So then she's defined a being, but *does her definition tell us what the properties of a being are?*

MARK Not definitively. They're either the properties of an animal, *or* the properties of an association of beings.

MAEVE But then *what are* the properties of an association of beings? Oh, yes, *number* —because every association has a *number* of members. But are there other emergent properties?

MARK We talked of this before. Since there are two kinds of beings in her definition, an association could be uniform: all animal, or uniform: all association, or mixed.

MAEVE Arrgh! Mixed! Look, that doesn't give us any idea about the kinds of things we'd like to know about a being, like its *behavior.* We'd like to know about properties that emerge from how beings behave in association.

And we haven't finished defining what a being *is.* So the definition is still circular. Nadia was just playing a trick with words in her definition.

MARK If you accept a definition, you accept whatever's needed to make it work. If you can't see it clearly, you'll be at the mercy of the authority that made the definition.

NADIA Well, my idea of a being was based on behavioral properties.

And, to tell the truth, I have never actually seen an association of angels, nor one of unicorns, so I have no idea of whether either of those would have the *behavioral* properties that would move me to call it a *being.*

So if I implied that an association of *beings* is a being, I'm sorry. I'll take it back.

But I will assert that an association of *animals* is a being, and not by the fallacy of composition, but by observations of its behavior.

If you'd ever seen a colony of army ants as a dark shadow slithering along the forest floor, you'd understand it to be a being. Not just a being, but a carnivore. It extends itself in columns like pincers that surround and envelop any insect or small animal not agile enough to get out of its path, and it simply *ingests* it.

At night, it curls itself up into a ball like a possum and hangs from a fallen branch and becomes inert. You might want to say it's sleeping.

You might even want to call it an animal. And it would be that, but for the fact that each of its hundreds of thousands of cells provides its own locomotion.

MAEVE But that's just a *perception.* It's still a *society*, not an animal.

NADIA No, it's not an animal. But what is perceived, and what defines it as a *being*, is its behavior. The behavior of the colony cannot be seen in the behavior of an individual ant. The aggregate behavior is of a different order, and so must be attributed to a different entity.

MARK It's a being because if its emergent behavioral properties.

MAEVE I can see how that might be a perception for colonies of ants —or bees, or termites. But I don't see it for animals of higher order.

NADIA And what distinction would you make to deny it? Yes, mammals are more complex than insects, their groups are smaller in number, and they have different mechanisms of coordination.

But a wolf pack is an association of wolves, just as the army ant colony is an association of army ants. In each case the behavior of the aggregate is not that of the individuals. And so it's a being.

MAEVE But with a higher order animal —a mammal— we can understand its motivations. A wolf hunts when it gets hungry. So it's expected that the wolf pack hunts also.

NADIA We use the word *hunt* for the activity of both a wolf and a wolf pack. But their actions are different. A lone wolf will chase a rabbit for a meal, but won't try to attack a moose.

MAEVE You don't think a wolf would attack a moose?

NADIA The wolf is looking for a meal, not a fight. Those antlers could injure him, and an injury that impairs his ability to hunt could be fatal. Would you go to a restaurant where you had to fight the headwaiter to the death to get a table?

MAEVE Probably not very often…

NADIA But the wolf pack can safely attack a larger animal, because it can surround it, and then attack from the rear.

What the wolf pack does is not the same as what a lone wolf does. The pack is a being, but an abstract being, not an animal.

And, from antiquity, collective beings have been given distinctive names —a skein of geese, a flock of sheep, a covey of quail, a pride of lions, a pack of wolves, a shoal of fish.

We don't just say 'group of lions' and 'group of wolves', because they have different behaviors, different personalities. A pride of lions doesn't hunt in the same way a wolf pack does.

For each species of social animal, the collective being involves the animals in their totality, and serves the survival needs of the species.

MAEVE Of course, that would be true for human beings also. The natural group is the family.

NADIA You should worry about using word *natural* for anything concerning human beings. Nothing about society is free of human influence, so it can't be truly natural.

MAEVE But families exist in all societies.

NADIA Even so, this *natural* grouping varies with culture. We don't believe a family even exists unless it's sanctioned by a religious ritual or legal ceremony.

But the significant point is that our influence on each other through language has enabled the formation of many other types of collective beings, which are based on —and serve— only selected human characteristics. There are all kinds of human organizations.

MAEVE Yes, and the collective of human beings would be a diluted form of human being.

MARK No, it's a *being*. Don't call it a *human* being.

NADIA And there's no reason to say *diluted*. *Whatever* sort of being it is, it's more particularly *that* sort of being because its members are selected for particular characteristics.

Think of a football team as an abstract being. Its *purpose* is to win football games. The members are selected for size and athletic skills. If you were to broaden the selection criteria to include eloquence, musical talent and skill at macramé, you could still have a team, but one with less chance for postseason play.

And considering the diversity of human characteristics, you'd be hard pressed to make generalizations that cover the diversity of collective beings.

MAEVE Well, there *are* theories of social organizations or societies, and no lack of generalizations.

NADIA Any theory of social organization requires a theory of human nature, whether or not it's explicitly stated. And there's the problem.

MARK Karl Marx analyzed society as an economic system, so he considered a person to be an economic being.

NADIA And that's a major flaw in the theory of communism.

MAEVE On the other hand, if a corporation is a being, it certainly *is* an economic being.

MARK So Karl Marx said a person is an economic being, and now the Supreme Court says an economic being is a person. Does anyone think this is progress?

NADIA The ideologies of both communism and capitalism are based on ideas, or idealizations, of human nature.

MAEVE But, Nadia, I'm sure you meant that to have a *valid* theory of social organization you need *valid* theory of human nature.

NADIA Of course, but the problem is circular reasoning. Each idea validates the other. Our view of human nature is shaped by society, and society is shaped by our view of human nature.

MAEVE So you can't think your way out of this.

NADIA You might get some insight by considering human behavior in great generality, as an abstraction beyond the apparent form of the activity. A child growing up is constantly faced with new challenges, and it seeks to overcome them by attaining more capability, skill, influence, control. In a general sense, it's seeking to increase its *power*.

But personal development doesn't end when physical growth ends. The mature individual goes through many phases too, encountering new vistas with new fears and new threats, and constantly tries to overcome by gaining influence and control —power over him or herself, over the environment, over others.

This quest for personal development takes many different forms, which vary with innate disposition, social position or individual experience, and which are mediated by society. But the generality, beyond the form, is power-seeking.

MARK   It's a broad generality, and vague enough.

MAEVE   I don't see how it applies to associations.

NADIA   Well, why do people join associations? For as many different reasons as there are human motivations. In the most general sense, though, they want to increase their power; they are motivated by self-aggrandizement.

MAEVE   Yes, but as a rule, in joining an association you have to *give up* certain powers or freedoms that you have outside the association. It's a loss as much as a gain.

NADIA   Sometimes. But security, freedom, influence, power, take many forms. The personal freedoms given up are not valued by the individual as much as the forms of power gained, so it's perceived as a net gain.

MAEVE   But if your view of human nature is simply power-seeking, what does that say about the association? If you claim it also has power-seeking behavior, that would seem to be simply the fallacy of composition.

NADIA   People are motivated to join associations to increase their power, but it shouldn't be assumed that membership always satisfies the need. People vary — some would still want greater power.

MAEVE   They can join another, more powerful association.

NADIA   Or, they could gain power by seeking a leadership position within the association.

Now, if the association chooses its leaders on the basis of seniority, for example, you should not be surprised to find that the only new initiatives it undertakes are those that were novel when those leaders were young.

But most leadership positions are chosen through influence among the members —members who joined in their quest for power. In the competition for leadership, the only winning strategy is to advocate more effective, or more aggressive policies to achieve the purposes of the organization.

So you could conclude that any association is motivated to increase its effectiveness, or power. That's not the fallacy of composition.

MARK   And that's nothing *at all* like saying that an association of persons *is* a person.

NADIA   Of course not. The forms of power an organization can wield *cannot be the same* as those of an individual.

The association's power will be more formal, using the law, publicity and mass action. A boycott or strike by an individual is meaningless. As a person, carrying the power of your one vote, you can try to influence your congressman, but that is not at all the same as what a corporation does. It sends lobbyists, bearing the corporation's inducements and threats, to meet with the congressman.

MAEVE   But the lobbyists are people.

MARK Yes, but agents of the corporation.

NADIA And they're sociable people too. They smile and laugh at the congressman's jokes and flatter his wife and ask about his children, share stories of their own children and indulge *all* the congressman's opinions. But they're agents of the corporation, paid to use their personal charms to enable the *corporation* to get what *it* wants.

The association itself can't influence others with emotional connections, by empathy —by inducing a true feeling of kinship or friendship, or intimacy. An association can't coax, entreat, challenge, goad or cajole a person, using insights gained by self-knowledge.

MAEVE But an organization can transmit human emotion, by videos.

NADIA Yes, of course, it can simulate and stimulate emotions. But, don't you see, that although that *appears* to be a personal interaction, it is an *artifice*. There is the intervention of professionals here, who have the technical knowledge, the technology and the techniques to *simulate* human emotions. And not only simulate, but amplify, with lighting, makeup, camera angles...

MARK They also have control over the frame, the background, scenes of violence and terror, or the security of family and home, or patriotic images of national power and glory.

And the background sounds that stir emotions beneath any conscious awareness —a baby crying, a terrified child pleading, angry, threatening voices, or else the subtle soothing violin...

NADIA That's all emotional manipulation. The simulated human emotions can be projected on the platforms of power, by professionals acting dispassionately, without the *real* human emotion actually existing, anywhere.

When emotional appeals are made by an individual, they may or may not be sincere, but when made by an organization, they are guaranteed not to be.

6. THE YANKEES

(The front door opens. A 16-year-old boy enters, removing his backpack.)

KEVIN Hi, Gramp. Hey, Maeve!

MAEVE Hello, Kevin.

KEVIN I gotta hang out for a while. Mom's picking me up.

MAEVE Sure.

NADIA Hi.

MAEVE *(to Kevin)* You know Nadia, don't you?

KEVIN Oh, yeah. Hi.

MARK How was soccer practice?

KEVIN It was okay. *(He goes to the far end of the table in the dining area and sets up his laptop computer.)*

MAEVE Are you hungry? I could make an omelet.

KEVIN No thanks, I'm good. *(He sits and focuses his attention on the computer.)*
   (The others regard the boy. He seems absorbed with the computer.)

MAEVE Anyway, … so I guess we've solved that problem.

NADIA I'm glad we did. What problem was that?

MAEVE The Supreme Court's announcement that a corporation is a person.

NADIA *A corporation is a person*? I don't think so.

MARK Nobody thinks so. It's an absurdity.

MAEVE *(Noticing Kevin's attention.)* Kevin, what do you think? Is a corporation a person?

KEVIN I don't know.

MARK You don't *know* if a corporation is a person?

KEVIN I mean, that's just … like, a figure of speech, isn't it?

MAEVE You mean like a simile?

KEVIN Yeah, like a simile.

NADIA Or is it a metaphor?

KEVIN Right, it's a metaphor.

MAEVE It's like when you say life is just a bowl of cherries.

KEVIN Yeah.

MARK *Is* life a bowl of cherries? What do you think, Kevin?

KEVIN It could be, if you cherry-pick the good parts.

MAEVE Hey, good one, Kevin.

NADIA But after the good parts, it's just the pits.

KEVIN Hey, good one, Nadia.

MARK But if you were asked, "What is life?" Could you really answer, life *is* a bowl of cherries?

KEVIN It depends on what the meaning of *is* is.

MAEVE Hey, Kevin's got the chops of a real politician.

MARK You understand, Kevin, that when we say that one thing *is* another thing, the plain meaning is that the one thing has *all* the properties that define the other thing.

KEVIN Sure.

MARK But when we mean that the one thing has *one* outstanding characteristic of the other, that's a metaphorical use of the word *is*. It should never be confused with the primary meaning.

KEVIN Yeah. So, '*a corporation is a person*' is a metaphor.

MAEVE Right.

MARK But it's no longer *just* a metaphor. It's now a legal ruling —the highest law in the land.

NADIA I never supposed legal rulings were based on poetic language.

MAEVE They're not *supposed* to be.

MARK No, but there's also some pseudo-logical argument behind it that muddles the distinction between the singular and the plural. It's guaranteed to lead to more absurdities.

NADIA You mean more tough questions for the Supreme Court to resolve.

MAEVE Yes, and all of them *constitutional* questions —beyond the authority of Congress.

KEVIN I don't see how you can mix up the singular and plural.

MARK I don't know either, Kevin. Suppose I asked you this: Who *are* the New York Yankees?

KEVIN Well, Derek Jeter,...

MARK Right, Derek Jeter and whoever else they re-sign...

KEVIN Hey, Hideki Matsui, World Series MVP!

MAEVE I'm not sure that's good enough anymore, Kevin.

MARK Okay, now I'll ask a different question. What *is* the New York Yankees?

KEVIN Uh, ... a team.

MARK Yes. The New York Yankees *is* a major-league baseball team. It's the team that in the past had the players Babe Ruth, Joe DiMaggio, Mickey Mantle, and currently has Derek Jeter and some other guys.

But the players are not the team. Players come and go. The team goes on.

MAEVE I believe the New York Yankees is also a corporation.

MARK Right. And the Supreme Court says a corporation is a person, so now there's no *legal* reason why the New York Yankees couldn't put the New York Yankees in at second base and batting third in the lineup!

KEVIN What? That's crazy!

MARK It is, it's totally crazy!

(*The doorbell rings. Maeve opens front door. It is Charles, the lawyer.*)

MAEVE Hello Charles.

CHARLES Maeve. Hey, Mark. How are you?

MARK Fine. Come on in.

CHARLES Hey Kevin, how you doing?

KEVIN Hey, Charles…

MAEVE We haven't seen you in a while.

CHARLES Been busy. I don't get back here very often.

KEVIN Hey Gramp, tell Charles what you just said.

MARK About the Supreme Court decision?

KEVIN Yeah, Charles —he said it means the New York Yankees can put the New York Yankees in to play second base.

MARK Or any position, really.

MAEVE Not shortstop though.

MARK Well, of course not.

CHARLES What are you talking about?

MARK The Supreme Court ruling. The *Citizens United* case.

CHARLES Oh, yeah.

MARK Have you heard about this ruling? The Supreme Court says a corporation is a person.

KEVIN And because the New York Yankees is a corporation, they can put the New York Yankees in to play second base.

CHARLES That's ridiculous.

MARK It is, isn't it? It's *totally* ridiculous.

CHARLES No, what *you* said is ridiculous.

MARK What *I* said? *I'm* not the one who said a corporation is a person.

CHARLES You know it's just a legal designation. A corporation is a person in the eyes of the law, with the same rights as a person.

MARK Like the right to play second base?

CHARLES There is no *right* to play second base. You have to be a natural person to play in a baseball game.

MARK Really? Where does it say that?

CHARLES There are league rules.

MARK Oh, thank God for the league rules.

MAEVE Charles, why did you say *natural* person?

KEVIN You have to be a natural to play shortstop.

CHARLES In legal terminology, the word *person* could refer to an organization, like a corporation. So the term *natural person* is used to designate a human being.

MAEVE Oh, so if you say to one of your lawyer friends, "I met a person on the street yesterday…," he would have to ask, "Was it a natural person or a corporation?"

CHARLES (*with a hard look at Maeve*) You don't meet a corporation on the street.

MARK Okay, but suppose your lawyer friend tells you, "I'm representing a person contesting a tax assessment," you would ask, "A natural person or a corporation?"

CHARLES (*with a withering look at Mark*) First of all, he would have said, "I have a *client* …" And secondly, when I said it's legal terminology, I meant it's what's written in legal documents —for precision— but we can actually *speak* the language of the people.

MARK Okay, okay Charles, I assume you're right about the league rules, but have you actually checked? Because they might just say '*person*' instead of '*natural person*,' and so that wouldn't keep the corporations off the field.

CHARLES Come on, just use some common sense, would you?

MARK Charles, the Court just said a corporation is a person, and you're making an appeal to *common sense*? The common sense barrier has been trampled!

CHARLES Come on, that's such a naïve reaction. You're not aware of the legal context.

MARK A corporation is *not* a person— it's a completely different thing! What legal context changes that?

CHARLES A corporation has legal rights, and the courts have to deal with that. It was necessary to resort to the legal fiction that it's person in order to retain the consistency of the law.

MARK A legal *fiction*!

CHARLES Yes, that's actually a well-established legal concept. Justice Harlan F. Stone wrote, "…**fictions are sometimes invented in order to realize the judicial conception of justice**… "

MARK A *fiction*!

CHARLES It's done out of a legal necessity.

MARK So they just *make things up*!

CHARLES Not just *anything* —there must be consistency with precedents. You just don't understand the law.

MARK That's for sure, for sure. But what worries me is that you *think* you *do*. Can you explain how this bizarre idea got into a law?

CHARLES It's not a new idea. It was decided a long time ago, in an interpretation of the Fourteenth Amendment, that a corporation has equal protection of the law. This decision just extended it to the First Amendment.

MARK Just like that! Just extended it back a hundred years to when the Bill of Rights was written —when most people had never even heard of a corporation— and then claim that the Bill of Rights was written for corporations!

CHARLES I don't think the Court claimed the Bill of Rights was written for corporations. That would be *original intent*. But that's not the modern doctrine.

MARK Oh, original intent —you mean the idea that the Constitution means what the people who wrote it intended to mean? That's got to be a *doctrine*?

CHARLES Look, constitutional interpretation is not as simple a matter as you think. Society changes, and so the Constitution's meaning to society must change, too.

MAEVE It seems its meaning to the Supreme Court is changing a lot faster.

CHARLES Well it's obvious that over the years the Court's expanded its power of judicial review.

MARK Really! And that makes it okay? And you go along with it?

CHARLES Well, they're the Supreme Court, so you have to agree. But it was an activist interpretation.

MARK *Activist* is not the word! Oh sure, the law journals will have a lot of serious handwringing about judicial activism and judicial restraint, but none of them will be able to say what happened here because they haven't got the vocabulary for it.

CHARLES The *vocabulary*?

MARK They won't use the only word that properly describes it...

CHARLES And that would be...?

MARK *Bullshit*! It's plain bullshit. Not even high-quality bullshit!

KEVIN Hey, Maeve —Gramp said bullshit!

MAEVE Watch your language!

KEVIN Yeah, Gramp, you're not allowed to say...

MAEVE I was talking to you!

KEVIN But I was just telling you...

MAEVE I don't care what he said! I don't want you using that language.

KEVIN What about my First Amendment rights?

CHARLES Bullshit is not a legal term.

MARK Exactly! That's exactly the problem! That's why there's no legal explanation for this decision! You don't have a word for a concoction of asininity and deceit that comes down from the highest authority!

CHARLES Mark, you can say you disagree, you can say you don't like it —but there's no need to use obscenities.

MARK You should be using the word obscenity for this *opinion.* Your legal language is worn out! What word do you have for political deception in the highest court in the land, that usurps the constitutional power of Congress and the President, through the *sham* of constitutional interpretation? Obscenity is a good word...

MAEVE Mark, Mark —excuse me ... you know Nadia... needs to do her laundry, and you've still got a load in the machine.

   (*pause*)

MARK (*sighs*) Hshss... (*Mark walks off, through the kitchen.*)

CHARLES Maeve, I've never seen him get so upset. What is his problem?

MAEVE He sees the distinction between the singular and the plural being muddled. He believes that distinction is profound not just in language, but in logic and reasoning —and when it is muddled, clear thinking is impossible.

CHARLES Oh, you mean what *he* calls clear thinking.

MAEVE You think it's so subjective? I think if it's clear, it must be capable of being communicated. People will follow, if it's clear, because our minds seek clarity.

NADIA Well, not always. If the reasoning threatens the core of one's reality, that's frightening. Fear will interrupt logic.

MAEVE Oh, that's true, too. *"It is difficult to make a man understand ... when his salary depends on his not understanding."*

CHARLES Lawyers can understand it. Lawyers can follow the reasoning.

NADIA Really? That's such a comfort to me. And I'm sure all Americans will be pleased to know that we don't have to worry about our constitutional rights —and why even bother making the kids learn about it?— because the lawyers can understand it.

MAEVE He's a lawyer, Nadia. I don't think he hears the irony.

CHARLES No, I get it Maeve. But Mark doesn't appreciate the difficulty of interpreting the Constitution. He's off in his ivory tower, tilting at windmills. He doesn't understand how things are done practically.

NADIA He may be right, Maeve. In this practical world it's all about power. Those who can shout the loudest win the argument.

CHARLES It's not about *shouting*, it's about dealing with reality.

NADIA Reality is created by repetition. Those who have control of the media create reality. This is the way things are done.

CHARLES That's what you have to deal with, then.

MAEVE Mark's point was that we need consensus on definitions when we deal in abstractions. The only *reality* of collective nouns is in the *consensus* of our understanding.

CHARLES What does he mean by *collective* nouns?

MAEVE You know, they're the words that are used in the singular, but refer to more than one object.

CHARLES Oh, you mean like *pair*? Like a pair of shoes?

MAEVE I suppose. He was talking about associations, but *pair* is a collective also.
  (*Mark returns, through the kitchen, carrying a laundry basket.*)

CHARLES So, Mark, what is it you were saying —that a pair of shoes is not real?

MARK It has no *physical* reality. It's all conceptual.

CHARLES A pair of shoes?

MARK Right. Or socks. Here, look... (*He reaches into his basket and pulls out a pair of shorts.*) ... ah, here's a pair of shorts. We *call* it a pair, but it's a physical object. (*He drops it on the table, then pulls out another and drops it on the table.*)

CHARLES Mark, there's no need to air your dirty laundry.

MARK It's not dirty. Fresh out of the dryer. I even put some of that fluffy stuff in... (*He pulls out another pair of shorts and sniffs it.*) You want to smell?

CHARLES I'll pass.
  (*Mark drops it on the table, pulls out another and drops it on the table.*)

MARK Okay, there's four pairs of shorts. Physical objects, not much more to say. (*He stuffs the shorts back into the basket.*)

  But pairs of socks have a different reality. (*He pulls out socks, sequentially holding each one up to show it, then tossing it on the table.*) … Here's one sock (*a white sock*) … two (*a brown sock*) … three (*a dark grey or navy sock*) ... four (*a black sock*).

  Now, how many *pairs* of socks are on the table?

MAEVE Well, there's only one *pair*.

NADIA No, look closely. One's black, the other's navy. There aren't any pairs.

MARK Well some of these are cheap socks, and the color fades. One might have gone through a wash cycle and got a lighter shade while the other was hiding under the bed.

NADIA Well ...

CHARLES I'd call it a pair.

MARK Kevin, how many pairs are on the table?

KEVIN Two. You got four socks. That's two pairs.

CHARLES Well *technically*, a pair is just two socks.

NADIA No, they've got to match.

MARK That's just a fashion statement isn't it?

MAEVE You can't wear one white sock and one black. People will think you're nuts.

MARK You've got to be bold. Tell them it's the latest style.

MAEVE If it were, the stores would sell them that way.

MARK So how many pairs are there?

NADIA None.

MAEVE One.

KEVIN Two.

MARK Apparently, we need some authority to tell us what a pair of socks is.

CHARLES Okay, Mark. So what do you say the *real* answer is?

MARK Six.

MAEVE & NADIA What?

MARK Six pairs.

MAEVE But there are only *four* socks!

MARK Yes, but six *pairs*. I'll show you. (*He holds up the white sock with the brown sock*) ... one pair ... (*He drops the brown sock, then holds up the white sock with the navy sock*) ... two pairs ...

CHARLES Wait, ...

MARK (*He drops the navy sock, then holds up the white sock with the black sock*) ... three pairs ...

CHARLES Wait —you're counting the same sock more than once!

MARK I'm not counting *socks* —I'm counting *pairs*.

CHARLES But a sock can't be in more than one pair!

MARK Yes it can ...

MAEVE & NADIA No, it can't!

MARK Yes, every other sock you pair it with makes another pair.

CHARLES Mark, those are pair-*ings*, not pairs.

MARK What's the difference?

CHARLES A *pairing,* is a potential pair, not a real pair.

MARK Oh. So what's a *real* pair?

NADIA Well, not all of the *parings* can be real pairs.

MARK Which ones can't be?

CHARLES Well, as long as you're following the rule that any two socks makes a pair, then any of the pairings *could* be a pair, but not all of them at the same time.

MARK I'm asking how many pairs are on the table right now.

MAEVE Well, then there are none, because you haven't paired them up yet.

MARK I showed you ...

CHARLES Those were pair-*ings*, not real pairs!

MARK So what's a real pair?

CHARLES A real pair is determined when you actually put the socks on your feet. A sock on one foot only makes a real pair with the sock on the other foot.

MAEVE Or when you fold them together. That's equivalent to wearing them.

CHARLES So that a sock you're wearing is only *paired* with the sock on the other foot, and its *pairing* with a sock on the table can't be a real pair.

   (*pause*)

KEVIN Yeah, but then you could put that one on too.

MARK Put two socks on one foot? Yeah, sure, I could do that.

CHARLES Oh, so then you're wearing *three* socks, and you want to claim you're wearing *two* pairs?

MARK No, I want to claim I'm wearing *three* pairs.

MAEVE Three?

MARK Two pairs with the socks on different feet, and one pair on one foot.

CHARLES You can't have a *pair* of socks on one foot!

MARK Why not?

CHARLES Because two socks on one foot are not a pair, because that's not how a *pair* of socks is worn. By putting two socks on one foot, you're effectively *stipulating* they're not a pair!

MARK (*Stares at Charles*) ... Is this a principle you learned in law school?

CHARLES It's a principle known to people who are not idiots.

KEVIN But you can make a pair by folding socks together.

CHARLES Two! Only two! Two socks folded together make one pair.

MARK Then I can put that pair on one foot.

CHARLES No, not as a pair, you can't ...

MARK Yes I can, yes I can! The Supreme Court says so!

CHARLES *What?*

MARK The Supreme Court says a pair of socks is a sock!

CHARLES You're nuts.

MARK   The Supreme Court says an association of persons is a person, so an association of socks is a sock! It's a *constitutional* principle.

MAEVE   I don't believe the Constitution says anything about socks.

MARK   It doesn't matter what the Constitution says. It doesn't say anything about associations of persons either. So where does the idea come from? The Supreme Court is asserting it as a principle — *a universal truth.*

CHARLES   Come on, Mark — really? The Supreme Court's opinion is a profound legal ruling — nuanced reasoning in the context of a body of precedents. And you're comparing it to your problem of matching up your damn socks?

MARK   Do you understand the concept of a principle? If an association of persons is a person as a matter of principle, then an association of socks must be a sock by the same principle. And if it's not, then what is the principle actually, that would make it true in one case but not in the other?

CHARLES   Every principle has its limits, Mark. You can push *any* principle to ridiculous extremes, to make it appear ridiculous.

MARK   But if it's stated as a principle and limited to just one example, then it is not a principle at all, but a deception. So I'd like to know, where was this principle established? And what logic created it, and what limits were stated for it?

CHARLES   You're asking for easy answers to profound legal questions. Maybe if you'd study law for five or ten years, you'd be capable of understanding it.

MARK   We're talking about the Constitution, here! And you're telling us that we must either become lawyers to learn what it means or else trust lawyers to tell us?

CHARLES   Well, you can read it and get its *broad* meaning. But as far as following *all* of its implications — yeah, I think that's your choice.

MARK   Then the lawyers become the ruling class.

CHARLES   See, that's just your *paranoia.* You don't know the law, you can't follow legal reasoning, and you won't respect the judgments of those who can. So you're paranoid — implying that the entire legal profession is corrupt.

MARK   I never said corrupt. Complacent, maybe. Uncritically acquiescent. Subservient. Enabling.

CHARLES   *Who's* enabling?

MARK   The judiciary, with all its groupies and wannabes. The legal establishment as a whole takes it for granted that Congress and the Presidency are power-seeking branches that can't be trusted to limit themselves to their constitutional roles.

   Yet it applauds the Court for expanding its own power far beyond its constitutional authority, through the *sham* of constitutional interpretation.

CHARLES   No one's applauding. That's your paranoia, because you don't understand the legal processes or the legal culture. You can't understand the complexities of science or technology either, but you don't call those disciplines corrupt.

MARK   Did you entirely miss the point of my problem of matching up my damn socks? We couldn't agree on what constitutes a pair —because there's no physical reality to a pair of socks. No scientific experiment can identify a *pair*.

Now if it mattered enough, we *might* have argued it out and come to an agreement —a consensus— on what constitutes a pair of socks. I don't know what it would be, but I can guarantee you it would *not* be that a pair of socks is a *sock*.

And there's no physical reality to an association of persons either, yet the Supreme Court is asserting that an association of persons *is* a person.

So tell me, how can this be? What's the difference?

CHARLES Obviously, the difference is that a sock is a physical object, but a person —*in the law*— is a larger concept than just a natural person.

MARK In other words, the Court's reasoning involves no physical reality *at all*. It's just abstractions encountering abstractions —ideas and other ideas. And yet you want us to trust legal reasoning as if it were —like science— grounded in physical reality and verified in repeatable experiments.

MAEVE But, Mark, mathematics is metaphysics, too. Just ideas and other ideas.

MARK Yes, its reality is the reality of consensus, too. And that's why in learning mathematics you spend so much time practicing the rules of reasoning, and studying definitions —clear, unambiguous, universally-accepted definitions.

You can't make an idea morph into another just by muddling a definition.

CHARLES Well, legal reasoning has its own discipline. It's just different. You're just paranoid in your distrust.

MARK Is legal reasoning grounded in any reality? If it's the reality of consensus, whose consensus? How can we understand this?

CHARLES I think we have a consensus that *you* don't understand it. So why don't we just leave it at that?

MARK We can't, because the Court's reasoning defies logic. A metaphysics that muddles the distinction between the singular and the plural has fundamental contradictions. It cannot sustain a universal consensus.

CHARLES What universal? There are different disciplines. There's no universal.

MARK Look, our original Constitution had that same sort of muddle built into it. I wouldn't call it a political deception, but an artifact of the compromises necessary to get the Constitution ratified —and it was papered over.

It was inevitable that the contradiction would have to be resolved, but it took a lot of bloodshed to do it. Now the Supreme Court is perpetrating the same sort of muddle.

I hope we get off easier this time.

CHARLES Bloodshed? What *are* you talking about?

MARK The Civil War. Or, as it's called in the South —The War Between the States.

CHARLES How does that have anything to do with this?

MARK I think Kevin can answer that. Hey, Kevin, what *are* the United States of America?

KEVIN What do you mean? They're states. You want me to name them?

MARK Yes. Try it in alphabetical order.

KEVIN Ah, umm — Alaska, Arizona, Alabama ... —wait, Alabama ...

MARK Okay, that's close enough. Now here's a different question. What *is* the United States of America?

KEVIN Our country.

MARK Right, a great nation on the North American Continent.

KEVIN And the world's only remaining superpower.

MAEVE (*singing*) *"We are the champions, my friend ..."*

NADIA What do you think —should that be our national anthem?

MAEVE It's the perfect mixture of triumphalism and belligerence.

KEVIN But Queen is British...

NADIA Irony, Kevin.

MARK Charles, you do perceive a difference between *states* —in the plural— and *an association* of states —in the singular— don't you?

CHARLES Of course.

MARK But if you follow the logic of the Supreme Court, that would mean the United States —as an association of states— must *be* a *state*.

CHARLES But the United States *is* a state.

MARK But then you see, you're perpetuating the muddle by using the same word for different *things*. The United States is not the same *thing* as one of the states, because first of all, it is an association of states, and a state is not.

But more importantly, there's the matter of sovereignty. Before the Civil War —or the War Between the States— there were two ways of looking at it. Either the United States was sovereign and the states were not, or the states were sovereign and the United States was not. Either way, they cannot *both* be sovereign.

But now if you follow the Supreme Court's reasoning, the United States must be a sovereign state *because* it is an association of sovereign states.

That makes no sense at all. It's the fallacy of composition —on steroids.

CHARLES Listen, Mark, it was a limited ruling. And the game you're playing here is just extending it to ridiculous extremes.

MARK The ruling is *fundamentally* illogical. It will lead to nothing but more befuddlements.

And it's a transparent political rip-off. By extending the Constitution to associations of persons, the Supreme Court has given *itself* the power to overrule Congress on any issue involving the regulation of corporations.

CHARLES That's just your uninformed opinion. You're ignorant of how precedents work in establishing the common law.

7. SOCRATES

MARK Arrgh! (*Agitated, Mark rises and paces*) Look, we ought to be able to use *logic* to straighten this out. *Socrates* taught us how to do this. You know about Socrates, don't you, Kevin?

KEVIN Oh, uhh ... (*typing rapidly*) ... Soc-ra-tes, ... sure ... the Greek philosopher... 370 to 299 BC.

MARK In Socrates' time, twenty-four centuries ago, there were *two* (*holds up two fingers*) kinds of beings that walked on the earth —men, and the gods.

KEVIN You mean, that's what the people believed.

MARK Well, everybody believed it, so it was true.

KEVIN Just because everybody believes it, doesn't mean it's true.

MARK Of course it does, Kevin. ... *Men* and the *gods*. Of course, the gods were bigger and stronger, and they could do things men couldn't, so naturally, they controlled things. When they could, that is. They had lot of troubles of their own.

KEVIN Did the people ever *see* the gods?

MAEVE Kevin, they had pictures and statues. They knew exactly what the gods looked like.

KEVIN Yeah, but did they ever *see* them?

MAEVE Sure. Every so often Zeus would throw a tantrum and come by in a dark cloud and —zap-boom!— throw lightning bolts down on them. You've seen his picture, haven't you? With the lightning bolt in his hand?

MARK Anger management issues and lightning bolts. Watch out.

MAEVE Naturally, the people took cover. They knew it was dangerous to make eye contact.

KEVIN Yeah, but they never actually *saw* any of the gods themselves, did they?

MARK Kevin ... (*stares at Kevin*) ... have you ever actually *seen* a corporation?

KEVIN Uh ... no, but ...

MARK Of course not. Nobody has. And yet you believe they're real.

KEVIN Yeah, but corporations *are* real.

MARK Of course you believe that. Everybody believes it.

KEVIN What — *you* don't believe it?

MARK Of course I do. Didn't I just say everybody does? And so they're real.

MAEVE Kevin, the gods were real to the people. They knew all the stories, the fights and the marriages, the murders and the love affairs and the illegitimate children, all of it, and the people had their statues and heard their voices ...

MARK How did they hear their voices?

MAEVE At the oracles. At Delphi, the god Apollo spoke through the voice of a young priestess up on a pedestal. She sang in the language of the gods.

MARK I'm sure she had a sweet voice and made some strange sounds— "equal protection, equal protection," she might have been singing. But of course that would have been all Greek to the people.

MAEVE No, it wasn't all Greek to them, it was the language of the gods. So they needed the priests to give the *interpretation*, and the priests told them what Apollo wanted them to do.

KEVIN But that wasn't Apollo ...

MAEVE And then they would sacrifice a kid —I mean a young goat kind of kid— and the priest would examine the entrails.

KEVIN The entrails?

MAEVE The intestines, the guts.

KEVIN Euch ...

MAEVE Because the priests were skilled at *interpreting* the squiggles in the entrails, and they could tell whether Apollo was pleased with the sacrifice.

KEVIN C'mon, they were faking it.

MAEVE No Kevin, they weren't *faking* it. They'd been *indoctrinated*. They'd studied for years the doctrines of interpretation and the personalities of the gods. And everybody knew that a priest who had attained the exalted position of Oracle could *divine* the message in the entrails.

MARK Everyone believed it —including the priests. And so it was true.

MAEVE It was understood, Kevin, that divination is a spiritual capability, achieved through a career of spiritual refinement.

MARK It's not a matter of logic.

MAEVE The priests at the oracle would have been outraged at the suggestion that they should reveal the logic of their interpretation, or that such spiritual insights should be accessible by logic.

NADIA True, but perhaps a young priest, approaching the altar with trepidation for his very first interpretation, might have been seized with panic at tangle of intestines, because the doctrines of interpretation that he'd learned gave confusing and contradictory signals. But no priest had ever stepped down and said he couldn't see it. And the crowd was waiting, so he just took a stab at it— and for an instant he might've *felt* like he was faking it. But the crowd all seemed to agree that it was the right interpretation. And Apollo did not rebuke him.

And for days afterward he might have replayed in his mind his triumph in his crisis of faith, and he would have exulted to himself —joy is the overcoming of fear. And from then on he had the confidence that he had the power of the gods; the power was *within* him.

MAEVE And of course, he never again felt like he was faking it.

MARK But Socrates was familiar with the gods, too. He knew all the history —the feuds, the affairs, the marriages, the incest, the illegitimate children, the murders, the battles between the gods and between men, and between the gods and men.

He thought deeply about all these accounts, and he had a profound insight, a universal and inflexible rule: some gods are *mortal* and some gods are *immortal* ...

... but *all men* are mortal.

It was an interesting theoretical observation, and he might've had the idea of writing a short paper on it to present at the Athens Philosophical Society.

MAEVE Socrates never wrote anything.

MARK So apparently he decided not to. But then, maybe still ruminating on it while putting on his toga to go out to dinner, he had a disturbing thought...

MAEVE A *disturbing* thought?

MARK Not really a thought, but a qualm, a frisson, a wisp of anxiety. Now a lesser philosopher might have shrugged it off — "Hey let's get some souvlaki." But Socrates was always curious about what went on in his mind, so he let the idea form into words:

Socrates is a man.

It seemed to him to be a strangely foreign and fearful idea. Then the reasons for that formless anxiety became clear, as the next idea came crashing on down him:

Socrates is mortal!

Now that was *not* the conclusion that he expected, *not* the conclusion that he wanted at all, and if there were any way to squirm out of it, he would have been glad to do so. But he realized that his truths must be self-consistent, and for that, the conclusion was determined, unavoidable —*ironclad*:

All men are mortal.

Socrates is a man.

Therefore, Socrates is mortal!

He was certain of the truth of this syllogism; he had to accept it. For him, it was bad news, but it has been a model for logic —for clear thinking— for over two thousand years!

MAEVE I don't know where you're going with this, but bear in mind that Socrates was sentenced to death for his kind of thinking.

MARK Perhaps the ruling powers are offended by clear thinking.

NADIA History might offer more evidence on that point.

MARK But Socrates' logic has stood for over two thousand years, and it's still valid for the modern age, isn't it? We should be able to use his clear thinking to resolve this problem.

Of course, we'd have to update it a bit— lose the sexist language. These days we'd say:

All *people* are mortal! Sure, we've made great advances in medicine, but I think that's still true, isn't it? And now we also know:

A corporation is a *person*! So says the Supreme Court. Therefore, we must conclude:

A corporation is mortal!

I think the logic is ironclad.

(*pause*)

CHARLES No, a corporation exists in perpetuity.

MARK Indeed, in perpetuity!

KEVIN Per-pet-*chew*-ity.

MARK So it lives forever?

CHARLES That's right.

MARK So what happened here? Did we finally refute Socrates' logic?

CHARLES No —come on. That's ridiculous.

MARK Or is it perhaps that one of the premises is not valid?

CHARLES No, no. Look, the Court didn't say a corporation is a physical person — it's only *legally* a person. Only in the eyes of the law.

MARK So, *legally* a person, but not *mortal.* So in the eyes of the law, a person is not mortal.

CHARLES Well ... yes, that's right.

MARK What? You're kidding. Come on, you've got to be kidding. With all the laws we have about death... wills, inheritance, estate taxes... ?

CHARLES Those laws only apply *if* a person dies. The law doesn't say a person *must* die.

MARK (*stares at Charles in amazement, then bursts out laughing*) Oh, Charles, I had no idea you lawyers had this worked out so well. The law doesn't require you to die!

CHARLES That's right.

MARK The laws have all been written for immortal persons, and dying is optional! Hey, Kevin, were you planning to live forever?

KEVIN Sounds good to me.

MARK Well, good news— it's not against the law! What do you think, Maeve?

MAEVE Well, I don't know... think of the Medicare expenses.

MARK No, no, really. You have the right to live forever, just like a corporation.

But seriously, Charles, is that part of the legal theory? Were there briefs on this? Was this argument presented to the Court?

CHARLES You don't understand how the law works.

MARK Apparently not, because it seems to me the law has gone off into bizarro land... or maybe I'm just getting stupid.

CHARLES We can't discount that possibility.

MARK Okay, so our Constitution says that corporations and natural persons must have equal protection of the law. So does a corporation fill out a 1040 —a personal income tax form on April 15?

CHARLES No, of course not form 1040. A corporation pays corporate taxes.

MARK Uh-*huh*! So why don't *I* pay corporate taxes?

CHARLES Because you're not a corporation.

MARK Okay, okay... (*slowly, loudly*) *I* don't pay *corporate* income taxes because *I'm* not a *corporation*! And a *corporation* doesn't pay *personal* income taxes because...

CHARLES Because it's not that kind of a person.

MARK Because it's not *any* kind of person, because it's not a person!

CHARLES Well, it's not a *natural* person. It's a legal ruling, it's in the eyes of the law.

MARK Oh, the eyes of the law.

Okay, in the eyes of the law, a person is either male or female. And that is so because, in most states, you know, when you marry, you must certify that the person you're marrying is of the opposite gender. And marriage certainly *is* a legal matter. You ever been divorced, Charles?

CHARLES No.

MARK Then you don't appreciate that about marriage. You get the best view of the legal aspects on the way out.

CHARLES I'll try to remember that.

MARK So, in the eyes of the law: A person is either male or female!

And, in the eyes of the law: A corporation is a person!

Therefore, in the eyes of the law: A corporation is either male or female!

CHARLES No, no.

MARK Well, what is it? Not that *kind* of a person, again?

CHARLES That's right. In the eyes of the law, a *natural person* is either male or female, but not a *person*.

MARK And it's not really my problem, but if two corporations want to marry —in a state that doesn't allow same-sex marriage— would they be allowed to do it?

CHARLES That's stupid. Corporations can't marry.

MARK Well, what happened to equal protection of the law then? If natural persons can marry, why not corporate persons?

CHARLES Because it would be absurd.

MARK The absurdity barrier has been breeched —and *obliterated*! They have *rights*, from the Bill of Rights. They are persons in the eyes of the law, and marriage is a legal matter! Why can't they marry?

CHARLES They don't want to marry. They can have mergers.

MARK A merger is a *composition* of corporations, resulting in one corporation. A marriage is an *association* of persons.

CHARLES Corporations can join in partnerships, too.

MARK So are you saying that all the laws of marriage and divorce apply to corporate partnerships? I seriously doubt it. But even so, does the law allow natural persons to merge, like corporations, to make one person?

CHARLES You know you're being absurd.

MARK But the Supreme Court has said, without any sense of absurdity, that the Constitutional demands legal equality between corporations and natural persons. So where is the equality?

CHARLES It obviously doesn't apply where it's not physically possible.

MARK But a principle that encompasses physical impossibilities is not a principle at all. Certainly not a constitutional principle.

And it doesn't even apply where it is possible. What about holding companies? One person owning another person? Wasn't slavery banned by the Thirteenth Amendment?

CHARLES That's inane.

MARK Yes it is, it's inane. And yet it's a logical result of the Supreme Court decision. So what is it that's actually inane?

CHARLES It's so easy for you, taking cheap shots to make a mockery of the decision.

MARK *I'm* making a mockery? I'm not the one that said...

CHARLES Yes, yes —you're not the one, but legal complexities are beyond your understanding, so all you can do is conjure these ignorant cartoonish syllogisms.

MARK Cartoonish syllogisms, you call them now? The Court used the *principle* that a corporation is a person, in order to give corporations the rights of the Bill of Rights. And it asserted that the principle is a *constitutional* principle, so it can overrule the will of Congress —striking down laws passed by Congress.

The Supreme Court has *usurped* the power of Congress, on the basis of a principle that is nowhere in the Constitution, and is so fundamentally illogical that it makes the law nothing less than a fun house of cartoonish syllogisms.

CHARLES I don't think you even understand your own game. You're applying the principle literally —and ridiculously— outside of the legal precedents. But it's not a universal. It's a legal concept, valid in the eyes of the law.

KEVIN Hey Charles, has anybody ever *seen* the eyes of the law? Because you know, whenever you see Justice —with the scales— she's got a blindfold on.

MAEVE That's Justice, that's not the law.

KEVIN So how is Justice related to the law?

MARK Good question, Kevin...

MAEVE Sister-in-law!

KEVIN (*laughs*) Good one, Maeve.

MARK Charles, you tell him— what color are the eyes of the law?

CHARLES 'The eyes of the law' is just a figure of speech.

KEVIN Like a metaphor.

MAEVE It *is* a metaphor. It's *like* a simile.

MARK So what's the meaning of the '*eyes of the law*' metaphor? Is it as if people are blue polka dots and corporations are green polka dots but the law can't see the difference because it's color-blind?

CHARLES That's an idealization of it.

MARK No, it's *nonsense*. The differences are every bit as apparent in the eyes of the law as they are in any other eyes.

CHARLES In many cases they are, but you're not seeing the legal context. There are legal precedents that have defined what a corporation is as a *legal* entity.

MARK The law can define a corporation to be any sort of abstract being, but it can't *define* it into being a person, because a person already exits as a physical being — not in a definition!

CHARLES That's naive. The law does define a person —a legal person, a *juridical* person. '*The eyes of the law*' is in reality that body of law that supports that definition.

MARK Now the metaphor is a *body of law*? As if it were a tangible, persistent, substantive body?

CHARLES Of course it's not a *physical* body.

MARK Of course not. The law exists in a realm beyond physical reality, a realm of rules, decisions, principles, opinions, ideas, ideologies, allusions, doctrines, arguments and the magical fairy dust called *legality*.

It's all ethereal, only as substantial as the opinions of the judges whose opinions constitute the law.

Where is the *substance* of the law? Where are the bona fides, the bedrock assurances that the law will always preserve liberty, rather than becoming a tool for control and oppression?

CHARLES The bedrock is the Constitution. And the substance of the law is consistency. Judicial decisions must be consistent with precedents. That's what actually motivated this decision.

MARK Consistency? That's your indoctrination, your *ideology*, speaking. But it's an illusion. You can't graft consistency onto a fundamentally illogical proposition.

And your indoctrination makes *your* bedrock not the Constitution, but the unlimited power of the Supreme Court. A court with unlimited power has no need to persuade or convince —and so no need for consistency, or for the laws of logic or reason.

Yet we Americans defer to the law because we believe that law and justice are synonymous. Isn't the law administered in the Department of Justice? But history tells us that the law can be used to subjugate, to subdue, to keep the people under the control of those who control the law.

CHARLES Mark, you're going off the deep end, now,. You're scaring me. I fear for your sanity.

MARK You fear for *my* sanity? You think it makes *sense* that a corporation is a person, and you fear for *my* sanity?

CHARLES But you have no understanding of the context.

MARK I understand the context! It's a flat-out deception —a fraud, a political rip-off!

CHARLES You need a reality check. You're not a lawyer, yet you think you know the Constitution better than the Supreme Court. But your real delusion is to think your ranting can change anything.

MARK But change *is happening* and it's going to happen, one way or the other. If we can't get together to limit the power of the Court, then we're acquiescing to the absolute and arbitrary power of judges, through the sham of constitutional interpretation.

And we are guaranteed to get more of it. And you— *you* will defend the Court's self-aggrandizement no matter how absurd the ruling.

When the Court says that the Constitution says that the moon is made of green cheese, you'll be the first to explain to us that of course it doesn't mean that the moon is *really* made of green cheese, it's just *legally* made of green cheese. So the Constitution requires us all to *act* as though it were made of green cheese.

CHARLES You should just hear how ridiculous you sound.

MARK Okay, it's ridiculous, but enlighten me— exactly what would prevent the Court from making that ruling?

CHARLES They just wouldn't, it's stupid.

MARK They *wouldn't*. You didn't say they *couldn't*.

CHARLES No, they couldn't. The Constitution doesn't say anything about the moon or green cheese.

MARK That's no obstacle! It doesn't say anything about corporations or associations of people or campaign contributions either, and it doesn't stop the Court from saying it does...

Because the Supreme Court can say the Constitution says whatever they think it *ought* to say —whatever they *need it to say*— so they can make the ruling they want, to overrule Congress. And the Court can't be overruled by any power in or out of government.

MAEVE Mark, you're shooting yourself in the foot with a ludicrous example. Nobody could take that seriously.

MARK So you think '*a corporation is a person*' is not ludicrous enough? Of course, the Court wouldn't rule *now* on the substance of the moon, but only because there's no political payoff in it.

But someday, maybe sooner than you think, when the Food Corporation and the Minerals Corporation are butting heads over rights to the moon, the Supreme Court could very well make a landmark decision —overruling Congress based on what *the Constitution says* about the moon.

CHARLES Mark, you're paranoid.

MARK Then let me explain my paranoia. When you allow your words to be robbed of their meaning —as when metaphors become literal— you lose your ability to *think*. And when we're unable to think, particularly about the source of the authority of the law, despots will be sure to appear, to do our thinking for us, and tell us what the law is.

CHARLES You're calling the Justices despots?

MARK Oh, excuse me, that's not polite, is it?

MAEVE I think '*law-givers*' is the acceptable term these days.

MARK Charles, can you strip away the metaphor and try to think clearly? The reality is, that for the sake of convenience or efficiency in certain aspects of *business* —such as owning property, entering into contracts, and being responsible for torts— the law has been applied to corporations in the same way it applies to persons engaged in those business activities.

That's a long way from saying that a corporation *is* a person, or even that it is a person *in the eyes of the law*.

Because by *that* sort of reasoning, you could say that a dog is a person *in the eyes of the law*.

CHARLES A dog, really?

MARK Yes, really. Because the law treats a dog and a person the same.

CHARLES I'm a lawyer, and I never heard that.

MARK Sure, if a dog is hanging out where he doesn't belong, he's trespassing, so he can be arrested and put in jail, just like a person. Therefore, a dog is a person in the eyes of the law.

CHARLES So if your dog pees on my shoe, can I sue him?

MARK No, of course not.

MAEVE He's not that *kind* of person.

MARK No, no —it's because he's a person so he's protected by the First Amendment.

CHARLES What, the First Amendment? Freedom of speech?

MARK Of course. A dog is a person in the eyes of the law, so his freedom speech is protected by the First Amendment. And he expresses his opinion by urinating —it's the same thing as speech.

CHARLES That's absurd.

MARK Yes, yes it is. And we know it's absurd, because even a one year-old baby knows what a dog is and what a dog is not.

But the Supreme Court offers the same *absurd* reasoning for corporations, because a corporation is a mystical shape-shifting megamorphagus that we see mostly through the rose-colored lenses provided by corporate public relations departments.

8. CORPORATIONS

CHARLES Everybody knows what a corporation is.

MARK Really, *everybody*? What do you think a corporation is, Kevin?

KEVIN It's some hard-working people, bringing you the products you want and need and love.

MARK But it's not the *people*!

KEVIN No, but like, the *team*.

NADIA Of course, the people of the corporation are team players.

KEVIN Yeah, but they don't wear uniforms.

MAEVE Do they need to? Why do teams wear uniforms?

KEVIN So you can identify them.

MARK And so the team members can identify themselves.

MAEVE So *each* team member can identify *all* the team members —including him or herself.

KEVIN You mean identify himself to the other team members.

MAEVE And also to himself or herself.

KEVIN What, identify himself to himself?

NADIA Of course, to identify oneself to oneself as a member of the team.

MAEVE That is, to identify *with* the team. So the person's identity will be the team identity.

NADIA The corporate people are team players —without the uniform, yet with the corporate identity.

KEVIN The corporate identity is, like, a logo.

MAEVE Yes, when you *wear* a logo, it's a bit of a uniform. A vestigial uniform.

MARK So you can be on the team.

MAEVE And the corporation also pays famous athletes to wear its logo.

NADIA So when you wear the logo, you identify with the team.

MARK Right, if you wear the *sploosh*, you're on the same team as... as *Dennis Rodman*!

MAEVE What's a sploosh?

MARK It's a logo —you see it all over.

KEVIN Who's Dennis Rodman?

MARK *Sic transit gloria mundi.*

KEVIN Who's Gloria Mundi?

MAEVE I think she's someone Dennis used to date.

NADIA The logo is branding, creating a favorable attitude by identification. Giving you the feeling of being part of the family.

MARK It's public relations, but it's not the corporation. And neither is it the people. Can you *describe* a corporation, Kevin?

KEVIN It's like a vacuum cleaner, that sucks up money. And concentrates it and then it spews all out...

MAEVE A vacuum cleaner doesn't spew.

KEVIN No, but then it's like a volcano spewing money.

MAEVE Volcanoes spew rocks and ash, killing everything below.

KEVIN Or it's like a thunderstorm raining money down.

MAEVE What about those big chunks? When thunderstorms drop hail the size of melons, it's very destructive.

KEVIN No, but the big chunks don't come down. They get stuck up there and melt, and trickle down. That's called the trickle-down theory.

MARK How can you know what goes on up there?

KEVIN You have to climb the corporate ladder.

MAEVE The corporate ladder is like the side of a pyramid. The rungs get narrower as you go up.

MARK So when a lot of people try to climb, it gets crowded.

MAEVE People begin using their elbows to get some room.

MARK Or to knock back the competition.

NADIA But from the outside, all you see up there is the corporate veil.

MARK The corporate veil is what makes a corporation a unit —a single entity in the eyes of the law. Isn't that right, Charles?

CHARLES That's the common metaphor. The law doesn't care to look behind the veil to see who's responsible for the corporation's acts. It holds the corporation — as one body— responsible.

MAEVE But when a corporation's criminal activity is too morally offensive to be paid for with just a fine, somebody's got to go to jail.

KEVIN You can't put a corporation in jail.

CHARLES Right, so there are times when it's necessary for the government to *pierce the corporate veil.*

MARK The prosecutor will pierce the corporate veil to find the one or two of rotten apples in the bushel of ripe, healthy apples, and pluck them out.

MAEVE But finding the rotten ones won't be easy, because they're all team players.

CHARLES Sure, sure —but look, those are all just metaphors. In reality, the corporation is just people doing business.

MARK Now you're saying it's just *people* —in the plural? You're giving up the idea that it's a *person*?

CHARLES That's just another way of looking at it.

MARK So sometimes you chose the singular, sometimes the plural, by whim? But isn't it a legal principle that a corporation is a unit? Its components are hidden behind the corporate veil, and *it* is a singular entity.

CHARLES Okay, yes. Then you'd say it's an *association* of people.

MARK And an association doesn't have any of the properties of the members of the association. It's simply a common logical error —*the fallacy of composition*— to suppose that it does.

CHARLES I don't see how that applies.

MARK Let's understand it clearly. If every owner, director and employee of a corporation were a fat bald man, that would not make the corporation a fat bald corporation —let alone a fat bald *man*.

And if some skinny blonde women bought all the shares of the FatBaldo Corporation and replaced the directors and employees with skinny blonde women, it would still be the *same* corporation...

KEVIN They could change the name to SkinnyBlondo, though.

MARK ...and even then, it would be the same corporation, and neither fat nor bald nor skinny nor blond...

KEVIN Nor gloom of night.

MARK ...nor a man nor a woman nor a *person*, nor protected by the Bill of Rights. Because an association does not have the properties of the members of the association.

CHARLES Well, of course it doesn't have the *physical* features, because it's not a natural person.

MARK So why must it have the abstract features of a natural person?

CHARLES It just does, in the law.

MARK But our laws are made by Congress, which has never passed a law that says every legal association is the same thing as its members.

CHARLES Yes, that's the statuary law, but the courts must interpret the law.

MARK Just because *some* laws have been written or *interpreted* to apply uniformly to corporations and human beings, that does not mean that a corporation *is* a person. And the Constitution certainly does not say it.

MAEVE Charles, we know that corporations are creatures of the law. Not to belabor the obvious, they were *created* by the law. So I would think there must be a legal definition.

CHARLES I can cite what John Marshall wrote: quote, "**A Corporation is an artificial being, invisible, intangible, and existing only in contemplation of law. Being the mere creature of law, it possesses only those properties which the charter of its creation confers upon it, either expressly or as incidental to its very existence.**"

MARK There you have it —an *artificial being*, but not a human being!

CHARLES But that's just another metaphor.

NADIA No, that's not a metaphor! It *is* a being, a life form, active, energy-consuming, perpetuating its own existence. It was called an *artificial* being only because it was created in the law, brought into existence by an act of the legislature. But it *is* a being, a powerful and intelligent being.

KEVIN It can't be a being, if it's just people.

MAEVE No, Kevin, it's not plural. It's an entity, a singular thing.

NADIA It also has an abstract structure —laws, rules, policies, positions and responsibilities.

CHARLES That does not make it a machine, though. *People* control the corporation.

MARK It's always a comforting illusion to think you're in control, but that's mostly backwards. The corporation controls the people! The corporation pays the people, so the people do what the *corporation* wants.

MAEVE He who pays the piper calls the tune.

CHARLES No, the corporation can't force people to do what they don't want to do.

NADIA But it has no need to! It simply matches people with job requirements. For whatever the corporation needs to have done, it will *always* be able to find *some* person willing to do it —*for money*.

MAEVE And if upon occasion the corporation puts the wrong person in a position —for example, a person whose ethical concerns interfere with his or her job performance— the corporation will find a way to remove that person, and fill the position with someone who can focus on getting the job done. Someone who'll let someone *else* worry about the ethics.

NADIA If the job is believed to be both legal and necessary to achieve the corporation's goals, *and it pays*, it will be filled.

CHARLES That's a very cynical view. Anyway, the corporation can't act at all without people, so they define its actions.

MARK They certainly *perform* its actions, but the corporation defines the *roles* for the people.

Consider the role of corporate spokesperson. When a corporation finds itself in a situation that's damaging its reputation, it calls on a spokesperson to repair its public image. That role calls for a well-groomed, trustworthy-looking type, a person of moderate temperament, who exudes responsibility, sincerity and good intentions.

NADIA And if you don't think about the *role* of the spokesperson, you might very well accept the spokesperson —a human face, a human voice, with human emotions—

as the *embodiment* of the corporation.

CHARLES Oh come on, nobody believes that.

NADIA Nobody who *thinks* about it believes it. But when the spokesperson's speaking, the issue on everyone's mind is the unfair accusations against the corporation. And that's the issue because that's how the spokesperson's framed it.

And then, with the demeanor of a martyr, the spokesperson will nobly accept on the corporation's behalf full responsibility for the situation —even though it was not really the corporation's fault, and was absolutely unforeseeable, and nothing like it will ever happen again.

And you feel sympathy for... the corporation.

CHARLES I'm sorry, no. Everybody knows the spokesperson is a human being. Nobody's going to think of him as the corporation.

NADIA Now that we're talking about it, no. But you know, we are all so accustomed to fictional experiences, we allow ourselves the make-believe that an actor playing a role actually *is* the character he's playing. We like to understand the character by supposing that his opinions and emotions are genuine. The spokesperson exploits that supposition.

CHARLES And so? What– are you implying that the spokesperson's job is lying?

NADIA No, not lying —*acting*! You don't accuse an actor of *lying* when he is playing a role.

CHARLES Yes, that's because of the *setting*. It informs us that it is just an act.

NADIA Well then, the setting is a press conference. The spokesperson addresses reporters. Now, are you saying that there can be no acting, because this is a not a venue for make-believe? Or are you saying that if there is any acting, it is deception?

CHARLES Well, both.

NADIA But how could there not be acting? The spokesperson is portraying, with his human voice, image and personality, the views and attitudes of a corporate being, which has no physical reality, and no emotions.

And no one who *thinks about it* would insist that the opinions he expresses must be his own personal opinions. He is giving the corporation's position. He's playing the role that the corporation requires him to play —*acting* the part of the corporation.

CHARLES Well, the spokesperson has a unique role. The CEO has control over the corporation.

MARK Yeah, that's certainly the image the CEOs want to cultivate. If you've read any of the books by retired CEOs, you're sure to be familiar with the image of the powerful executive, smart and tough and no-nonsense, because that's the way you've got to be at the top, in the rough-and-tumble Darwinian competition of the free market economy. There's no place for sentimentality, it's dog-eat-dog, big fish eat the little fish, eat or be eaten. You've got to be hard-nosed, two-fisted, bare-knuckled, take no prisoners. You've got to be sharp, quick, opportunistic, and paranoid.

The executive knows all, controls all.

But every time a corporation gets caught in criminal activity, and the corporate veil is pierced to bring executives to trial, we discover that they knew nothing — *nothing!*— about scams going on right under their noses.

CHARLES Well, of course they're lying.

MARK I wouldn't be so sure. An executive knows he can be held responsible for whatever he knows about, even if he doesn't actively participate. So if he becomes suspicious —based on nothing that could be called a fact— that illegal activities are afoot, he could call for an investigation —or, *raise a big stink.* But that might bring about retaliation by his associates or superiors, and he could lose his job.

It might be more prudent for him to let it be known that he doesn't want to know about it — a sentiment he expresses in the words, "I don't want to know about it."

CHARLES That's an absurd idea of an executive attitude.

MAEVE It's no more absurd than the idea that one person can control the actions of thousands of employees, giving commands like a drill sergeant, and layers of shrewd and self-interested people will march in lockstep.

CHARLES Well, the CEO at least exerts enough control to establish the corporation's moral and ethical cultures.

MARK And is *that* the reason you think a corporation is a person? Do you think that it acts —like a person— in a social network, with the same social constraints as guide human behavior?

Look at the reality. The corporation interacts with its environment —the physical, social, financial, legal environment— in many complex ways, and the laws it encounters are not as simple as stopping for a red light. So when an executive is uncertain about the legality of an operation, he'll check with the legal department.

And here —wait, we have that quote from that robber baron. Maeve, who was it that said, "**I do not want a lawyer to tell me what I cannot do. I hire him to tell me how to do what I want to do**"?

MAEVE You're quoting J.P. Morgan.

MARK See, I think that quote should be the credo of the corporation's legal department. Corporate lawyers don't get paid to read the law like a country bumpkin lawyer. They get the big bucks for *thinking outside the box.*

And what is the box? It's the way ordinary people think about the law; it's the context that includes the reason for the law —the evils it was meant to prevent. It's the consensus view, the *spirit* of the law, even your mother's admonition, "*What if everybody did that?*" Now, if you wash all that away with cynical acid, you're outside the box.

Then you can see the law as the corporation sees it: nothing but a text. If the text forms an obstacle to its goals, the corporate lawyer must find an interpretation that removes the obstacle.

So he asks, are there alternative definitions or different senses of the words? What is the narrowest sense of a word that conveys a restriction or prohibition?

What is the broadest sense of a word for an allowance or exception? Can the corporation's activity be relabeled —perhaps by making a new distinction or a cosmetic change in practice— that will separate it from the language of the prohibitions, or include it in the exceptions?

Then with new insights, the corporate lawyer will write an interpretation of the law as a *possible* position for the corporation to take. Note that he is not certifying that it is his own personal belief —presumably, he can still understand the law from a human perspective— but as an interpretation that *might* be accepted by a court, *if* the corporation is ever required to defend its actions in court.

If possible, he'll avoid putting his own name on the opinion, but in any case he'll surely include a few formal-sounding caveats to let himself off the hook in the event of repercussions.

But the CEO is a man of action. He'll interpret the memo as, "*We got the go-ahead from Legal.*"

CHARLES Mark, you're slandering an entire profession, with no experience at all, no first-hand knowledge of what corporate attorneys really do.

MARK I'm not *slandering*. I'm not saying they do anything illegal. Even if a court rejects the company's position and imposes huge fines, the lawyer's part will be found to be completely legal. *Completely legal*! That's not slander. To a lawyer, it's high praise.

CHARLES You're speaking out of ignorance— just appealing to stereotypes.

MARK I'm not talking about all or even most lawyers. I'm just not going along with the implied assumption that passing a bar exam guarantees ethical sensibilities that outweigh the desire to make money.

And by my understanding of human nature, when a learned profession is practiced in a competitive environment with large rewards, those that excel will be those who can push principles beyond what others assume to be their limits.
If the game is to interpret laws to the benefit of the corporation, the best corporate lawyers will be very good at it.

CHARLES You can't even give me one example.

MARK Well, I can imagine if a law said the corporation must print certain disclosures, a corporate lawyer might notice that the law didn't say what size font must be used, or that it shouldn't be written in technical jargon in convoluted syntax, that will make it all but impossible to understand.

So the disclosures are printed, to comply with the law, while the corporation retains its objective —which is to avoid upsetting the customers.

CHARLES That's pathetic.

MARK Well, I'm not a corporate lawyer. I don't get paid the big bucks.

  (*pause*)

KEVIN Hey, *Maeve*! Shadrach wants to know the purpose of life.

MARK Who's Shadrach?

MAEVE That's his friend. He's chatting.

MARK Does he have any brothers?

MAEVE That's funny, that's what I asked.

KEVIN He's writing a paper. He needs to know the purpose of life.

MAEVE Tell Shadrach it's to build pyramids.

KEVIN Build pyramids?

MAEVE Yes. Tell him.

NADIA I don't think that's the answer he was looking for.

MAEVE I don't think it matters.

MARK Can't he just *Google* it?

MAEVE Look at you —down with the tech stuff.

KEVIN Shadrach says get serious.

MAEVE Seriously? That's human nature, isn't it? A person asks to know the purpose of life, and when you give him the answer, he rejects it.

NADIA And so the purpose of life remains an eternal enigma.

CHARLES Well, there was a time when building pyramids *was* the accepted answer.

MAEVE Maybe. Who knows if they'd even thought of the question?

NADIA Thought is shaped by language. If your language doesn't have the words to form the question, it doesn't get asked.

CHARLES Tell Shadrach the purpose of life is to make as much money as possible.

MAEVE Ah, that's a much better answer. That *building pyramids* was really stupid.

KEVIN Shadrach wants to know how.

NADIA So there are *two* problems with the question. The first is that a person won't believe the answer, and the second is that he will.

MARK Ah, thesis… antithesis. Now we need…

MAEVE I'm sure Nadia has the synthesis.

NADIA I can only think it's just a lack of linguistic restraint. We use words in one context and adapt them to another; we let metaphors leach into primary meanings; we tolerate encroachments in meaning, in which each new variation seems consistent with the last, yet fresh, more interesting.

   Do we have any reason to believe that the purpose of life here, *now,* is any different than it was in the last generation, or the many generations before? If the purpose of life exists now, it is the same as before language had the word purpose? Or is it that purpose didn't exist until the word appeared?

MAEVE Nadia, I have no idea what you are talking about.

NADIA I'm trying to understand his question by imagining how it might have been asked before language had the word *purpose.*

   Imagine yourself as a child in a time far, far back in antiquity, watching your father sharpen a stick with the jagged edge of a stone. You might have asked, "What is that?" and he might have answered, "I call it a spear". But that was not what you wanted to know, so you might have asked, "Why is that?" and, "How is that?" and none of the answers satisfied you. And then your father admired his finished work and said, "Now when the wolf comes, I don't run away. I stick him with the spear."

And that was what you wanted to know.

Then you might have seen your mother shaping a lump of clay and you might have asked, "What is that?" And she might have said "I call it a cup," but that is not what you wanted to know, so you asked, "Why is that?". And then your mother...

...well, to move the story along, let's imagine she had inordinate linguistic skills. So she said, "Kid, you seem to be asking about an attribute of this creation for which we do not yet have a word. So let's call it the purpose. The purpose expresses the use we intend for the object. So the *purpose* of this cup is to hold water, so you can have a drink without getting your face all wet."

And that is what you wanted to know.

Then you saw another object, a stick with a rock fastened to one end. And you said to your mother, "What is the purpose of that thing?" And your mother said, "I don't know, go ask your uncle Ogg. He's the one who made it."

Later, perhaps, seeing the leaves skittering in the breeze, you might've asked your father, "What is the purpose of the wind?"

Now maybe your father didn't like to say "I don't know" to any of his kids because he was afraid of sounding... ignorant. So he might have said, "The purpose of the wind is to blow the evil spirits away." It sounded good to him, because the wind lifted his spirit, and anyway, what did the kid know?

That's the way it likely would have gone.

Do you see the lack *linguistic restraint* here?

If he had exercised linguistic restraint, he would have answered, "Kid, you're misusing the word. The wind doesn't have a purpose, it just is —it just *blows*. We use the word *purpose* for *our* creations, for the things that we make, to express our reason for making them. It's our intention for their use. If you want to know the *purpose* of anything, you must ask its creator."

(*pause*)

KEVIN So ... you're saying life has no purpose?

NADIA No, Kevin. I'm saying that without reference to the creator of life, Shadrach is simply misusing the word *purpose*. He's forming an ungrammatical question, like asking about the price of a cloud, the color of a number — or the religion of a left-handed pipe wrench or the weight of a purple sunset.

Maybe there is some other word —perhaps one we haven't yet developed— that expresses what he really wants to know.

KEVIN Yeah, but he needs to know the purpose of life.

NADIA Then he must ask the creator of life, wherever or however he can find him, her, it or them.

And if it seems to him that he, she, it or they have created life that is capable of understanding that purpose, but by intention or inattention omitted revealing it to his, her, its or their creation, then that creation —being capable of knowledge that it is not given— is incomplete.

Then it would be the privilege of the creation itself —with no disturbance of the creator's purpose— to complete the creation, for the purpose —invented, discovered, or obtained by whatever means the creator has endowed it with— of the creation itself.

But that is what makes him a special kind of being —a *human* being— capable of conjuring a purpose to complete the creator's creation.

KEVIN (*typing*) Yeah, yeah... But he's not going to use that.

MAEVE Then he ought write about the purpose of things *we* have created.

NADIA Non-human beings. Like corporations.

MARK Of course. A corporation doesn't have such concerns about its purpose, because it knows who its creator is, and its purpose is found in its charter. Kevin, what is the purpose of a corporation?

KEVIN It depends on what kind of corporation it is.

MARK The kind of corporation we're talking about is a business corporation —a private, for-profit corporation, whether privately or publicly held.

KEVIN It's whatever its product is.

MARK Well, what is its product?

KEVIN I don't know.

MARK You ought to. The purpose of a for-profit corporation is to *make money for the investors,* so its product is *profits*.

All the stuff produced along the way —the cars, the basketball shoes, the chicken wings, the shrink-wrapped plastic, the shampoo, the wrinkle-erasing cream, the vacation timeshares, the mortgages, the collateralized credit default options, the ten-o'clock news, the Super Bowl and the half-time show and the ads, the sitcoms, the breakfast cereal, the mocha lattes, the fresh vegetables, the frozen vegetables and the boxes that hold them and the freezers that hold *them*, and the electricity that run *them*, and generators that produce it and the coal that fuels them, and the carbon dioxide emissions, the canned vegetables and the cans that hold them, the tin, the open-pit mines, the slag heaps and all the other stuff.

All— *all* of these are simply *byproducts*. Necessary side effects to the production of profits and growth.

MAEVE I read in the newspaper that the Chief Justice said a corporation has many interests, just like a person.

MARK It's amazing —isn't it?— the effectiveness of corporate public relations. They seek publicity through the channels of officialdom and authenticity. But this is extraordinary —getting the Chief Justice to propagate their propaganda!

CHARLES What propaganda? He's just stating a fact.

MARK It's a fact, sure —as long as you don't elaborate! A corporation does have many interests —*like a person*— but they're not the *same* interests as a person. A corporation's interests all serve its *purpose*, which is to make *profits* for the investors.

And profits are obtained by lower costs and greater revenues. Wages, for example, are on the expense side of the ledger, so a corporation has an interest in low wages. That means an interest in a low-cost, readily available labor supply, obtained by a high unemployment rate, with the competition for jobs keeping pay rates down.

Also, an interest in laws that hamper and dismantle unions, and in laws that allow employees to be considered contractors, so it can avoid paying benefits. And an interest in exemptions from wage laws for some classes of workers —interns, prisoners— and an interest in eliminating minimum wage laws entirely.

It has an interest in laws that allow operations to move to low-wage labor markets offshore, and an interest in unlimited work visas for foreign professionals, to bring down the wage structure for all professionals.

It has an interest in automation, the replacement of all forms of labor — not just repetitive manual labor— with robots and artificial intelligence.

It has an interest in minimizing all operational costs. That means an interest in defeating or rolling back laws that require costly measures for product safety, worker safety, and environmental protection.

That is not to say that it has no *concern* for these issues, because obviously, the lawsuits and negative publicity from a disaster would be harmful to profits, but that self-regulation will enable it to achieve these ends in a more cost-effective manner. But just in case a disaster occurs in spite of its efforts, it has an interest in laws to limit its exposure to lawsuits, and in laws that will limit negative publicity.

And a corporation has an interest in eliminating all corporate taxes, but until that is realized, it will have an interest in tax exemptions for any imaginable reason. And it has an interest in flexible accounting rules, and tax laws that will enable it to shield income from taxes, and to move revenues to wherever the lowest tax rates are found.

And, because tax exemptions lose their effectiveness at a certain point —the point of zero taxes— a corporation always has an interest in *subsidies*. Any corporate activity undertaken for profit that can be said to yield an incidental social benefit, such as the employment of a disadvantaged class of persons, or an improvement to the community infrastructure, must be subsidized by the government.

Or if a particular industry is not profitable, or insufficiently profitable, corporations would have an interest in a government subsidy as the obvious solution. And of course, if the corporation is on the brink of bankruptcy, it would surely have an interest in a government bailout.

But that's already on the other side of the ledger, where the corporation's interest in greater revenues. This means an interest in broadening patent and intellectual property law, and in laws that establish new rights, creating new forms of property, such as business models, human activities, DNA sequences —your own chromosomes!— and the laws of nature, which can then be owned by the corporation. Or, to be fair, they may be owned by any person who owns a science laboratory.

A corporation has an interest in eliminating government research laboratories and government-sponsored university research, to be replaced by corporate-sponsored research, so that the corporation would own the resulting intellectual property. Do I need to add that a corporation would also be interested in government subsidies for sponsoring such research, or is that being redundant?

And a corporation is interested in advertising. We know, we're immersed in it. We all think we're immune to it, but corporations wouldn't spend billions on advertising if it weren't working for them. So it has an interest in laws that will protect rather than regulate advertising.

It also has an interest in public relations. In order to maintain control over its public image, it is interested in laws that protect its privacy —laws that restrict access to its facilities and prohibit photographing and reporting on its operations.

A corporation is interested in tougher bankruptcy laws, so that natural persons won't be able to escape their debts to the corporation.

And it has an interest in laws that will facilitate mergers, and in rolling back anti-trust and antimonopoly laws. A corporation is always interested in growth —and in being too big to fail.

And it has an interest in *foreign policy*, for both sides of the ledger. To lower its costs, the corporation wants all foreign nations to allow it access to their natural resources —ores, oil, lumber, agricultural products, and labor.

And to increase revenues, it wants them to allow its products access to their markets, and to allow investment in their companies and industry.

But of course, only the government can secure these objectives, through treaties, trade agreements and international law. So the corporation must seek influence in the government.

And for those nations that might remain uncooperative, the corporation must use its influence in the government to apply stronger measures — economic sanctions, covert action by the espionage agencies, and military force.

CHARLES That's a totally unsubstantiated allegation.

NADIA But the public also has some influence in the government, and might not approve of foreign intrigues undertaken for the benefit of corporations. So the corporations have an interest in advancing an ideology that justifies such government action.

The people must be made to believe that capitalism and democracy are one and the same, and that socialism is equated with dictatorship.

And to preserve the purity of this ideology, examples of capitalist dictatorships must be obscured. And examples of socialist democracies must be hidden or declared evil —or if possible, eliminated.

MARK Oh, yes —one more interest. Corporations in the arms industry and services to the military —companies that often have the U.S government as their only customer— always have an interest in *war*, which is dependably good for their profits.

MAEVE And corporations have always been interested in the law. They are, after all, *creatures* of the law.

NADIA And they've lately developed an interest in writing laws — *actually writing the text* of bills they want their legislatures to pass, so that the language of the law will suit their purposes.

MAEVE Language the legislators won't even understand.

MARK So those are just a few corporate interests we've noticed in the newspapers, but there are so many more. And they're all driven by the corporation's *purpose* — profits and growth.

CHARLES It's obvious that *your* interest is to slander corporations.

MAEVE But Charles, can you explain this? Did the Chief Justice actually mean that having many interests —*just like a person* has many interests— qualifies the corporation to *be* a person, with the rights of the Bill of Rights? Even though its interests are not the same as those of a person?

CHARLES Look, there are lots of ways you can think about corporations, and their interests. But you folks just aren't getting it, because you're not focusing on the *legal* aspect— the corporation as a *legal* person.

MAEVE No, no. A *legal* entity is an entity recognized by the law and *subject* to the law. If you call it —metaphorically— a legal *person*, just because it's recognized by the law and *subject* to the law, you should not lose sight of the metaphorical nature of that usage.

But a *legal* entity is not a *political* person —not even metaphorically. A *political* person is one having the rights of citizenship —the right to participate in *creating* the law.

Aliens —foreigners, even if living in the United States— do not have the right to vote, nor to use their money to influence elections. They do not have *political* rights.

And corporations —artificial beings created by legislatures— were not created with *political* rights.

NADIA The *metaphor* of a corporation as a person does not extend to the *political* rights of a person. What justification could there be for it?

A corporation has no parents: it never was raised with their love and discipline, nor will it ever feel any responsibility for the care of aging parents.

It's neither male nor female, so it's untroubled by sexuality, sexual orientation, gender identity, or personal relationships. It can't marry, so it has no concern about either marriage or divorce.

It has no family and can't have children, so it has no concern for the health, safety, or education of children. And, being immortal, it does not worry about its own health or welfare in old age.

It has no religion, so it will never need to resolve conflicts between its own beliefs or practices and its role in civil society.

It's not a citizen, so it can't take any civic responsibility. It can't vote, nor serve on a jury to judge its peers.

It can't join the armed forces, nor shed its own blood in the defense of the country. Being immortal, it will never make the ultimate sacrifice for the country. Its patriotism, if you can call it that, is limited to supplying the country with arms —for a price.

That's the corporation in the eyes of the law. The question is, why would anyone want to call *that* sort of creature a *person*?

MAEVE Or, why would *our Constitution* say it has *political rights*?

CHARLES You folks aren't getting it. You're conjuring an image of a corporation as some kind of nefarious *being*, but that's not the *legal* view. In the eyes of the law, it's just a *legal* person —not a physical being.

MARK That makes no sense. It can't be a *person* unless it is first of all a being.

NADIA A natural person is a *human* being; an association is an *abstract* being.

9. THE FOURTEENTH AMENDMENT

MARK Charles, how did this nonsense get into the law? The Constitution says nothing about corporations at all. What authority does the Supreme Court have to give them constitutional rights?

CHARLES It's nothing new, Mark. The *'equal protection of the law'* clause of the Fourteenth Amendment has been interpreted to apply to corporations.

MARK That's just bizarre. It *couldn't* be what the Fourteenth Amendment is about.

CHARLES Well, it's been held to mean that. It was decided a long time ago, and it's settled law.

NADIA (*Looking over the bookshelves.*) Mark, do you have a copy of the Constitution here?

MARK It's in a couple of books. Look at the end of that shelf.

Anyway, Charles, I never heard of any amendment that mentioned corporations. I know the Thirteenth Amendment was passed right after the Civil War, 1865. It ended slavery. But, Maeve, what was the Fourteenth Amendment about?

MAEVE It was passed in 1868, to deal with issues left over from the Civil War and the end of slavery. Representation was one problem. The original Constitution said that each state's representation in Congress would be based on its population; but population was to be computed as the total number of "*free* persons," plus 3/5 of the number of "other persons."

These "*other persons*" were of course *slaves*, but a sense of decorum —or shame— kept them from using the word *slaves* in the Constitution.

NADIA (*Taking a book from the bookshelves.*) It doesn't say *unfree persons*?

MAEVE Nope, just "free persons" and "other persons."

Anyway, with the slaves being freed by the Thirteenth Amendment, the population count for the representation of the Southern states would automatically be increased by that 2/5 of the population of *other persons* that wasn't previously counted.

But by the state's rights guarantee of the Tenth Amendment, each state decides on its own who gets to vote. So the Southern states were getting increased representation — but they weren't giving the newly freed slaves the right to vote.

So the Fourteenth Amendment changed the rule. A state's representation in Congress would no longer be based on its total population, but on the part of its population that has *voting rights*.

This gave each Southern state a choice. If it denied the former slaves the right to vote, it would *lose* the representation it previously had in counting of 3/5 of them. But if it gave them the vote, it would *gain* representation by counting the remaining 2/5.

But that's all in Section Two of the Amendment. After that are a few more sections about the aftermath of the war, prohibiting officers of the Confederacy from ever holding Federal office, and preventing lawsuits against the US government for damages due to the war.

NADIA (*paging through a book*) So we're interested in Section One.

MAEVE Yes, that's the part about human rights. After the Thirteenth Amendment freed the slaves, the Southern states enacted laws to keep the former slaves in the same social status —without property or political rights— so they'd have to keep working on the plantations to survive. Section One guaranteed them citizenship and equal protection of the laws.

MARK And that's the section that supposedly applies to corporations?

CHARLES Yes —that is the interpretation.

MAEVE Of course, the word *corporation* doesn't appear there at all. Or anywhere else in the Constitution.

MARK Okay, I want to look at it…

NADIA I found it. I've got the Constitution right here.

MARK You found the Fourteenth Amendment?

NADIA I'm looking at it. This is Section One, listen, (*reads*) "**All persons born or naturalized in the United States and subject to the jurisdiction thereof, are citizens of the United States and of the state in which they reside.**"

MARK And that "**persons**" is supposed to be a reference to corporations?

CHARLES Well, corporations aren't citizens.

MARK That's not what I'm asking. Does the word *persons* here include corporations?

CHARLES Well, yes, the word *persons* is interpreted as '*natural persons or corporations.*'

MAEVE No, no, Charles. *This* particular reference to *persons* couldn't have that meaning. If it did, the sentence could be read, "**All** *natural* **persons** *or corporations* **born or naturalized in the United States…**" And that wouldn't make sense: corporations aren't born.

NADIA Or naturalized.

MAEVE Well, they were certainly never included in any legal process for obtaining citizenship.

CHARLES Yes, yes —but they're not citizens because the Supreme Court *ruled* that they're not.

MARK What? You're kidding! The Supreme Court had to make a *ruling* on that?

CHARLES Yes, there was a case that decided it. The Supreme Court wrote an opinion that this clause does not give corporations citizenship.

NADIA But, Charles, you're missing Maeve's point. She's saying that if *corporations* were included in the meaning of *persons,* it makes the clause nonsense. If the subject is '*corporations,*' the phrase "**born or naturalized**" doesn't have any meaning. It's just an ungrammatical —nonsense— arrangement of words.

That's how we know *persons* here can mean only *natural persons*.

CHARLES But that's not the *legal* interpretation. The *important* point is that the Supreme Court has *ruled* that a corporation isn't a citizen.

MAEVE But that *ruling* is superfluous. You can tell from the context that *natural person* is the only possible meaning of *person* here. Corporations aren't citizens because they're not included in this statement.

CHARLES No, they *are* included —in the definition of *person*. But they're not citizens because the *Supreme Court* has determined that they're not.

MARK So how did the Court come to that conclusion?

CHARLES I don't know the details. But look, corporations clearly don't meet the specified condition: they're not "**persons born or naturalized in the United States**."

MARK Yes, because they're not *persons*!

CHARLES No, they *are* persons, just not "**persons born or naturalized in the United States**."

NADIA But it makes no sense to consider whether they're *born or naturalized in the United States* when they can't be *born or naturalized* at all. Those words just don't apply to corporations.

MAEVE So, Charles, are you saying that what the Supreme Court decided was whether an event that can't happen *at all* could happen in the United States?

MARK Wouldn't you agree that's absurd?

CHARLES It's not so absurd. It might have been argued that the word *born* refers to an origin —a *beginning*. It's a common usage. An understudy gets a chance to play the lead, and suddenly a *star is born*!

MARK This is not about a *star* being born, it's about a *person* being born! That has a very specific meaning —involving *obstetrics*, not *dramatics*!

CHARLES No, but you have to consider its meaning for a corporation, too.

MARK So then a metaphorical use of the word *born* would get legal status as a primary meaning —and change the meaning of the Constitution?

CHARLES But, no, *it didn't happen*! The Supreme Court *rejected* that interpretation.

MARK But considered it! Some corporate lawyer came up with idea that his corporation would benefit from citizenship, and the Supreme Court took it seriously enough to hear this nonsense!

CHARLES Well, it would have to, because it had previously ruled that *person* means *natural person or corporation*.

NADIA But, Charles, that can't be true of *this* instance of the word *person*. Can we take it one step at a time?

There are two conditions for citizenship here: "… **born or naturalized in the United States**" and "**subject to the jurisdiction thereof**." If a person meets both, then he or she —or it— must be a citizen. But the Supreme Court ruled that corporations are *not* citizens, so it must be that corporations don't meet one of the conditions.

It's not the second condition. The Court couldn't be claiming that corporations —if they are persons born or naturalized in the United States— are not subject to its jurisdiction.

So it has to be the first condition; that they're not "**born or naturalized in the United States.**" And it's not a question of *where* it might happen. If they *could* be born or naturalized, it could happen in the United States as well as anywhere.

So what Supreme Court had to be ruling is that corporations are not "**born or naturalized.**" The words just don't apply to corporations.

CHARLES Yes, but the words don't apply to corporations because the Supreme Court has *ruled* that they don't.

MAEVE No, it's *not just* because the Supreme Court ruled it. It's because everyone knows what the words *born* and *naturalized* mean. And anyone who doesn't know can look up the meanings in the dictionary, and will not find any reference to *corporations* there.

CHARLES So what are you saying, then? That the Supreme Court can't make a ruling because it's clear to *you* what the ruling ought to be?

MAEVE I'm saying it's absurd to make a *ruling* on words whose meaning is so obvious.

NADIA But, in taking the trouble to affirm the obvious —that the words *born* and *naturalized* do not apply to corporations— the Court is also affirming that corporations are *not* included in this instance of the word *person.*

CHARLES But I told you —they *are* included.

MARK Arrgh!

NADIA (*sigh*) If the words *born* and *naturalized* do not apply to corporations, then "**All** *natural* **persons** *or corporations* **born or naturalized**" is simply a nonsense arrangement of words. It is ungrammatical —it doesn't make sense.

MAEVE And the Constitution does not include non-*sense*. That's how we know that the word *persons* in the phrase "**persons born or naturalized**" does *not* include corporations.

CHARLES It's not nonsense. Look, why are you obsessing about the word person in *this* clause? It's a moot point. We all agree that a corporation can't be a citizen.

NADIA Don't we all believe that there is a need for consistency in the interpretation of a text? If one instance of a word has a particular meaning, then all instances of the word in that text must have the same meaning.

MAEVE Or, Charles, are you saying the Supreme Court can just cherry-pick its way through the Constitution, giving a word one meaning here, another meaning there?

NADIA That is arbitrariness —twisting the document's meaning to whatever the Court wants it to be.

CHARLES It's not arbitrary. The different clauses deal with different issues, and so different doctrines of interpretation are used.

MARK So what rule is used to determine the *doctrine* to be applied?

CHARLES That's a judgment call. It depends on the subject matter.

MARK Arrgh!

NADIA What about *your* opinion then? When you read, "**All persons born or naturalized in the United States...**", do you think the intended meaning is 'All *natural persons or corporations* born or naturalized in the United States'?

CHARLES My opinion doesn't matter.

MARK So you no longer have an opinion on the Constitution, because you're afraid it might not agree with the Supreme Court's?

MAEVE Clearly, *this* particular reference to *persons* couldn't include corporations.

CHARLES Well, it's a moot point, because they can't be citizens anyway.

MARK Arrgh!

CHARLES Stop making such a big deal about it.

MARK So, what comes next, Nadia?

NADIA Okay, next, (*reads*) "**No state shall make or enforce any law which shall abridge the privileges or immunities of citizens of the United States**; ..."

MAEVE The reference is to *citizens*, so this doesn't apply to corporations.

MARK So with these "**privileges or immunities**," it's clear that this *equal protection* idea —which we haven't gotten to yet— isn't going to apply between citizens and non-citizens.

CHARLES No, the privileges or immunities of citizens are not included. I mean, '*equal protection*' covers all persons, regardless of citizenship.

MARK Really? But only *some* persons who are not born in the United States are allowed to become citizens. There's no equal protection in terms of legal qualification for citizenship.

CHARLES Well, there are *requirements* for citizenship, but they apply uniformly to all.

MARK No, they *don't* —we just covered that point. The Supreme Court has *ruled* that corporations cannot become naturalized citizens. So if they're persons, they're an inferior type of person. Where's the legal equality?

CHARLES You're bringing up cases that just don't apply. Equal protection in access to citizenship is just between natural persons.

MARK Don't apply? The whole point of the *Citizens United* ruling is that *equal protection* is equality *between* corporations and natural persons. But the principle is already refuted right here, in equal access to citizenship.

CHARLES You just don't understand the scope of the ruling.

MARK No, I surely don't. Nor do you. Nor does the Supreme Court. Because it's nonsense, and nonsense *cannot be* understood.

   Nadia, let's move on.

NADIA (*reads*) "… **nor shall any state deprive any person of life, liberty, or property, without due process of law; …"**

MARK And *that* reference to *persons* is supposed to include corporations?

CHARLES Yes. That's the *due process* clause.

NADIA So if *person* means '*natural person or corporation*', then the clause should make sense if the word *person* is replaced with either '*natural person*' or '*corporation*.'

   Suppose it said, "**nor shall any state deprive any** *natural* **person of life, liberty, or property…**" That would make perfect sense, right?

   (*pause*)

   But try it this way, "**nor shall any state deprive any** *corporation* **of life, liberty, or property…** " It doesn't make sense. Just like corporations aren't born, they can't be deprived of life or liberty. They can't be executed or put in jail.

CHARLES Well, then those words —*life, liberty*— just wouldn't apply to corporations.

NADIA Then those words *couldn't* apply to the word *person* if the word person included corporations. That's how we know *corporation* is not part of the meaning of the word *person* as it's used here. If you try to shoehorn it in, the sentence becomes nonsense.

MAEVE The people who wrote this were not stupid. They didn't write nonsense.

   (*pause*)

NADIA Next is this, (*reads*) "… **nor deny to any person within its jurisdiction the equal protection of the laws."**

MARK Now if *person* were to include *corporation*, that could be read, "**nor deny to any** corporation **within its jurisdiction the equal protection of the laws.**"

   And then the phrase "**within its jurisdiction**" doesn't make sense. A corporation is not a physical being. It has no *body,* and no physical location. So it can't be within any state's jurisdiction.

CHARLES But in the law, it certainly is.

MAEVE Isn't its location just the physical location of its headquarters?

MARK A corporation may own or lease physical offices —as well as factories, warehouses, and stores— in many locations, in different states. But those physical facilities *are not* the corporation, and their locations are not the location of the corporation. And the designation of one office as 'headquarters' is just an idea, and not a necessary one.

MAEVE Wouldn't it be where the CEO works?

MARK That's one idea. But maybe he likes to work at home, in his pajamas, and in a different house, in a different state, or country, each season. And a corporation doesn't even have to have an officer designated as CEO.

It doesn't have to have a headquarters. It's not located in any state.

MAEVE But it has to be *incorporated* in one state. Wouldn't that be a *legal* designation of the corporation's location?

MARK Well, a huge number of companies are incorporated in Delaware, because it offers the best deal for incorporation. But many of those corporations have no facilities there, nor do any business there —at all. So, Charles, does Delaware have jurisdiction over all of these corporations?

CHARLES Well, it has a form of jurisdiction. Jurisdiction over corporate governance, for example.

MARK You mean states have different *forms* of jurisdiction over corporations?

CHARLES Well, it would have to be so, because corporations have different sorts of interactions with states.

MARK But there's no hint of different *forms* of jurisdiction in this clause. And with them, the statement doesn't make sense. A state can't possibly provide *equal protection* to different entities if it doesn't have the same jurisdiction over them.

CHARLES Well, of course it would mean that it must provide equal protection within each form of jurisdiction.

MARK Within? But the "*equal protection*" of this clause is being claimed to hold between a corporation and a *natural* person. A state clearly doesn't have the same form of jurisdiction over both, so the equal protection can't be *within* a form of jurisdiction.

CHARLES There are still laws that overlap different forms of jurisdictions, and that's where there must be equal protection.

MARK Such tortured rationalizations, just to avoid the obvious. The *equal protection* of this clause was never intended to be between corporations and natural persons. It's an *impossible* meaning of the text.

CHARLES That's simply your failure to imagine it.

MAEVE I can't imagine it, either. You're saying that by the Supreme Court's interpretation, the laws of Delaware, which provide protection to each individual living in or visiting Delaware, must provide the same protection to a company incorporated in Delaware but doing all its business in California ...

as well as the same protection to a company incorporated in New Jersey with a factory in Delaware ...

as well as the same to a company incorporated in Texas that sells its wares in Delaware —and reports its revenues as accruing to a subsidiary in the Cayman Islands ...

as well as the same as to a bank incorporated in Switzerland with a branch in Wilmington ...

... because they are all *persons within the jurisdiction* of Delaware?

I'm sorry, Charles, that interpretation of "**person within its jurisdiction**" is just impossible.

CHARLES Well, these things have been worked out in the law.

MAEVE Undoubtedly, cases have been resolved, but *not* with the equal protection that you claim this clause demands, because that's an impossibility! And the people who wrote the Amendment couldn't have meant that. They were not stupid.

MARK It's obvious that the authors of the Amendment and the state legislatures that ratified it never intended or considered the word *person* to mean *corporation*.

CHARLES You don't know what they intended! You don't know the original intent. This was written over a hundred years ago!

MARK It was written by educated people with excellent English language skills. Their intention —what they meant— is right there in the text, and it's quite clear.

NADIA We can still read Mark Twain, Henry James, and Henry David Thoreau, and we believe we understand them.

CHARLES But you don't know the *law*. You don't know the *legal* definition of the word *person*. Do you have a legal dictionary?

MARK No. Why should I?

CHARLES I have one in my car. Wait— I'll show you.

MARK But I don't think that's ...

(*Charles goes out the front door.*)

MARK What was that all about?

MAEVE He's going to prove his point.

MARK He wants to insist that the Constitution is a legal document, so it's in his bailiwick.

NADIA Isn't the Constitution a legal document? It's been called a *Covenant*. That's a contract, isn't it?

MARK It's an agreement, in the form of a contract, between the government and the people.

MAEVE But the question is, is it written in legal language?

MARK A contract doesn't have to be written in legal language.

MAEVE Isn't it just that a *meeting of the minds* is required?

MARK That's what I thought. But if one party believes a contract's written in the people's language and the other party believes it's written in legal language, what are the chances for a 'meeting of the minds'?

MAEVE So why would the guy with the legal dictionary win the case? Why not show him your dictionary?

MARK Seriously, I'm afraid to look. The legal definition may have leaked into my dictionary too.

MAEVE So then it's a case of *everybody knows* a corporation is a person.

MARK Everybody knows. The media pounds it into our heads. Nobody knows what it means but everybody knows it's true.

MAEVE That's the way it'll be accepted.

(*Charles comes in the front door, dictionary in hand, another volume under his arm. He opens the dictionary as he approaches.*)

CHARLES Just a minute, I'll show you.

NADIA What's this book?

CHARLES Just some more legal references. Here. (*He hands the reference book to Nadia and pages through the dictionary.*)

CHARLES Okay, this is Black's Law Dictionary, Eighth Edition. (*He hands dictionary to Mark, and shows the definition.*) Read it.

Mark: (*reads*) **"Person. One - A human being. Also termed natural person.**

Two - The living body of a human being: contraband found on the smugglers person.

Three - An entity (such as a corporation) that is recognized by law as having the rights and duties of a human being. In this sense the term includes partnerships and other associations whether incorporated or unincorporated."

Okay, that's *three* definitions of *person*.

CHARLES No, there's more.

MARK Okay, then there is a sub-entry. (*reads*) "***artificial person***. **An entity, such as a corporation, created by law and given certain legal rights and duties of a human being: a being, real or imaginary, for whom the purpose of legal reasoning is treated more or less as a human being. An entity is a person for purposes of the due process and equal protection clauses but is not a citizen for purposes of the privileges and immunities clauses in article 4 section 2, and in the 14th amendment.**

What...?

CHARLES You see?

MARK "...**for purposes of the due process and equal protection clauses... in the Fourteenth Amendment...**"?

CHARLES You see?

MARK This is incredible... and in the *dictionary*. I can't believe it.

(*pause*)

George Orwell warned us.

NADIA Well, he tried.

CHARLES Come on. Now you're making your ignorance of the law into a melodrama.

MARK Charles, Charles — *look*. We're trying to decide, is it possible to interpret the word *person* in the equal protection clause of the Fourteenth Amendment to mean *corporation*? So to prove it is, you show me a dictionary entry that says that the word *person* in the equal protection clause of the Fourteenth Amendment means *corporation.*

And you don't see anything wrong with this?

CHARLES You see, you don't understand. This is a *legal* dictionary, and so this is the *legal* definition.

MARK Not definition— *interpretation*! No, not even interpretation— *redefinition*! Not the original meaning!

Look, look —suppose you begin reading the Bible. In Genesis one, verse one, you read, **"In the beginning, God created the heavens and the earth."**

Now you're not too sure of your theology, so you go to the dictionary to look up the word *God.* You find a definition about a Supreme Being. But also, an alternative definition that says: In the book of Genesis, chapter one, verse one, '*God*' refers to ... the Big Bang.

CHARLES What? It's not the same thing.

MARK It's exactly the same thing! You'd say to yourself —*wait a minute*! This can't be right! This is not the definition of a *word*, but a definition of a particular *instance* of the *use* of a word.

And this definition of an *instance* of a word could *not* have been in the dictionary at the time that instance was written —because the dictionary couldn't refer to an instance that had not yet been written.

This is completely obvious, isn't it? That definition was not in the dictionary at the time the word was written, so it's *not the author's definition*!

And furthermore —*furthermore!*— the only reason a definition would be needed for an *instance* of the use of a word is to replace —or *displace*— the definition the word had at the time it was written. Someone else —*not the author*— has imposed his own interpretation on that instance of the word, to change the meaning of the text.

CHARLES But the interpretation that's being *imposed* —as you put it— is the Supreme Court's opinion. So that's the legal definition of the word in that instance of use.

MARK But the Constitution is not written in legal language...

CHARLES Of course it is. It's a legal document —the foundation of the entire structure of our government, and the highest law in the land!

MAEVE Mark, didn't you say the Constitution was a contract between the people and the government?

MARK I said it had the *form* of a contract...

CHARLES Well, a contract should be written in legal language, to clarify the conditions and be precise about the obligations.

MARK *Precise*? *Clarify*? You've got to be kidding! You just showed me in your legal dictionary *three* —no, *four*— definitions of the word person! So how does having multiple definitions of a word make for clarity and precision?

CHARLES Well, you have to understand the context.

MAEVE And *that* —the context— removes all the ambiguities? But the context for this amendment is the social and political problems resulting from the Civil War and the end of slavery. Nothing about *business*.

CHARLES Well, business is a factor affecting social conditions.

MAEVE There's no mention of it in the Amendment.

MARK Wait —look. Suppose you had looked in your *legal* dictionary —before the Supreme Court altered it— you'd find three different definitions of person. Which one applies? You say you decide from context.

The first definition is a human being. Of course, it fits the context perfectly.

The second definition is the living body of a human being. From the example —*the smuggler's person*— it's the human body as an object owned by the human being. That's obviously not it, from either the large context or the grammatical context.

The third definition is a corporation or association. It doesn't fit the large context of the document, which is political rights, voting rights —human rights. And it doesn't fit the immediate contexts. It has no meaning with the phrases "**born or naturalized**", "**life, liberty**" or "**within its jurisdiction**" —either. That's obviously not it.

So you'd come to the same understanding of the text as any non-lawyer reading the English language.

Maeve. Why didn't the Supreme Court look in the legal dictionary when it interpreted the Amendment?

Mark. Obviously, the Court wanted its own definition. But after the Supreme Court's alternate meaning is put into the legal dictionary, the text of the Constitution becomes a code —not just legal language, but gibberish —*goat entrails*— that only courts can interpret, and whose meanings only lawyers —the ones who've been properly *indoctrinated*— can understand. The *people* have no access to its legal meaning.

CHARLES But this is what the Court ruled. The Constitution itself says it's the highest law of the land —and laws must be interpreted.

MARK That's certainly the Supreme Court's view of it. That puts it into their bailiwick. But where does the Constitution get its authority? The essence of the Constitution, the *bedrock* authority of it, is in the common understanding —the agreement, the covenant, the meeting of the minds— between the people and their government.

The reason the people respect it —revere it!— is because it's our only bona fide guarantee that our government won't be taken over by despots who will impose their own ideas of what our freedoms should be. The authority of the Constitution is in its first words, you know what they are?

CHARLES "We the people..."

MARK "We the people!" Notice, not "we the lawyers." It's written in the language of the people and the people don't use words according to definitions in a legal dictionary. The word *person* here means human being.

MAEVE *"When I use a word, it means just what I choose it to mean, neither more nor less."*

MARK Who are you quoting?

MAEVE The great semanticist Humpty Dumpty. From *Through the Looking-Glass.*

MARK Humpty Dumpty! *Humpty Dumpty* wouldn't have put up with this scam!

Changing a dictionary definition after the word was used is like backdating a document, or altering the text of a contract after it's been signed —a fraud! Where is the Supreme Court's authority to change the Constitution?

CHARLES They didn't *change* the Constitution, they just interpreted the text.

MARK Interpreting is assigning a *meaning*. And the meaning the court assigned was quite clearly not the meaning in the minds of the authors, nor the large number of the people's representatives in the legislatures that ratified the Amendment.

MAEVE And it seems to me, it's unconstitutional. If the Court changes the meaning of the Constitution —even if it puts the change in the dictionary rather than the text— it's bypassing the amendment process that the Constitution specifies. That's unconstitutional.

MARK Of course it's unconstitutional. But saying it means nothing, because the word *constitutional* has been stolen from us. You and I —We The People— have no authority to say what is constitutional, nor have our elected representatives — Congress and the President.

The word now means only one thing: *by order of the Supreme Court*!

10. THE LIVING CONSTITUTION

CHARLES Calm down, Mark. You don't appreciate the role of the Supreme Court in holding the government to the Constitution. Can you imagine the dysfunction if everybody could decide for themselves what powers the Constitution gives them? It would be *chaos*.

And you don't appreciate the difficulties of interpretation. Your "*meeting of the minds*" idea, for example —it's just naïve. The original meeting of the minds —or *original intent*— of the Constitution, is going to erode over time *necessarily*, because society evolves —its *values* are constantly changing.

Look, I'll give you an example. Maeve knows this. With the ratification of the Fourteenth Amendment, the states were required to provide "**equal protection of the law**." So the Southern states passed laws that provided facilities for African Americans that were separate from whites, but that were claimed to be "separate but equal." That was segregation. And the Supreme Court found those laws to comply with the Amendment: they were constitutional.

That was a narrow interpretation of the *equal protection* clause. It didn't require much in the way of equality.

But then in 1954, in *Brown v. Board of Education*, the Supreme Court overturned that interpretation with a broader one. "Separate but equal" was not equal enough, and the laws of segregation were found to be unconstitutional. What had changed? Society's values had changed.

NADIA This is the notion of the *living Constitution* isn't it? The idea that the Constitution continually changes its meaning, to adapt to changes in society?

CHARLES It's been called that.

MAEVE What a marvelous doctrine for the Supreme Court to assert for itself! With the Constitution continually changing its meaning, the whole messy amendment process becomes totally unnecessary! Why should the people bother trying to say what they want their government to be, when the Supreme Court has anticipated their needs, and changed the meaning of the Constitution to meet them!

MARK More to the point, the Supreme Court is *compelled* to reinterpret the Constitution in order to *preserve* the meeting of minds between the people and the government.

CHARLES If that's the way you want to look at it —and if you could lose the ironical tone— yes, that's the general idea. *Tempora mutantur.* The changes in the tenor of the Constitution are the changes wrought by time.

MARK So, *when* did the Court rule that the *equal protection* clause in the Fourteenth Amendment applied to corporations?

CHARLES It was 1886. The case was *Santa Clara County v. Southern Pacific Railroad.* The railroad was disputing taxes by the County.

MARK So, 1886? And the Fourteenth Amendment was passed in 1868. That's eighteen years.

So what are we supposed to believe here, that America's values changed so radically in eighteen years, that the Fourteenth Amendment had to include corporations? Maeve, was the country swept by a great pro-corporate fervor during this period?

MAEVE Those were Reconstruction years, with a lot of turmoil. At first, the South was occupied by Federal troops, and there was a lot of anger at opportunists — carpetbaggers— finding ways to profit from the Federal government's attempts to reconstruct the social institutions of the defeated South.

And later, there was also a lot of anger at the abusive practices of corporations —particularly the railroads, which had grown very powerful. Congress passed some important measures at this time to control them.

NADIA Hey, look what I found in Charles' book. *The Interstate Commerce Act*, 1887...

MAEVE Yes, that was major legislation regulating the railroads.

NADIA Yes, but here's an example of the text, from Section 13, quote, (*reads*) **"That any person, firm, corporation, or association, or any mercantile, agricultural, or manufacturing society, or any body politic or municipal organization..."**

(*pause*)

MAEVE So?

NADIA Oh, the rest is all about appeals to some Commission. I was just pointing out the *language* —how the law applies to **"any person, firm, corporation, or association..."**

MAEVE Oh, right! Charles told us that the *legal* definition of '*person*' includes corporations and associations. Now if that were true, Congress wouldn't write a law that said "any *person, firm, corporation, or association.*"

CHARLES Well, there's redundancy. They were just making it clear.

MARK *Clear?* You're kidding! Have you seen that sign at the playground that says, "No Dogs or Poodles Allowed"?

CHARLES No. What is it, some sort of joke?

MARK Why would you think it's a *joke*? Don't you think the *redundancy* just makes it *clear* that poodles are included among the dogs not allowed?

CHARLES Well, it's just a joke.

NADIA Not to spoil the joke, but the humor is in the *clear* implication that a poodle is *not* a dog.

MAEVE Or, Charles, can you imagine a legislature passing a law about children's welfare, saying a decision is to be made by 'the child's *parent or mother*'?

CHARLES What? No, they wouldn't ...

MAEVE Of course they wouldn't. If you say '*parent or mother*' to make it *clear* that mother is included in the law, you're actually implying that mother is *not* included in the word parent. Or possibly even that *mother* and *parent* are synonyms, implying that a father is somehow not included. It's a muddle.

MARK The legislators writing the laws were not stupid. When they wrote "**person, firm, corporation, or association,**" the word *person* clearly meant human being, and nothing else.

NADIA And here, I found the Sherman Antitrust Act, 1896. Section eight, quote, (*reads*) "**That the word 'person,' or 'persons,' whenever used in this act shall be deemed to include corporations and associations existing under law.**"

CHARLES There, you see?

MARK See? What are you talking about? That clause is included in the act because without it, '*person*' would mean what it has always meant —*natural person*! In the law as well as in common language.

MAEVE The Fourteenth Amendment has no such clause.

MARK *Nowhere* in the Constitution is there such a clause.

NADIA Surprising —isn't it?— how hard it is to get clarity back, once the meaning of a word has been muddled.

MARK But it ought to be absolutely clear! Nobody could seriously believe this Amendment was intended to be about corporations!

CHARLES Original intent is not the modern doctrine of interpretation.

MARK So the Court doesn't think it matters what the authors meant, or what the people thought it meant, or what legislatures that ratified it took it to mean?

CHARLES The modern doctrine of interpretation, textualism, focuses on the text itself, not the author's *intention*.

MARK But the *text* of the Fourteenth Amendment clearly doesn't have *anything* to do with corporations!

NADIA True, Mark. But what hope do you have of changing it? The Justices won't be able to see it as an error … or deception.

MAEVE *It is difficult to make a court understand … when its power depends on its not understanding.*

NADIA Absolute power depends on infallibility. To admit to an error would deny the legitimacy of its absolute power.

CHARLES That's ridiculous. It's *settled law*, that's all. It's the interpretation the courts have been using for over a century. You're not going to change it.

MARK So we've got a Constitution corrupted by a shyster lawyer's trick, and the Supreme Court's just doubling down in it —legitimizing the corruption.

CHARLES That's nothing but a slander! That's your real motive.

MAEVE But, wait —*wait a minute*! Why don't we just *read the opinion* and see how the Supreme Court explains why a corporation is *necessarily* a person?

MARK Of course! The Supreme Court's opinion in the case! Nadia, can you find it in that book?

MAEVE He said it was *Santa Clara County v. Southern Pacific Railroad*.

CHARLES No, you won't...

MAEVE I'm sure there's some soaring rhetoric, resonating with the eloquence of Oliver Wendell Holmes.

CHARLES No, it's not in my book.

MARK No? Why not? This has got to be a landmark ruling, establishing the *personhood* of corporations.

CHARLES No, actually, there's nothing about that in the opinion.

MARK Nothing about what?

CHARLES Equal protection for corporations. It's not mentioned at all.

MAEVE What? How can that be the Court's ruling then, if it's not in the opinion?

CHARLES The Chief Justice, Morrison Waite, issued a statement before the oral argument. He said that the Court would not hear arguments on the question of whether the equal protection clause of the Fourteenth Amendment applies to corporations, because, he said, " ...**we are all of the opinion that it does.**"

MAEVE Would not hear arguments? How is that even legal?

CHARLES The Court had considered it while preparing for the case.

MARK Oral argument was not allowed? Not even one rumpled lawyer on the salary of Santa Clara County was allowed to stand before the Supreme Court and defend the Constitution —and all humankind— from the invasion by corporations?

CHARLES I'm sure it was considered, in chambers.

MAEVE But then why didn't they write it into the opinion? Isn't a court's opinion supposed to give the legal authority for a ruling, so that everyone can see that the court is not just acting arbitrarily?

MARK And isn't an opinion supposed to explain the legal reasoning, for the guidance of the courts that must decide future cases? Where is the instruction about what this actually means?

CHARLES Well, the Court found other reasons that decided the case. The decision didn't rely on the equal protection clause, so it didn't have to discuss the principle.

MARK So it was just an *announcement*...?

MAEVE It was my understanding that the place of Court opinions in our legal system was established when George Washington first took office as president. He asked his Chief Justice, John Jay, to advise him about the law. And after conferring with the entire Court, Jay turned him down. He said you'll know what the law is when we write our opinions in real cases.

Clearly, Chief Justice Jay was asserting that the Court will make law —common law, that is— through *decisions* in *cases*.

But if this principle wasn't used to decide a case, it's nothing more than an *edict* by the Chief Justice. How could it be considered law?

CHARLES I'm not a constitutional lawyer. But, you know, legal standards have evolved since that time.

MARK Okay, so the Court didn't use the principle it announced. But let me take a wild guess: the Court decided the case in favor of the corporation anyway.

CHARLES Well, yes.

MARK Surprise, surprise.

CHARLES So now you're insinuating the Court was biased.

MARK Charles, the Court accepted the position the corporation wanted —equal protection for corporations and individuals— which is an *absurd* interpretation of the Fourteenth Amendment. And then it wouldn't hear any argument about it, and left no record of the reasoning. And you don't think there's any bias?

CHARLES That's just speculation. You don't know all that the case involved. There's just no point in rehashing it now.

MAEVE But this is the principle —now called a *constitutional* principle— that's enabling the Supreme Court to overrule Congress on the regulation of corporations —today!

NADIA Listen to what I found —a quote from Thomas Jefferson, writing about the Justices. Here's what he thinks. (*reads*) **"Having found from experience that impeachment is an impracticable thing, a mere scare-crow, they consider themselves secure for life; they skulk from responsibility to public opinion, the only remaining hold on them, under practice first introduced into England by Lord Mansfield. An opinion is huddled up in Conclave, perhaps by a majority of one, delivered by a crafty Chief Justice as if unanimous, and, with the silent acquiescence of lazy or timid associates. He sophisticates the law to his mind by the turn of his own reasoning."**

CHARLES Thomas Jefferson? Come on, that had to be half a century earlier. And his animosity toward the Court is well known.

MARK But was that it, Charles? A crafty Chief Justice? How did he *sophisticate the law to his mind*, and what was *the turn of his own reasoning*?

CHARLES Look, I'm sure the entire Court considered it, and had a reason.

MARK Of course, you mean to imply a *valid* reason. Besides lazy or timid associates, what about the traditional corruptions —bribery, extortion, threats, sexual enticements, blackmail, dementia, ideological zealotry?

CHARLES See, now you're showing your real motivation —to slander the Court.

MARK No, no —I'm not *accusing*. I don't *know* what happened. And in the absence of any explanation, neither do you. I'm just offering alternatives to expand your thinking.

NADIA Human beings are corruptible. I don't believe an exception has been made for Justices.

CHARLES There's no reason to call it corruption! The Supreme Court is not corrupt!

MAEVE But then, is this your idea of valid legal reasoning? The Supreme Court delivering an *edict*, with no explanation? Charles, you're a lawyer —how do you justify it?

CHARLES Look, I don't have to justify it. This is the Court's interpretation. Maybe they made a mistake, but they're still the Supreme Court.

MARK Oh? Okay, so you think the Supreme Court might have made a mistake.

CHARLES If you think it's wrong, all you can say is they made a mistake. There's no proof of any corruption.

MARK No, certainly no way to prove it.

CHARLES No.

MARK Still, to take a corporation for a person, that's ... quite a mistake.

CHARLES So? Anybody can make a mistake.

MARK I mean, if you took General Grant for General Lee —that would be a mistake...

 ... but to take General *Motors* for General Lee... that takes *mistake* to a new level.

CHARLES So now you're implying that the Court is stupid?

MARK No! Making a mistake doesn't mean you're stupid. Anybody can make a mistake.

CHARLES Even you, huh?

MARK Sure, I've made mistakes. Making a mistake is not stupid...

 ... true stupidity requires *repeating* a mistake to pretend it wasn't a mistake.

CHARLES Uh-huh.

MARK So how come the Court didn't follow up with a decision that corrected it?

MAEVE Well, clearly, if you're *supreme*, you don't ever need to admit to a mistake.

NADIA If you're *supreme*, you *can't* admit to a mistake.

11. STARE DECISIS

CHARLES Come on, you're being ridiculous. It just shows you're not familiar with the doctrine of *stare decisis*.

MARK *STAR-ay de-CY-sis*! Whenever you lawyers need to sound profound, you trot out the Latin. What does it mean, *stare decisis*?

CHARLES Let the decision stand.

MARK Oh. Okay, so what is the *doctrine* of stare decisis?

CHARLES That the court should let a decision stand.

MARK That's it? That's not a doctrine, that's a slogan! It's like, Remember the Alamo! Or, carpe diem! Hell, *carpe diem* is more of a doctrine!

CHARLES You'd rather make a mockery of it than try to understand it.

NADIA No, Charles, why don't you just explain it to us?

CHARLES Then listen. *Stare decisis* is a fundamental rule —a *necessity* for any society that purports to be governed by *laws not men*. Everyone must know and agree on what the law is.

MARK Well, that's what we have legislatures for.

CHARLES Yes, in a democracy, the law is the will of the people, so the people's representatives in the legislatures write the formal laws —the *statutes*. That's statutory law.

But that's not *all* the law. Because, no matter how comprehensive and clear the statutory law is, there will always be *some* circumstances that give rise to a difference of opinion about how, or whether, a law applies, or even which of several laws might apply.

It's these differences of opinion that bring disputes into court. And in deciding those cases, the *court* determines what the law is.

MAEVE Okay, that's what's called the common law. But courts can't write opinions contrary to the statutory law. That would usurp the function of the legislature.

CHARLES Right, the statutory law prevails. But when there is none, or its meaning is disputed in a case, the court must resolve the controversy using principles of *equity* — concepts such as *fairness*, *evenhandedness*, and *justice*.

MARK Right, but *whose* concept of justice?

CHARLES Just like the statutory law reflects the will of the people, the court's commitment to the principles of *equity* will reflect social norms.

MAEVE So it's *society's* standard of fairness that shape the common law.

CHARLES Of course. Even when writing statutory law, if a legislature can't nail down requirements precisely, it'll resort to the concept of *reasonableness* —an appeal to what a reasonable person would expect or do. That reflects the social norm.

The legislature assumes it will be clear enough in most cases, and for the particular cases when it's not, it trusts that the courts will make it clear.

NADIA We're all reasonable persons here, so we should be able to understand the common law.

CHARLES Of course, that's exactly what I'm telling you! So in a court case, the judges must examine the relevant law —if there is any— and the essence of the dispute, and then find a principle deriving from *equity* that is *necessary* in order to resolve the case with justice.

That principle is the *rationale* for the decision. If you need the Latin for it, it's *ratio decidendi* —the reason for deciding.

MAEVE So when the court finds the *rationale,* it's creating *law* for that case.

CHARLES Yes, the law that *holds* for that case. The rationale is also called the *holding* for the case.

Now I'm sure we agree that fairness in the law requires *consistency.* If a court decides a case one way —with a particular rationale— and then decides a similar case differently, it's being *arbitrary.* That allows the perception of bias — that the decision is actually being made on the basis of *who* the parties to the lawsuit are.

So the rule of *stare decisis* is to ensure consistency. It says that once a case is decided with a certain *rationale,* if another case of the same type —with the same circumstances— is later brought to court, it *must* be decided according to the same rationale.

The earlier case would be a *precedent* for the later case. And in being decided by the same rationale, the later case is said to *follow the precedent.*

MAEVE But why would a case with *the same circumstances* come to court, anyway?

CHARLES Right, right —it very likely wouldn't. But that's precisely *because* of the *stare decisis* rule, don't you see? If it weren't for that, courts could simply ignore precedent cases, and then the parties to every dispute would have to go to court to see how it would be decided *in their case.*

But since the rule of *stare* decisis *requires* a court to follow the rationale of the precedent, the disputes for which there is a precedent case will be settled out of court.

MAEVE Sure, since both parties would know how the court would rule.

CHARLES Yes, how it *must* rule, because of *stare decisis.* In other words, they know what is held to be the *law* that governs that particular controversy.

MAEVE That's the common law. So when a court announces a rationale for a case, it's not just deciding that case, but all cases of the same type.

CHARLES Not exactly —it's not *deciding* other cases. A court's only responsibility or authority is to provide justice in the case being heard. Future cases will be decided by the courts that hear them.

MAEVE But for similar cases, those courts *must* follow the same rule —the same rationale.

CHARLES Yes, that is *their* responsibility. *Stare decisis* is a rule for *following* precedents, which means looking back to see what has previously been decided. It doesn't mean looking forward, to anticipate and preempt judgment of future cases.

Because, as you said, that's the function of *statutory* law, which is the legislature's domain.

MAEVE But a case that's exactly the same as a precedent *would effectively* be preempted, by being settled out of court. Because both parties would know how the court would rule.

CHARLES That is the way it works. But no two cases can be *exactly* the same. The question in any case is whether its similarity to a precedent would require following the precedent's rationale, or whether the court will see a reason to *distinguish* the case from the precedent. If the court —guided by the principle of *equity*—finds a reason to *distinguish*, the case can be decided with a different rationale.

But then, the rule to distinguish the case from the precedent will also become part of the common law. Then courts that hear later cases *must* distinguish from potential precedents in the same way, if it can be done.

NADIA So the doctrine of *stare decisis* turns a court's decisions into rules that courts must follow ... which is, effectively, law...

MAEVE That's the common law.

NADIA ...but only to fill in the gaps where the statutory law is missing.

CHARLES Yes, but not just to fill in gaps. Sometimes there are *overlaps* in statutory law, where more than one law may be claimed to apply. Then the court must construe *the laws*—that is, decide which law best applies to the circumstances of the case.

NADIA And what rule is used for that?

CHARLES There are quite a few rules. The court will choose the law that's more relevant to the case, the law that comes from the higher authority, the law that's more specific, or more recent.

NADIA So the common law fills the gaps where the statutory law is missing or ambiguous, and will resolve conflicts within the statutory law...

CHARLES Yes, exactly.

NADIA ...and then successive additions to the common law make finer distinctions among cases, filling in the gaps between precedents. And that progressively develops the law, filling the areas in which there is no law, or where it's unclear.

CHARLES Yes, it tends toward that effect. But there's no end to the variety of circumstances that are brought up before the law. There will always be new disputes, and the need for new common law.

(pause)

MARK Well, that doctrine of *stare decisis* certainly makes for a neat *theory*.

NADIA Yes, it's the common law complementing the statutory law —both reflecting social norms.

MAEVE Doesn't it just make you all warm and fuzzy inside, to think how they work together to serve the will of the people?

MARK A beautiful theory.

NADIA *Beauty is truth, truth beauty.*

MARK It may be the beautiful theory you learned in law school, Charles, but it has absolutely nothing to do with the *reality* of what happened here.

The principle announced in the *Santa Clara* case —that equal protection in the Constitution applies to corporations— was not the *rationale* of anything. It wasn't used to decide the case.

It wasn't demonstrated to be a *necessary* principle of equity. And in fact, equating a human being and an abstract being is an impossibility, so it has nothing to do with commonly understood principles of *equity*.

And it isn't a principle for *distinguishing* cases, either, but *exactly* the opposite! It *denies* the right of a court to use a perfectly obvious distinction —whether a law applies to a human being or a corporation— as a means of distinguishing cases.

And if it were a principle of common law, it would be limited to the type of case for which it was found to be the rationale —the rationale deemed *necessary* in order to achieve justice. But this principle can't be limited to the type of case in which it was announced —because it wasn't even used in that case.

So the cases to which it does apply are not specified. It's an open-ended principle, a generality to be to used to decide cases that the courts have not yet seen. But that's the domain of *statutory* law. This edict clearly intrudes on —it *usurps*— the legislature's authority to write statutory law.

MAEVE Charles, I think that's right! If the principle announced in *Santa Clara* wasn't used to decide the case, and its *necessity* was never demonstrated, it certainly *couldn't* have been cited as a *precedent.*

CHARLES Well, I understand your point, Maeve, but it's a bit naive. It was cited. Two years later, in *Missouri Pacific Railway v. Mackey*, the Court affirmed that equal protection in the Fourteenth Amendment applied to corporations, and it cited *Santa Clara* as the precedent.

MAEVE But —*wait a minute!* What could they possibly have cited? You said it was an *oral* announcement.

CHARLES Yes, it was, but it was published. The company that publishes the Court's opinions presents the essential facts of each case in a *headnote* before the opinion. The Chief Justice's statement was included in the headnote.

MARK But that wasn't written by any Justice.

CHARLES Well, no, but it was spoken by the Chief Justice, and stated the Court's opinion.

MARK It was the Chief Justice's opinion.

CHARLES He said, "...**we are all of the opinion**".

MARK Maybe he was the crafty kind Jefferson warned about, who "... **sophisticates the law to his mind by the turn of his own reasoning.**"

CHARLES There you go again —slandering the Court.

MARK No, just look at the *fact* —it's nothing but an edict. It's a ... what do you call it —an *obiter*?

CHARLES The Latin term you want is *obiter dictum*. Anyway, about your insinuation that the Court is biased, you should be aware that this time the Court ruled *against* the railroad.

MAEVE What...?

MARK So apparently, we've got to add to your doctrine of *stare decisis* that an *obiter dictum* by a court is just as good as a *rationale*.

NADIA Here's the definition of *obiter dictum* in Charles' law dictionary. Listen, (*reads*) "**obiter dictum**... **A judicial comment made while delivering a judicial opinion, but one that is unnecessary to the decision in the case, and therefore not precedential (although it may be considered persuasive).**"

MARK Not *precedential*. It can't be used as a precedent! And you said Maeve was *naive* for supposing exactly that— that the dictum in *Santa Clara* couldn't be used as a precedent.

CHARLES Well, yes, but look— that's just a dictionary entry, it's not *law*. Anyway, the Court considered it persuasive.

MARK Persuasive? An edict, with no explanation? Oh, but the only Justices it had to persuade were precisely the ones that had announced it two years earlier.

MAEVE But wait, Charles —*wait a minute!* The *principle* that we're talking about here is that corporations must have equal protection of the law, right?

CHARLES Yes.

MAEVE So obviously, a corporation would argue for it. But you said that in this *Mackey* case, the principle was *affirmed* and the railroad *lost*. So ... I don't get it.

Was the railroad arguing *against* the principle?

CHARLES No, no. Of course the railroad wasn't *against* it.

Look, here's the case. The railroad was appealing a judgment against it in a lawsuit brought by an employee who was injured on the job. The judgment was based on a California law that applied only to railroads. So the railroad argued that the law was unconstitutional —violating the Fourteenth Amendment— because it didn't provide equal protection to railroad corporations.

But then the Court ruled that the equal protection principle did not prohibit the legislature from passing laws that applied to one type of corporation but not another. So the railroad lost.

MARK What? Wait —*wait*. That doesn't *affirm* the equal protection principle —that *denies* it!

CHARLES But, no, the *principle* was explicitly affirmed. The Court wrote, "**It is conceded that corporations are persons within the meaning of the amendment**," — citing *Santa Clara*. But the equal protection clause didn't apply in this particular case.

MAEVE So again, the principle wasn't used to decide the case.

CHARLES Well, it didn't determine the final decision... but it was used in the reasoning. The Court just found the principle to be narrower than the railroad had argued, so the railroad lost.

MAEVE But if the Court didn't say *how* narrow the principle is, it could be so narrow that it doesn't exist at all.

CHARLES What? No. I don't see your point.

MAEVE The Court accepted the principle, citing *Santa Clara*, where it hadn't been used to decide the case, then wrote that it affirmed it, but then narrowed it so it didn't decide this case either. It wasn't a *ratio decidendi* for either case.

CHARLES Well... yes, that's true.

MARK But in the written opinion, it's explicitly affirmed as a principle of law.

MAEVE But it *can't be* a principle of common law —it wasn't a rationale.

NADIA And, Charles, if the *Mackey* case was about an injury to an employee, how could the Court cite *Santa Clara* —where a railroad was disputing its *property taxes*— as a precedent?

CHARLES Well, it was just the principle that was cited. That the Fourteenth Amendment applies to corporations.

NADIA So you're saying a court can simply pluck a principle of out of one case, where it wasn't even a *holding*, and use it *as law* in an entirely unrelated case?

CHARLES It's not a matter of *plucking*. The principle was broad enough to apply to both cases.

NADIA It's broad enough to apply to *any* case where a law restricts a corporation.

MARK So in spite of your theory of *stare decisis*, a *precedent* case is not a *similar* case at all, but just a case where a court happens to announce a broad and vague principle.

MAEVE Yes, it's clear that the principle of equal protection for corporations was announced and then affirmed ...

MARK And then it's doctrine —*settled doctrine*.

MAEVE ... without being used to decide either case, or ever demonstrated to be *necessary* to achieve justice in a case. This is *not* the way common law is supposed to work.

CHARLES Well, yes, there have been a few anomalous rulings. The law is not perfect.

MARK Anomalous? Oh, a small perturbation that's of no consequence to our Constitutional system? One tiny imperfection just disappears when you look at the big picture?

MAEVE Charles, you know very well that the Constitution gives the Supreme Court only one authority —the power to decide *cases.* That is, the power to decide whether it's the plaintiff or the defendant that's in the right in a case, according to the law. Read Article III of the Constitution.

CHARLES Yes, yes, of course. Yet it's absolutely *necessary* for courts to *construe* or laws in order to decide cases.

MARK Sure, when there isn't a clear law for deciding a case, a court may improvise a rule —creating common law— using the principles of equity.

But that's *not* what the Court did here! The principle it announced was not *necessary* to decide the case. It set a precedent based on an edict, a *dictat*. The Court just ignored —*trampled over*— the rules for making common law!

CHARLES Well, it was an anomaly —an aberration.

MARK Then why didn't they fix it?

CHARLES You just do not appreciate how the tradition of *stare decisis*, is a *necessity* for impartial jurisprudence.

MAEVE You said *stare decisis* means "let the *decision* stand." The decision was that the railroad didn't have to pay the County taxes for its fences. That can stand. It doesn't mean you have to let stand as law an announcement that has nothing to do with the decision.

MARK What, is there a principle of *stare obiter dicta*?

NADIA Well, I can see that the Court absolutely violated the principles of common law, here. But it was just one case. Or two. Why is that such a problem?

MARK You don't see the *problem*, Nadia?

NADIA I'd like to hear it from the lawyer. Because, Charles, you did tell us that the common law is subordinate to the statutory law, didn't you? The courts must defer to the will of the legislatures.

CHARLES Yes, that's true, generally speaking.

NADIA Oh? By that, do you mean, *not always*?

CHARLES You understand that the judicial function is to interpret the laws to see how they apply to a case. It's also called *construing* the law.

MAEVE It's called statutory *construction*, isn't it?

CHARLES Yes, the word *construction*, in this context, comes from *construing*, not *constructing*.

And when two laws conflict with each other, statutory construction involves deciding which law holds. An important rule is that the law that comes from the *higher authority* takes precedence.

NADIA I can understand that. If one party in a case cites a law passed by a city council, and the other cites a state law —which might lead to a different result– the court should decide on the basis of the state law

CHARLES Right…

MARK Now, here's the problem —the *Constitution* is the highest law.

NADIA Is that right, Charles?

CHARLES The *problem* is only Mark's —but, yes, the Constitution is the highest law of the land. It says so itself.

So if a court determines that a statute —a law passed by a legislature— conflicts with some provision of the Constitution, the court can decide the case on the basis of the Constitution rather than the statute.

MAEVE And no legislature can reverse any court decision that cites the Constitution.

MARK And the court will not only decide the *case* on the basis of the Constitution, but will also judge the *law* to be null and void, not to be respected in *any* case, because of the conflict with the Constitution.

NADIA Okay, so in the big picture, there are actually *three* levels of law in our legal system. The lowest level is the *statutory common law*. That is, common law created by courts construing statutes.

At the level above that is the *statutory law*, written by legislatures, including Congress.

And the highest level is the common law created by courts construing the Constitution. That's *constitutional common law*.

CHARLES No, no, Nadia. That term is not used. It's just called *constitutional* law.

MARK But *constitutional common law* is exactly what it is. The Supreme Court considers all of its opinions that cite the Constitution to have the authority of the Constitution itself.

MAEVE And of course, it is common law. Their opinions interpreting the Constitution don't have to reference the Constitution at all, but simply cite a precedent opinion that's in the constitutional common law. That's any opinion in a chain of precedent opinions that leads to back to an interpretation of the Constitution.

MARK Or leads back to nothing but an *edict* —an *assertion* by the Supreme Court that the Constitution says what it clearly does not say!

Now, do you see the problem, Nadia? If the Supreme Court makes a false claim about the Constitution —either innocently or intentionally— then that's what the Constitution says.

It has set a *precedent*, enabling that falsehood to be used in future cases, and it will be propagated and elaborated throughout the law, overruling all legislatures —*forever*.

MAEVE Whatever the Supreme Court says the Constitution says, that's what it says.

KEVIN Wow. It's like King Midas. Everything it touches turns to gold.

MARK Right, if gold is power. Because there is no force that can make the Supreme Court give up a power it has *usurped*.

CHARLES No, that's absolutely not true. There's always the possibility of a constitutional amendment.

MAEVE But that requires supermajorities; two-thirds of Congress and three-quarters of the state legislatures. It means the entire population would have to understand the usurpation by the Court, and become agitated enough to act against it.

MARK But if just a third of the population can be *duped* into believing that the Court's corruption of the Constitution *works in their favor*, they won't act.

MAEVE If they believe it works in their favor, they won't be *capable* of understanding why it's wrong.

MARK How can they not see it? If the Constitution's turned into gibberish, and all power is concentrated in an undemocratic body, how can they not see that it ultimately undermines their own security?

CHARLES Stop the hyperbole. You're being paranoid. The Supreme Court is not the bogyman.

MARK (*rising*) Excuse me, I've got to go meet a class.

CHARLES We agree to disagree, then.

MARK *You* can agree. I'll just disagree...

(*Mark exits via the hallway adjoining the living room.*)

MAEVE Come on, Charles, how do you, personally —not as a lawyer, but as a citizen, presumably believing the Constitution preserves our liberty— how do you justify this interpretation, or this *edict*?

CHARLES I don't have to justify it. Look, I'm not saying I agree with it, and I fully understand that *you* believe the Court was wrong. But it's not a question of right or wrong, it's an *interpretation*.

MAEVE But it's not what the Constitution says, *at all!* It's not a possible interpretation. You can't make that interpretation without changing the meaning of words, and changing the dictionary. That's cheating, fraud. Where's the Court's authority for that?

CHARLES You're challenging their authority? They're the Supreme Court.

NADIA Just the word *Supreme*, means they have supreme power?

CHARLES Well, they have the power to make an interpretation of the Constitution.

NADIA So apparently, they can say anything at all, as long as they say it's an interpretation?

CHARLES Not *anything*. It has to be reasonable.

MAEVE And who decides what's reasonable? Oh, the Supreme Court. So they can say anything, if they say it's an interpretation and it's reasonable.

CHARLES Look, Maeve, I'll agree that there's some doubt that a *literal* reading of the Fourteenth Amendment would support the interpretation that a corporation has legal equality with a natural person. And I might not agree with it, but that doesn't make it an unreasonable idea...

MAEVE Wait —so you're admitting that it's *not* what the Fourteenth Amendment says, and yet you want to insist it's a constitutional principle anyway?

CHARLES I'm not *admitting* anything. I only said that there might be doubt that the *language* of the Fourteenth Amendment establishes the principle. But it's still the Supreme Court's call. The Court may have a holistic view, and see the principle in the overall *thrust* of the Constitution.

MAEVE The thrust? You mean they're making constitutional rulings from what they considerer the *spirit* of the Constitution? Not what the words say, not the author's meaning?

CHARLES See, you're still appealing to original intent. That's not the modern doctrine of interpretation.

MAEVE Why must it be a *doctrine*? It's just common sense. If you look only at the *text*, and it says *nothing* about corporations, then it's not about corporations.

NADIA Here's quote from Charles' book. This is from Justice Joseph Story, quote, (*reads*) "**It is obvious, that there can be no security to the people in any constitution of government, if they are not to judge of it by the fair meaning of the words of the text.**"

(*Mark reappears, wearing a coat and carrying a briefcase.*)

MARK Of course it's obvious. If any branch of the government has unchecked, unlimited power to say the Constitution means what they think it *ought* to mean, and then to overrule the other branches on that basis, the Constitution won't be anybody's guarantee of liberty.

And by acquiescing to that unlimited power —which the Supreme Court has awarded *itself*— we have enabled a usurpation of power, and the corruption of the Constitution.

And by the act of usurping power, the Supreme Court —the only non-democratic branch of the government— has demonstrated its *contempt* for the Constitution's authority to define and constrain its own powers.

And furthermore —here is a core *conservative* principle— if you do not oppose a usurpation of power, you are enabling it, and you will have more. The process of usurpation will not limit itself.

Power always seeks greater power. If it is not challenged, it will naturally enhance its own comfort, convenience, and security. If it is challenged, it will react —out of fear for its security— to repel the challenge, repress the opposition, and solidify its power.

CHARLES That's just paranoia, Mark.

(*Mark opens the front door, looks out, and pauses.*)

12. SLAVERY

MARK Oh, here comes Paul, now
(*Paul enters.*)

PAUL Hey.

MARK So now you can ask Paul. He's the proud owner of a corporation.

PAUL You going?

MARK Yeah, sorry. I gotta go. I'm already late.
(*Mark leaves.*)

PAUL Hey, how you doing, Kevin?

KEVIN Hi, Paul.

MAEVE Paul, you incorporated your business?

PAUL Yeah.

MAEVE But why?

PAUL My accountant told me to.

MAEVE Yes, but why?

PAUL So he could get the fees.

NADIA I don't think that's the reason he gave you.

PAUL He said it would insulate my personal finances from the business. And this is supposed to be good, because it makes his life easier, and I get to pay the fees.

CHARLES Your *business* pays the fees.

PAUL Right. That's the way he sees it. Like it doesn't cost me anything. Except it cuts into the business profit, which is my income.

CHARLES But now you have a separation between your personal wealth and the assets of the business.

PAUL So what? It's incorporated, but it's all mine anyway.

NADIA Now this is confusing to me. I thought the whole point of a corporation was to enable *shared* ownership of a business.

CHARLES That was the *original* idea. But it's evolved.

NADIA Evolution is a phenomenon of *nature*. Corporations are not natural.

MAEVE True, Nadia. And Charles has been telling us that legally, a corporation is an *association* of persons. Now it seems to have *evolved* into no association at all

CHARLES What, a corporation owned by one person? It's the same thing —it's just a degenerate form of association.

MAEVE Come on, Charles —it's *not* the same thing. One person does not make an *association.*

PAUL Oh, boy. What are you fighting about now?

MAEVE We're not *fighting.* We're having a discussion.

NADIA It's about the *Citizens United* case.

PAUL So what about it?

CHARLES Mark's been having a hard time with it. And he's gotten Maeve all upset.

MAEVE Paul, the Supreme Court has ruled that it is a constitutional principle that a corporation has freedom of speech.

PAUL Really. So *whose* speech does it have freedom of?

CHARLES *Whose* speech?

PAUL Yeah, whose? A corporation has the freedom of *whose* speech?

CHARLES Its own speech.

PAUL But it's owned. It is totally controlled by its owner. Like a slave. Does a slave —or *did* a slave— ever have freedom of speech?

CHARLES That's irrelevant. We don't have slavery.

PAUL But we did when the Constitution was written, and we're talking about a constitutional principle. I'd say it's relevant. *Did* slaves ever have freedom of speech?

CHARLES We're not talking about slavery.

PAUL It's the same idea. What could freedom of speech mean to a slave —or a corporation— that's owned and controlled by its owner?

CHARLES It's not the same!

PAUL The slave still wouldn't be allowed to voice any opinion contrary to its owner's, so what kind of freedom of speech is that?

CHARLES No, no —you're missing the *legal* issue here. *Legal* freedom of speech is simply what the First Amendment guarantees: that *Congress can make no law* abridging freedom of speech. And with the Fourteenth Amendment, it applies to state legislatures as well.

   So it means speech can't be restricted by any *law.* It doesn't mean there can't be *other* restrictions on speech that might occur for various other reasons.

PAUL So? So did slaves have the benefit of the First Amendment, so *Congress* couldn't pass laws abridging their freedom of speech?

CHARLES No, that's stupid. And it's irrelevant.

PAUL I don't think so. The First Amendment doesn't exclude slaves, so the High Court might have ruled that a slave *legally* has freedom of speech. And if the Court had made that ruling —without changing the slave's status of being owned and controlled by his owner— then *whose speech would the slave have had the freedom of?*

CHARLES The Supreme Court never ruled that slaves have freedom of speech.

PAUL But suppose it had.

MAEVE The question is, w*hose* speech would have benefited from the ruling?

CHARLES It's a stupid question.

MAEVE The slave's speech still wouldn't be free, so it would have to be the owner's.

PAUL Of course. But the owner already has freedom of speech. The ruling would've given the owner an extra dose —another voice beyond his own, with freedom of speech. And that's political power. The owner can have his slave tell everyone how he really enjoys servitude, with such a wonderful master. And no law could abridge the freedom of that speech.

CHARLES That's idiotic. And it never happened. Why would a court make such a stupid ruling?

NADIA *Why would* a court? Its motive couldn't be known! On its face, the ruling would've seemed to strike a blow for the *ideal* of freedom— who could be against freedom of speech? But in *reality*, it would've given greater voice —and political power— to the slave-owner, to maintain control and oppression.

CHARLES Oh, come *on* …

NADIA So if you ask *why*, it would be *either* because the Court is idealistic and naïve —blind to the real effect of the ruling— *or else* because it is cynical and shrewd— seeing and full well intending the real effect, while posturing at idealism.

PAUL Then even *you,* Charles, would have been asking, is the Court *stupid*, or *evil*?

CHARLES Come on, this whole *idea* is absurd! Look, there were contradictions in slavery. It was morally wrong, and completely contrary to all of our ideas of freedom. But it's over.

PAUL Well, it may not be morally wrong to own a corporation, but it's still contrary to our idea of freedom. A corporation is owned and controlled by its owners, so it doesn't have freedom. And if it doesn't have freedom, how can it have *legal* freedom of speech?

CHARLES It's different. The slavery analogy is just wrong.

MAEVE But it's not an *analogy*! The Constitution makes a distinction between "free persons" and "other persons." Now, the Supreme Court says a corporation is a *person* in the Constitution. But it's owned: it's clearly not a *free person*.

So what is the practical effect of the Court saying an *unfree* person has *legal* freedom of speech?

PAUL W*hose* speech does it have the freedom of?

CHARLES This is ridiculous. The distinction between *free persons* and *other persons* ended with the Thirteenth Amendment.

MAEVE Well, it certainly made a comeback when the Supreme Court announced that the *Fourteenth* Amendment made *corporations* persons.

CHARLES But a corporation's not a slave! It's not an independent person.

NADIA *Slaves* were not independent persons! And it was obviously in recognition of that fact that the Court never awarded them *legal* freedom of speech.

PAUL But now the Supreme Court says that my corporation —which I own and control— has *legal* freedom of speech. *Why?*

MAEVE More precisely, Paul, the Supreme Court says it is *the Constitution* that says that your corporation has legal freedom of speech.

PAUL *The Constitution* doesn't say anything about corporations!

MAEVE We know that, Paul. But it assigns rights to *persons*, and the Supreme Court says a corporation is a person.

PAUL What a load of bull! I own a corporation, so am I now going to be accused of owning a person? I am not a slave-owner!

CHARLES A corporation's not a slave.

PAUL Of course it's not —because it's not a *person*. I know what I own— it's a business, not a *person*.

MAEVE But with the Supreme Court's ruling, you now control the speech of *two* persons: yourself and your corporation.

CHARLES Yes, but the corporation's not your *slave*, because *in terms of its speech* it's just you.

PAUL That is like a slave. Its political speech is just its owner's.

CHARLES This is ridiculous. Oh, *wait* a minute —I see what you're getting at. You want to talk about *slaves* so you can imply someone's being *deprived* of their freedom of speech. But that's not what's happening here. No one is being denied freedom of speech.

PAUL Right, because there's no *person* there, other than me. How does my corporation qualify as a person?

CHARLES It's not a *physical* person. It's just a legal designation.

MAEVE Here's the reasoning, Paul. The Fourteenth Amendment says all '*persons*' must have equal protection of the laws. And the Supreme Court ruled that the word *person* includes corporations, so corporations are *legally* equal to human beings.

PAUL What bull! The word *person* in the Constitution means human being!

MAEVE I agree, but the Court ruled otherwise.

PAUL What? So they just changed the meaning of the words in the Constitution? To give corporations rights that the authors never intended?

MAEVE That was the ruling.

PAUL It's a sham, a deception! *Mendacity —a lie!* And for the sake of political power, to overrule Congress —to overrule democracy!

MAEVE Okay, Paul...

PAUL Can you imagine if *anyone* but the Supreme Court tried a brazen scam like that? They'd be crucified in the media! But, no, that can't happen at the highest level of power. *Nobody* can oppose the Supreme Court.

CHARLES No, Paul, calm down. This decision is actually supported by profound legal reasoning.

PAUL Really, *profound*? It's a profound *stupidity*!

Do you see how power and stupidity and go hand in hand? The Supreme Court has absolute power, so it doesn't need to *persuade* anyone through its rulings. They can be just plain stupid, and there's nothing anyone can do about it!

MAEVE Paul...

PAUL Nobody can believe how *stupid* the ruling is, so they can call it *profundity*.

CHARLES Take it easy, Paul. You're overreacting.

PAUL It just shows you what unlimited power does. *Power corrupts; absolute power corrupts absolutely*!

CHARLES No, Paul. Let me explain. It's not just a gimmick of interpreting a word in the Constitution.

PAUL Not *just* that? But the word *person* in the Constitution means human being!

CHARLES No, it's more than the word. You don't understand. It's a fundamental legal concept that's been affirmed in many judicial opinions. It's *effectively* true in all important respects —aside from the pithy expression of it as '*a corporation is a person.*'

See, that's where the problem is. Someone tries to put a sophisticated legal determination into a nutshell, then it becomes a cliché that lay people repeat —and then they *think* they understand it.

NADIA So it's too complicated for us *muggles* to understand?

CHARLES Look, do you think that just because people can say '*e* equals *m c* squared' that they *understand* the theory of relativity? That's nonsense. It's a lot more complicated.

NADIA Well, I don't claim to understand relativity, but I'm sure about one thing: if *e* does *not* equal *m c* squared, the theory is *wrong*.

PAUL And a corporation is *not* a person, so whatever theory your jurisprudence has for it, it's *wrong*.

MAEVE And saying it's *effectively* true because of judicial opinions does not make it a *Constitutional* principle. The *Constitution* has to say it.

PAUL Just claiming that the word *person* includes corporations— that doesn't cut it.

CHARLES No, no —you don't understand. That's just jargon —a shorthand way to denote a subtle legal concept. It's not even a *necessary* way to express the legal rights of corporations.

PAUL How does it work, then? If you're not going to claim a corporation's a *person*, how does it have freedom of speech?

CHARLES Well, it's really the *owner's* freedom of speech, just held in the name of the corporation. If the corporation's speech were to be restricted by law, that would be an abridgment of the *owner's* freedom of speech.

PAUL But I have full freedom of speech *without* my corporation, or *outside* of my corporation. There's no *necessity* for me to use my corporation for my speech. So where's the abridgment of *my* freedom of speech, if my corporation doesn't have freedom of speech?

CHARLES You're looking at it from the wrong point of view. Why should you be *required* to speak outside of your corporation? That —right there— is an *abridgment* of your freedom of speech.

PAUL It can only be an *abridgment* if you start with the assumption that I have a right to express all of my political prejudices in my corporation's speech. That's just an assumption, and it's not a *necessity.*

CHARLES Yes, it is a *necessary* assumption. Your freedom of speech is —first and foremost— *freedom!* Any law that would prohibit you from speaking in the name of your corporation is an abridgment of *your* freedom of speech.

PAUL I don't see where there's any abridgment. Before I formed my corporation I had total —unabridged— freedom of speech.

Now I create a corporation and let's suppose —as I actually did suppose— that the *purpose* of the corporation was to do business, for profit, not to be used for political speech.

So how was my freedom of speech *abridged* when I formed the corporation?

CHARLES Well, look, you've invested your money in that corporation. If you were restricted from speaking through your corporation, those funds would no longer be available to you for political speech. That's an *abridgment.*

NADIA So it's all about money? It's freedom of money?

MAEVE It would have to be. The Supreme Court decided long ago that money is speech.

PAUL Do you know how much I invested in my corporation?

CHARLES It doesn't matter how much. It's just the principle, that if a *law* prevents you from speaking, your freedom of speech is abridged.

PAUL But I'm not prevented from speaking. Listen, before I formed my corporation, I had other ideas. I actually wanted to buy a racehorse. I'd found a colt I thought had some prospects. But I was getting advice that this was too risky. I should keep my money safe— invest in Treasury notes.

Now if I'd invested in the horse, or even the Treasury notes, my investment wouldn't have freedom of speech —but that's not considered any *abridgment.*

So why would an investment in my corporation be an abridgment, if *it* doesn't have freedom of speech?

CHARLES Look, if you commit your funds to a form of investment in which you *know* you'll have no control over them, you have no *expectation* that they'll be available for political speech. It's not an abridgment, because it's your *choice* to invest that way.

PAUL But it's the same with my corporation. I made a *choice* to commit my money to the business, with no expectation of using it for political speech.

CHARLES That's just saying you're *unaware* of the abridgment. That doesn't mean anything. You still have control over your capitol in the business, so if you can't use it for political speech *for no reason except that a law says you can't* —that's the abridgment.

PAUL No, I still don't see how it abridges *my* freedom of speech. If the money's needed for the business, then *that's* the reason it's not available for political speech. And if it's not, *and I have control*, I can pull the money out of the business, and use it for political speech on my own.

CHARLES Yes, but if you had to withdraw money from the corporation in order to speak, you'd be taking profits, and you'd have to pay income taxes. That's an *abridgment*.

NADIA So this ruling is all about creating a tax avoidance scheme?

CHARLES Your *rights* can be abridged through taxation. If you're taxed in order to speak, that's an *abridgment*.

PAUL But anyway, you're wrong. My accountant told me to make my investment in the corporation in the form of a loan. So if I take money out of the corporation, it's just repaying the loan. I don't pay income tax on that.

CHARLES Yes, but that's just a temporary situation. After your loan is repaid, you'd have to pay income tax on the money you take from your corporation.

PAUL But you said the *abridgment* was that the money I'd *invested* is made unavailable to me for political speech.

CHARLES Well, yes, it *is* that, but not *just* that. If the form of investment you've made allows control over your investment funds, or revenues from the business, then you must have control. The *abridgment* is when you can't use the funds for speech *because of a law*.

NADIA I must say, I am simply *awed* by the *passion* Charles has for freedom of speech. He will brook no impediments, whatsoever.

CHARLES When the government attempts to suppress speech, you have to take your constitutional rights seriously.

PAUL Okay, so my corporation doesn't have freedom of speech *of its own* —it's *my* freedom of speech. But then just to be clear about it: *my* legal freedom of speech allows me to indulge my political preferences or prejudices in the speech of my corporation.

CHARLES That's right.

PAUL Even political speech that has nothing to do with the corporation's business.

CHARLES It's your freedom of speech.

PAUL Even speech that advocates policies *detrimental* to the business.

CHARLES Well, yeah.

PAUL And since this speech is actually money —used to fund campaigns for or against certain politicians— the expense might wreck the business, possibly leading to bankruptcy.

CHARLES Well now, that wouldn't be very rational, would it?

PAUL Does freedom of speech depend on the speech being rational? And who's to say what's rational? I may have reasons you don't know about. I may own other corporations that *would* benefit from that speech.

CHARLES Well, there is a presumption that the corporation's speech would benefit the corporation.

PAUL Presumption? Wait a minute. You couldn't be saying that this *presumption* forms any restriction or puts any requirements on my corporate speech. Because there's nothing in the First Amendment that says it's only for speech that benefits the speaker.

CHARLES Well, no ...

PAUL I mean, that's not the reason we have freedom of speech. I could speak in favor of laws that would only benefit other people. Or even laws that would make my *own* activities illegal.

CHARLES You could.

PAUL And since it's *my* freedom of speech, I could have my corporation campaign for laws that have nothing to do with its business. Or even laws that would harm it, or destroy the business. In spite of any *presumption* that a corporation wouldn't do that.

CHARLES Yes, yes, you could, if your corporation is fully owned by you. But it's a silly argument. Why would you want to do that?

PAUL Wait— freedom of speech doesn't require me to give any *reasons why* I'm advocating for anything. As I said, I may have my own private reasons.

CHARLES Yes, but you're basing your whole argument on a phenomenon that just doesn't happen.

PAUL How can you *know* that? Speech in which the speaker's motives are hidden— that happens *all the time.*

The *purpose* of political speech is to get the voters to vote the way you want. If you're campaigning for a candidate, you'll give the voters reasons why *they* should want him in office. And if you have a hard time making that case, give them reasons why they should *fear* the election of his opponent.

The reasons why *you* want the guy elected are nobody's business but your own. The voters wouldn't understand. You don't have to try to make them understand. Hey— if you publicize *your own* reasons, it may be *counterproductive* in motivating the voters.

So you give the voters the reasons that work best *on them.* You don't have to tell anyone *your* reasons.

That's what freedom of speech means.

CHARLES Well, that's...

PAUL Or, if you're advocating a policy, you give people reasons why *they* should want that policy. And if you hear any ideas that might get people to go for it, you run with those ideas— you publicize them. You don't have to scrutinize them.

Or, if necessary, hey— you just *make up* stuff. Stuff that *might* be true, *could* be true —who knows? Whatever works on the voters. Let them decide. If they're stupid enough to believe it, that's their problem.

You don't have to tell anyone *your* reasons. That's what freedom of speech means.

NADIA I must say, I am simply *awed* by the depth of Paul's commitment to the ideal of freedom of speech.

CHARLES No, he's taking it way too far...

PAUL And just incidentally, people will *guess* what you're after if they know what your interests are. So to keep your motives out of the discussion, you'll want to speak through a corporation.

Then folks would have to look for the motives of the corporation. After that, let them look behind it, see if they can find a person to hold responsible.

NADIA As the Wizard of Oz said, *"Pay no attention to the man behind the curtain."*

MAEVE The man behind the corporate veil.

CHARLES Well, that's pretty cynical.

PAUL It's just reality. What, are you going to pretend that speech —political speech— is the impartial dissemination of good beneficial information? Like it's all openness and honesty?

Come on, it's about winning elections. It's about getting what you want. It's about power.

CHARLES But you're basing your argument on a very cynical view.

MAEVE He has a point, Paul. The Supreme Court wouldn't lend its dignity to an argument tainted with cynicism. Not even to acknowledge it.

NADIA For the sake of its public image, it must project idealistic values.

PAUL Idealistic? Ruling that *unfree* beings must have legal freedom of speech? That doesn't defend the freedoms of *free* people. How is it idealistic?

MAEVE The Court might claim that *the Constitution says* that obscuring the source of the speech is fundamental to freedom, because it facilitates truth rather than deception.

PAUL What bull! The purpose of political speech is not *truth*, and it's not *information*, either. It's about getting the candidate you want elected.

CHARLES Look, Paul, your argument is just cynical. Really, are you saying this is what you do with your corporation?

PAUL Hell, no. I don't have the money. I mean, I might be able to use a quarter of one percent of my company's revenues for politics, but that wouldn't make the slightest ripple in any campaign.

But if my company had an annual revenue of, say, four hundred billion, a quarter of one percent is a billion. If I wanted some laws changed, I'd consider that expense. A billon a year for political campaigns could get me quite a bit of sympathy in Congress.

NADIA You surprise me, Paul. I wouldn't have questioned your ethics.

PAUL *My* ethics?

NADIA You're saying the only reason you don't buy influence in Congress is because you don't have enough money.

PAUL Power corrupts, Nadia. Didn't I already say that? If I had a company with revenues of four hundred billion, you wouldn't be talking to *me*, you'd be talking to a guy with a company that had revenues of four hundred billion.

And if you want to talk to *that* guy about ethics —well, you can't, because he's not going to talk to you. But anyway— he'd cite his *respect* for the gentlemen of the Supreme Court.

MAEVE The *Justices* are ladies and gentlemen.

PAUL Sure, and since they've *sanctioned* buying influence with politicians — because it's *sanctified* by the Constitution— he'd certainly fall in line with their ethics.

CHARLES That's not what this ruling is about.

PAUL No? But we still haven't got *your* legal argument clear, Charles. You're saying that since my speech is protected by the First Amendment, it's still protected when I speak through my corporation.

If that's true, *and if money is speech*, there could be no law limiting political spending by my corporation — not on the basis of the amount, nor the reason for it, nor the purpose of the corporation, and not the basis of whether it benefits or harms the corporation's profits or solvency.

CHARLES Well, yes —that is, *if* your corporation is fully owned by you, but ...

PAUL But that's not the *purpose* of the corporation. It isn't supposed to be just a channel for political views.

CHARLES Of course it's not *just* that. Its purpose is to make profits.

PAUL But with no limitations on political speech, the corporation could just become a tool for political propaganda by the owner.

CHARLES Come on, that's certainly not the usual case. And if it happens, it would be a small price to pay for freedom of speech. If the government could suppress that, it would open the door to government control of *all* speech.

NADIA I think this is where you make the slippery slope argument.

CHARLES Well, look, if the problem is that a corporation might spend too much on political speech, and the remedy is that it must lose its freedom of speech, the cure is worse than the disease.

MAEVE Wait —*what*? *Its* freedom of speech? *Its*? You were arguing that it's *Paul's* freedom of speech.

CHARLES Yes, yes, but suppose a legislature passed a law that abridged his freedom of speech, but the law *targeted* his corporation?

PAUL In that case, I'd have to take the funds out of the business, pay the income tax, and produce the speech myself.

CHARLES But the law is unconstitutional. Suppose your corporation —or some corporation— got hauled into court for violating that law. How would it defend itself?

PAUL I don't know. Why did it break the law?

CHARLES Because it's an unconstitutional law! And the corporation must assert that in court. The law abridged its freedom of speech, and so it must be declared unconstitutional.

MAEVE No —*no*! You were arguing that the law abridged *Paul's* freedom of speech.

CHARLES Well of course, if Paul were the defendant, *he* would obviously defend his freedom of speech that way. But the law restricted speech that the corporation produced, and it's the corporation that stands accused of violating the law. So it's a question of *standing*. The corporation is the legal entity with *standing* to defend its freedom of speech.

MAEVE *No* —not *its* freedom of speech! It's *Paul's* freedom of speech!

CHARLES Yes, but as the owner's surrogate, the corporation can defend his rights in court, but it legally *acts* in its own name. So right there you can see the necessity of the corporation having the legal freedom of speech in its own name also.

PAUL This is a shell game! After all your ballyhooing that it's *my* constitutional right to exercise *my* freedom of speech through my corporation, you make a quick shuffle —now it's about *standing*, and *whoops!*— First Amendment protection is under the corporation's shell!

And just like that, the corporation has *constitutional* rights!

MAEVE But, Charles, there's no *necessity* for it. If Paul's corporation were actually defending *his* rights, it would argue in court that *its* speech was really *his* speech, so that a law that restricted *its* speech was an abridgment of *his* freedom of speech.

And the court would have to deal with that claim.

All you've said is that it's simply *convenient* for the corporation to make this argument by speaking in its own name, but in Paul's voice —*as if* it held constitutional rights that are actually Paul's constitutional rights.

PAUL The cost of that *convenience* is the extension of the Bill of Rights to corporations. That's nothing less than a mutilation of the Constitution!

NADIA I'm sure a corporation would have no inhibitions about *claiming* constitutional rights, but *why would a court accept that claim?*

CHARLES It's obvious that a corporation can defend its rights.

MAEVE *Its* rights? Again —*its*? We're talking about *Paul's* rights!

CHARLES You're just not getting it.

MAEVE No, I'm certainly not. How did the Court's opinion explain how the *owners'* rights became the *corporation's* rights? And what was the case, anyway?

CHARLES What case?

MAEVE The case that *set the precedent.* The first case where a corporation claimed *its own* First Amendment rights, and the Court accepted it.

CHARLES There have been a lot of cases like that. I don't know which was first.

MAEVE But wouldn't you think it's a landmark case? It should be a celebrated case, with an opinion that demonstrates the *constitutional* necessity of freedom of speech for corporations.

NADIA And you're telling us the reasoning would not simply resort to the *edict* delivered in the *Santa Clara* case, that a corporation is a *person.*

CHARLES Look, come on —there have been a lot of opinions. I don't know of one that actually expresses it that way.

MAEVE What? But you said the corporation's right of free speech doesn't depend on the proposition that a corporation is a person.

CHARLES Yes, but it's just obvious, from commonly understood principles. The right of free speech for corporations is derived from the right of the owners.

MAEVE But you haven't shown us the *necessity* for Paul's corporation to have *legal* freedom of speech. *Paul's* speech is protected by the First Amendment —as anyone's is— outside of any corporation.

Your only *substantive* point is that if he's obligated to take his money out of the corporation in order to use it for political speech, he'd have to pay income tax on it. And you called that an *abridgment* of his freedom of speech.

But with other forms of income —salary, for example— there's no constitutional right to use pre-tax income for political speech.

CHARLES Yes, well, you don't see the *necessity* of it, because the distinction between the owner and the corporation is somewhat artificial when there's only one owner.

The *necessity* of the idea comes out of the reason corporations were created in the first place— in order to allow multiple owners.

PAUL So then the corporation is like a slave with multiple owners.

CHARLES No, it's not a slave! There's no *human being* that's being deprived of his freedom of speech. The corporation *is* its owners —it's *defined* as its owners.

PAUL But it's owned.

CHARLES People can't own *people*, so ownership is limited to the corporation's *material* assets. And having ownership shares is just a way defining the membership of the corporation.

PAUL And, ownership of the common shares —the voting shares— is the means of determining control. So it's controlled by its owners.

CHARLES Yes, but it's not a slave!

PAUL But it's controlled. It's not free. So if it has freedom of speech, *whose* speech does it have the freedom of?

CHARLES The owners!

PAUL But there are multiple owners, different individuals, independent voices — all sorts of speech. So *whose* speech does it have the freedom of?

CHARLES All of the owners. The consensus of the owners.

PAUL What *consensus*?

NADIA I don't understand this concept of *consensus* either. I own some stock in a public corporation, so I'm an owner. If the corporation has *my* freedom of speech, it must express *my* political opinions, just as I would.

CHARLES Come on, you're not the *only* owner, so that's entirely unreasonable. The corporation's speech must be the consensus of *all* the owners.

NADIA But if my speech must join a consensus, it's not my free speech. So the corporation would have *my freedom of speech* for speech that's not my free speech.

CHARLES It doesn't have *just your* freedom of speech. Its freedom of speech is derived from *all* the owners.

MAEVE But how? *How* is this right derived from all of the owners? Is it by the rule of corporate democracy?

CHARLES What do you mean by *corporate democracy*?

MAEVE The way corporate elections are held —for the board of directors, for example. Each owner votes the *shares* he or she owns. So each owner's influence is proportional to his or her ownership share in the company.

So if the corporation's *rights* were determined by the same rule, each owner's share in the corporate right would be in proportion to his or her ownership share.

CHARLES But... no, there's no accounting like that.

MAEVE Then, is the corporation's right composed of an *equal* amount of each owner's right, *regardless* of how many shares the owner has?

CHARLES What? That's crazy.

NADIA Maeve, are you imagining that rights can be quantified in *fractions* —as if there could be a quarter or a tenth of a right?

MAEVE But no —not fractions of rights for *entities*. Each *owner* has the full amount —one unit— of freedom of speech, and *if* the corporation has freedom of speech, it also has one whole unit.

NADIA A *unit* of freedom of speech?

MAEVE Whatever that might be —whatever. I'm just asking *how* the corporation's right is composed of the rights of *all* the owners. It couldn't be the *total* of them, because that's more than one.

And it couldn't be the right of just *one* of the owners, because the rights of the other owners wouldn't be included.

So the corporation's right has to be a *composite*, composed of a *part* of each owner's right. The question is, *how* is the composite formed?

CHARLES Maeve, that's crazy —you can't think of rights as being divisible, or adding up, like physical quantities. There's no law like conservation of matter for conservation of rights.

PAUL A right exists if the Supreme Court says it does. Period.

MAEVE But this is a *constitutional* right! The Supreme Court can't say a corporation has the right of freedom of speech unless the *Constitution* says it does.

That's why Charles was telling us that the corporation's *constitutional* right of freedom of speech is actually the constitutional right of the owners. *All* of the owners. I just want to know *how* that happens.

CHARLES But you can't break it down in detail like that. *All* the owners have freedom of speech, and it's the same for *all* of them, so the association of owners also has freedom of speech, no matter *how* you look at it.

What more of an explanation do you want?

(*pause*)

MAEVE (*sigh*) What I want to see, Charles, is how the right of freedom of speech always protects the *free speech* of the one who has that right.

PAUL In other words, if the corporation has the *freedom* of speech of all of the owners, it must be used to produce the *free speech* of all of the owners. If it can't do that, whose *speech* does it have the *freedom of*?

CHARLES By its very nature, a corporation with more than one owner must produce the *consensus* speech of the owners.

NADIA The consensus speech would not be my free speech, but an *abridgment* of it. That's an abridgment of my freedom of speech.

CHARLES No! Your First Amendment right simply protects against abridgment *by law*. But if speech is limited as a matter of *circumstance*, that's not an abridgment of *constitutional* rights.

NADIA But then how is this consensus formed? The corporation never asks me for my political opinions.

CHARLES It's just through the usual mechanisms of corporate governance.

MAEVE That's corporate democracy. Each owner votes the number of shares he or she owns. The owner with a controlling share of the stock has the power to elect the directors, so he or she has control of the corporate speech.

NADIA So the *circumstance* that limits my speech is *corporate governance*. Now, isn't that specified in law?

MAEVE Of course it is. The corporation is a creature of the law. Its governance is determined by laws passed by a state legislature.

CHARLES Yes...

PAUL So then those laws abridge Nadia's freedom of speech.

CHARLES No, no! Those laws weren't passed with the *intent* of limiting her speech. Their *purpose* is to allow the owners to control the corporation. So that's not an abridgment.

PAUL But the income tax law wasn't passed with the *intent* of limiting speech, either, yet you called *that* an abridgment.

CHARLES The income tax law *itself* is not the problem. The abridgment is the law that restricts the corporation's speech. It's because of *that* law that you'd have to pull your funds out of the corporation —and pay income tax— in order to exercise your freedom of speech.

MAEVE So it's about the *intent* of the law? But the First Amendment does *not* say, "Congress shall make no law *with the intent of* abridging the freedom of speech."

CHARLES But that's clearly the meaning. Look, it also doesn't say, "Congress shall make no law abridging *speech*."

What can't be abridged is *freedom* of speech —that's freedom from *intentional* government suppression.

There may be laws —like those of corporate governance— which, if you want to examine their effects, you may find some effect restricting speech. But if those laws legitimately have some other purpose, they do not abridge *freedom of speech*.

NADIA So this law of corporate governance is not an abridgment. Yet its effect is that *my* freedom of speech is being used to justify the corporation's freedom of speech *that isn't my speech*.

PAUL Like the case of a slave whose freedom of speech is the freedom of the speech of its owner.

CHARLES No, not a like slave! It's all voluntary. Nadia, you must realize that when you make an investment in which you don't have control, that's not a loss of your freedom of speech, because it's your *choice* to invest that way.

PAUL So you're saying if you don't have enough of an investment to control the board of directors, you should just forget about freedom of speech in your investment?

CHARLES Look, in this decision, the Supreme Court specifically said that the company must *disclose* its political expenditures. So with due diligence, you should know whether the corporation's political views are compatible with yours.

And you can chose to invest, or not, on that basis.

PAUL That's not the reason you invest! You invest for *profit*.

NADIA But I'm already invested. So not only can the company support candidates I oppose —not only can it justify it by claiming *my* freedom of speech, but it can use *my* money for it, too. I *own* a share of the corporation's funds.

CHARLES But it's not an abridgment of your freedom of speech, because it was your *choice* to invest that way.

PAUL And the owner with the controlling share of your corporation can use the corporation's speech just like I can in my corporation —to indulge his personal political prejudices or whims or ideological delusions —without limit.

CHARLES Oh, no, no, Paul. The majority owner has a major stake in the corporation, so he'll use its speech to advance *its* interests.

PAUL Among his other interests, yeah, I'm sure he'll support the campaigns of politicians who'll pass laws that allow the corporation to grow, increase revenues, decrease costs, escape regulation, hinder competition, enjoy privacy, and avoid taxes.

That's what you'd expect. It's all for the purpose of increasing profits.

But the point is, it's the owner's *freedom* of speech. *Freedom* —first and foremost. That *individual* could have many political passions —foreign policy, or social issues, family, morality, religion— or other financial interests that have nothing to do with the interests of the corporation.

Nothing in the principle says that his speech must be filtered or limited in content or amount when it's run through the corporation.

CHARLES Oh, no, no. That's all wrong. You'll find out, Paul, if you ever take your corporation public, that you're asking people to invest in your business, and they have a right to know its *prospects* for profit.

So you have to file a public *prospectus*. That's a document in which you must explain what your business is, and how you're going to use the funds invested in it for making a profit.

It's effectively a *contract* between you and the investors. So you can't just use the corporation's funds for your political speech.

PAUL But what about *my* freedom of speech, then?

CHARLES Well, you still have your freedom of speech, but the corporation's not just *yours* any more. The corporate speech must be the speech of all the owners.

PAUL That's not what we mean by freedom of speech! My speech must have freedom —no restrictions!

CHARLES But that's unreasonable for a shared enterprise. There are practical limits. You must realize that all of the officers of the corporation —including yourself, if you happen to be one— have a *fiduciary duty* to protect *all* of the owners' interests in the corporation.

So they can't just squander the corporation's funds on the political campaigns that *you* —or any owner— want to support.

PAUL See, now that's exactly the way *I* understood it. The corporation's *purpose* is to do *business*, not politics.

But *you said* that *my* freedom of speech extends to my corporation, so any law that restricts my corporation from supporting the politician that I want to support, is unconstitutional.

And *now* you're saying that if I sell shares to the public, the requirement of *fiduciary duty* limits the amount that I can have the corporation spend for my political speech.

CHARLES Of course it does. It must.

PAUL So that abridges my freedom of speech!

CHARLES No, no. Again, you're missing the *legal* issue. *Legal* freedom of speech is just protection against *laws* that restrict speech…

PAUL Yes, yes. So is this requirement for *fiduciary duty* written into law?

CHARLES Yes, of course there are laws…

PAUL Then those laws must be unconstitutional. They're *abridgments* of the majority owner's freedom of speech.

CHARLES No, *no*! Those laws weren't passed with the *intent* of limiting political speech. They're just *circumstance* —the necessary consequence of a corporation having multiple owners.

PAUL The *necessary consequence* of multiple ownership is that the corporation must have a defined *purpose,* and everyone should know what it is.

And legislatures can pass laws with the *intent* of holding a corporation to its purpose.

CHARLES Yes, but not to abridge its freedom of speech.

PAUL *Its* freedom of speech? Again —*its*? You were telling me it's the *owners'* freedom of speech.

CHARLES Yes, of course, it *is* the owners'. But after the reasonable requirement of consistency with fiduciary responsibility, no *law* can abridge the freedom of that speech.

PAUL But the owner's speech is already abridged!

CHARLES But it's not a First Amendment abridgment unless it's by a law *specifically intended* to abridge.

NADIA So, Charles, how is this *reasonable requirement* of fiduciary responsibility enforced?

CHARLES Well, the owners must be vigilant. If a stockholder sees breach of fiduciary duty, he can sue.

NADIA Okay, let me understand this. I own a few shares of a corporation, so I'm a minority stockholder. So when I see the corporation spending for political campaigns instead of using the funds for making profits, I can sue —who? The corporation?

CHARLES Well, you could try, but you're not going to get any sympathy in court. You'd be trying to win an award for yourself, through a judgment against the corporation. If you won, the other shareholders would just lose.

So you'd be harming the corporation for your own benefit, and the court won't accept that. The concept of fiduciary duty applies to the shareholders, too.

NADIA So if I sue the corporation for violating *its* fiduciary duty, I'd be violating my *own* fiduciary duty.

CHARLES In effect, yes. But fiduciary duty really applies only to the *individuals* that have responsibility for the corporation.

And as minority shareholder, you actually do have a remedy. First, you must work within the corporation: notify the corporate officers of the breach of fiduciary duty, and demand that they correct it.

If that's unsuccessful, you must notify all the shareholders of the problem, and try to get a majority of shares to vote for a change in policy, or to replace the board of directors.

And if that doesn't work either —and if you can attribute *that* failure to the internal problem you're trying to correct— then you can bring a lawsuit against the officers or directors that you hold responsible.

MAEVE That's piercing the corporate veil. Doesn't that happen only for the most serious allegations, like criminal activity?

CHARLES Ordinarily, yes. But this is a special kind of action —a *derivative* lawsuit. It's brought by the shareholder, but for the benefit of the corporation. If it succeeds, the judgment against the responsible officers will go to the corporation. The shareholder who sued will benefit only indirectly, as will the other shareholders.

NADIA So I've got to do all that, just to prevent the corporation from using *my* share of the corporate funds to elect a candidate I oppose.

MAEVE And I'm sure the officers will defend themselves by claiming that the support of political campaigns is a valid business expenditure.

CHARLES Of course they will. And the legal doctrine is that 'business judgment' is generally a matter beyond the competence of a court. If there's no evidence of a conflict of interest, it's assumed that the officers acted in good faith.

MAEVE You mean, as long as they didn't *personally benefit*, they're assumed to have acted in the best interests of the corporation —even if their decisions clearly harmed the corporation?

CHARLES Right. If it's bad business judgment, executives can be fired and directors voted out. But the *court* won't punish them for their business judgment.

PAUL But look, couldn't she demand that the officers *demonstrate* that it's a valid business expenditure? If it is, they should be able to produce a cost-benefit analysis for the strategy, showing exactly how —and by how much— profits were expected to increase as a return on the expenditure for the politician's campaign.

CHARLES No, no. As the plaintiff, the burden of proof will be on her —the shareholder— to show that there could not possibly have been *any* benefit. I don't know how she'd prove it anyway. There are intangibles, like good will.

MAEVE And if she does manage to prove it, it simply means the officers' *business judgment* was faulty, right? It doesn't amount to a breach of fiduciary duty.

CHARLES That's right. Unless she could show they got a personal benefit.

MAEVE And so there's no judgment against the officers. And so, no change in behavior.

CHARLES You could assume that.

PAUL And everybody knows that from the start.

CHARLES You might assume that, too.

13. MEDIA CORPORATIONS

NADIA Now I'm confused. I thought Charles was suggesting that the requirement for *fiduciary duty* would effectively *prevent* the corporation from spending for political propaganda.

MAEVE You'd think it ought to, but it clearly doesn't have any force. Political expenditures come under *business judgment*. No further questions asked.

NADIA But the law that was just invalidated —that prohibited political expenditures by a corporation— that was really just an explicit and quite particular enforcement of fiduciary duty. It required the corporation to stick to *business*.

CHARLES No, no, you're not seeing the whole picture. The law that was invalidated went far beyond simply enforcing fiduciary duty.

There are companies whose *business it is* to propagate political opinion. Their *product* is political opinion— in videos, books, magazines. Spending money to promote their product —political opinion— increases profits. It's perfectly consistent with everyone's *fiduciary duty*.

The law prohibiting political expenditures harmed their legitimate business.

MAEVE You're talking about media corporations. They're special cases, and I think the law considers them separately. And allows them to profit.

CHARLES But you can't consider them separately.

NADIA What do you mean, *can't*? Maeve said the law actually *did*.

MAEVE Yes, there is an exception for media corporations, isn't there?

CHARLES Yes, yes —Congress tried to make that exception. But it was struck down too, in the *Citizens United* ruling.

NADIA *Tried to*? But she said Congress actually passed such a law.

CHARLES Yes, but it was not an effective law.

NADIA Not *effective*? But that's certainly just a matter of opinion. The fact is, Congress actually passed the law, so it *can* be done. Saying it *can't* be done is disingenuous.

CHARLES No, that's not what I meant.

NADIA No, what you *meant* is that Congress *may* not do it —because the Supreme Court does not permit it.

CHARLES No, look, Congress can *write* the law, but it *can't* work. That's what I meant.

MAEVE What is this, a new doctrine of constitutionality? Does the Constitution say the Supreme Court can invalidate a law because it is —in the Court's opinion— *ineffective*?

CHARLES No, no. That law was unconstitutional because it tried to make a distinction between media corporations and others.

NADIA The Constitution says nothing about *any* kind of corporation, so how could that be an unconstitutional distinction?

MAEVE You know how it's done, Nadia.

NADIA Oh, simply by *declaring* a corporation to be a person.

MAEVE Oh, but wait a minute —wait!. Charles, remember, you told us that in the *Mackey* case, the Supreme Court *explicitly* said a legislature *may* write laws that apply to one type of corporation but not another.

CHARLES Yes, yes, that's true. *Particular types* of distinctions are possible, but this one *can't* work. There are just too many ways to get around it, legally.

NADIA Spoken like a true corporate lawyer.

MAEVE A corporate *constitutional* lawyer. JP Morgan would hand you a cigar.

CHARLES Be realistic about it. Look, if there were separate laws for media companies, any corporation could set up a subsidiary media company, or else acquire one, and then gain its privileges. So no distinction is going to work.

NADIA Or it could *merge* with a media corporation.

MAEVE Right. The boys in Mergers and Acquisitions wouldn't want you to forget that option.

CHARLES That's right. They could do it by merging, too. So it would be completely futile to try to make some distinction between media corporations and others.

NADIA *There's* the problem. Corporations can own each other, spawn offspring, divest, acquire, split, merge and invert. They're creations of the law, that have more shape-shifting tricks than any biological being.

MAEVE Is *that* the Court's logic, then? The *Court* will decide what *can* be done effectively, and what *can't* be done effectively? Because the *Constitution* prohibits Congress from passing laws that the Supreme Court considers ineffective?

NADIA But are you missing the irony here, Maeve? Charles is all on board with the Supreme Court's doctrine that corporations must have *legal* equality with natural persons.

Now he cites the *legal* qualities of corporations —shape-shifting tricks that are *impossible for a human being*— as the reason legislatures may not regulate them!

MAEVE Oh, right. Corporations can *morph* to get around the law, so where's the equal protection? Why can't I reduce my taxes by a legal *inversion* with a person in a low-tax country?

CHARLES Come on, that's just childish reasoning. You don't have the legal conception of a corporation.

PAUL You don't have the conception of the *stupidity* of this proposition that corporations are persons.

MAEVE We understand that it was the legislatures that *created* corporations and granted them their legal capabilities. And that by giving them *constitutional* rights, the Supreme Court has usurped the legislatures' right to regulate them.

NADIA Charles, that simply doesn't make sense.

CHARLES That's because you're obsessing about it from such a narrow view. You have to think about a corporation's rights in a broader sense, as rights that apply to *all* associations of citizens.

MAEVE But a corporation is *not* an association of *citizens.*

PAUL Right— you don't have to be a citizen to be a corporation owner.

NADIA You don't even have to be a human being.

CHARLES The courts will straighten that out. Look, it's a broad principle, and you're just obsessing about a nit-picking detail.

MAEVE The nit-picking detail we've been obsessing about is the *legality* of it —the legal *source* of the idea. If this principle —*not* in the Constitution and *never* passed by a legislature— is now the highest law of the land, what does that say about our legal system? How does it actually work,?

NADIA All you've shown us is the *edict* in *Santa Clara* —which mentioned *corporations*, not associations of citizens.

MAEVE And we've already seen the *legal* definition of a corporation, in John Marshall's ruling, "**... an artificial being, invisible, intangible, and existing only in contemplation of law. Being the mere creature of law, it possesses only those properties which the charter of its creation confers upon it...**"

CHARLES Yes, yes —but that was written *two centuries* ago. Corporations have evolved. Now they're significant forces in our society.

MAEVE So now you're appealing to *evolution*? This is hocus-pocus.

NADIA Certainly, evolution must be a wonderful thing, if it actually produced the wonderfulness of *ourselves.* But evolution actually has a rather poor record overall, with many more failures than successes.

MAEVE Many of its successes are not all that admirable.

NADIA Anthrax, tuberculin bacillus, salmonella, the Ebola virus, HIV... all evolved.

MAEVE So what is it about *evolution* that you find so compelling, Charles? Is it the *naturalness* of it, that it's not under human control?

CHARLES It's just reality. You have to accept it —it's just the way things are.

MAEVE Corporations did not become what they are through any *natural* process. They're products of the law —*statutory* law, written by legislatures.

CHARLES But they've developed by common law too, that's driven by social forces. Society evolves —it's not under anyone's control.

NADIA No one's control? It wasn't *nature* that made corporations legal persons.

PAUL And it wasn't legislatures expressing the will of the people.

MAEVE It was the Supreme Court that ordered it, citing the Constitution to overrule the legislatures. So we're asking, where is the *constitutional necessity* of it demonstrated?

CHARLES You see? This is what I mean. You don't understand how legal interpretation works. You're insisting on some narrative that *you* can understand, from a narrow-minded, *literal* reading of the text.

MAEVE I think we read the text fairly, and it clearly does *not* refer to corporations.

CHARLES Yes, it *could* —under a broader interpretation.

NADIA Then why not give us the clear logic of the interpretation, from a *reasonable* reading of the text? So that we —and everyone else— can understand.

CHARLES But that's an illusion. It's simplistic. It ignores all the complexities and ambiguities that occur in law. They must be resolved through constitutional interpretation.

Oliver Wendell Holmes wrote, "**The life of the law has not been logic; it has been experience.**"

NADIA The experience of the Supreme Court in delivering *edicts*?

CHARLES No, it's their experience in the development of the law, through judicial opinions. And observation of its effects in society.

NADIA So then there's no logic to the law?

CHARLES Of course there *is*, but it's not the *kind* of logic *you* want! It's not a thin line of didactic, mechanical logic. It's reasoning with a wider frame of reference —the broad mainstream of judicial thought that takes into account contemporary social attitudes.

MAEVE Then can you demonstrate how that *broad mainstream of judicial thought* makes a corporation a person? Without the hocus-pocus, smoke and mirrors?

CHARLES It *can* be demonstrated. Read the decision— I'm sure you'd find many, *many* precedents cited.

NADIA Perhaps so, but those cited precedents just cite other precedents. And you said the origin of all of them was *Santa Clara,* which had no reasoning *at all.*

MAEVE So you can trace it to a non-legal pronouncement, not a rationale, not a *holding* —not even an *obiter dictum.* It has no legal standing.

CHARLES Who are you to say it's not legal? It's been *accepted*, don't you see? You can't get around that. There may be hundreds of judges that affirmed it in their rulings.

PAUL Sure, but they *have to.* A judge that doesn't go along with the Supreme Court gets overruled by a higher court. That's a black mark on his career prospects.

MAEVE He's not in tune with the judicial *ideology.*

CHARLES No, no. Judges rule according to the law, not *ideology.*

NADIA But the judiciary is a hierarchical system, isn't it? The power is at the top. The way to rise in the hierarchy is to make the rulings that will please the Supreme Court.

CHARLES Oh, come on, now. The judiciary has a lot of independent-minded judges, who are not afraid to put their true convictions into their judicial opinions. They come to agree on this principle independently.

NADIA Really? But your lecture on *stare decisis* was all about how judges are *required* to follow precedents.

CHARLES Yes, yes —but look, there are still ambiguities that require judgments to be made —*nuanced* judgments— that depend on understanding the precedent cases, and the distinguishing characteristics of each case.

NADIA So, weren't any of these independent-minded judges capable writing a clear, coherent statement showing *why* references to *person* in the Constitution must include corporations? All we're hearing is hocus-pocus, abracadabra.

CHARLES It may seem so to you, but that's because you don't understand the nature of the judicial process. Cases are decided by close reasoning of facts, law and principles, under some doctrine of interpretation.

But a Justice can't write out an entire doctrine of interpretation in an opinion.

NADIA They're obviously not using the doctrine of *textualism*. We looked at the text, and there's no hint of corporations anywhere in it.

MAEVE Nor could they be using the doctrine of *original meaning*. When you have to rewrite the dictionary to give a text the meaning you want, you can't call it *originalism*.

NADIA So what *doctrine of interpretation* could possibly justify this?

CHARLES There are various doctrines, with many subtle variations. There's the pragmatic method of interpretation, too.

PAUL Pragmatic? That's just a fancy word for *practical*, isn't it? It means you only have to think about the *practical* consequences of your ruling —never mind the legal formalities.

CHARLES No, no— *practical* assumes you have a particular goal, and you do whatever you need to, to get to it. That's not a judicial attitude. The doctrine of *pragmatism* simply calls for *awareness* of the social effects of a ruling.

MAEVE William James, a founder of the pragmatic school, wrote, "**The pragmatic method means looking away from principles and looking toward consequences.**"

PAUL Sure, it's easy to see where that leads. The *consequences* of every important court decision are that one group is pleased, and another group is angered.

So in any case that pits the interests of the powerful against the powerless, the *pragmatic* decision will be the one that makes the powerful happy, and lets the powerless deal with the anger.

MAEVE Of course. If you make the powerful angry, look toward the consequences —they're the kind you don't want.

PAUL And if you make the powerless angry, they'll whine, but so what? No consequences.

CHARLES Come on, that's simplistic. And cynical. The strongest ethic of the judicial culture is *equity*. That comprises the principles of *objectivity, fairness,* and *equality* before the law.

NADIA *"The pragmatic method means looking away from principles and looking toward consequences."*

PAUL You can't deny that the *pragmatic* consequence of this *Citizens United* decision is more power to the billionaires that hold controlling interests in the corporations, so they can use the investments of the minority shareholders—*your money*— to support *their* politics.

CHARLES Well, there it is. I knew sooner or later you'd turn this into class warfare.

MAEVE No, no —there's no *warfare* going on here, Charles! *Warfare* is bullets and blood and bombs ripping bodies apart! Warfare is what we have in Iraq and Afghanistan.

   Here, we are merely having a *discussion!*

CHARLES Maeve, it's just a figure of speech.

MAEVE But why bring up images of *violence*? Isn't it simply to arouse the *fear* of violence in order to shut down a discussion of wealth inequality?

CHARLES It's just a commonly used term.

NADIA Then can you make your point without the scare language?

CHARLES Look, Paul's whole argument is just an attempt to stir up envy and anger at the wealthy.

MAEVE I think his anger is directed at the Supreme Court.

PAUL It all works together. Wealth buys power; power bestows wealth. They feed each other, spiraling upward— higher, narrower, ever more concentrated.

CHARLES That's absurd. There's no quid pro quo. The justices are not getting rich.

PAUL They're the sycophants for the moneyed interest, as a class. It's a class action.

CHARLES You don't know what a class action is.

NADIA Charles, the *pragmatic* effect of this ruling is to give more political power to the owners of the controlling shares of corporations. Would you deny that?

CHARLES But Nadia, that's the wrong way to look at it. A corporation is an association of private individuals. And the government has no responsibility —nor right— to meddle in its internal operation just to ensure that each member's voice is given equal weight.

NADIA We were talking about the doctrine of pragmatism —*looking away from principles.*

CHARLES You can't *assume* the Court employed any particular doctrine. And there are important principles that can't be overlooked.

   In any case, the pragmatic effect would be up to the organization. It's a *voluntary* association, so it's free to work out its political position on its own. If you don't think it fairly represents your views, you don't have to remain a member.

NADIA Oh, so I can leave. I can sell my shares. And then I don't share in the profits.

CHARLES Well, look, there's still the competition. If you think your corporation's wasting its resources on political campaigns, that would give the edge to the competing corporations that don't do that. So you'd be better off investing in one of those.

NADIA But not if a corporation that supports politicians gets better results on the bottom line, through some favorable treatment in the law.

MAEVE Of course Nadia's not suggesting this would happen because of any *quid pro quo* —because that would be *illegal.*

PAUL Right, *quid* for *pro quo* is illegal, so there won't be any written contracts. It's just *understood* that by supporting a politician's election, the corporation earns his *good will.*

MAEVE The politician couldn't overlook that while considering the corporation's legal interests. Nor overlook his or her prospects for continued support —and reelection.

CHARLES Look, there's nothing new here. That sort of influence has always been going on. It's all part of the rough and tumble of our political process.

PAUL Charles, this is not rocket science. There are two only possible justifications for a corporation to support a politician's campaign.

One is that it will benefit the corporation. This is buying favoritism in the government, for an unfair advantage. It's a form of bribery —even if the Supreme Court declares it to be legal.

The other is that it will benefit society. But a for-profit corporation has no *business* improving society. Its *purpose* is to make profits. That's the reason the investors invested, and that is its obligation —its *fiduciary responsibility*— to the investors. To divert any of its resources to *improving society* is a corruption of its purpose.

The two possible reasons for supporting politicians are both corrupt.

CHARLES No, no. The corporation's motivation *is* consistent with its purpose. It *is* motivated to make profits, but not *necessarily* by an unfair advantage for *itself.* It could be advocating for larger issues, for more efficient technologies or more effective economic policies.

PAUL You're telling me what its motives *could* be, but its actual motives can't be known. The law can't compel it to reveal its true motives.

NADIA But its *purpose* is known, and publicly stated, and that is to make profits for the investors. So it must be assumed that investments in the political sphere are intended to pay off in greater profits.

CHARLES But when you assume it's through an *unfair* advantage for itself, that's just a slander on the corporation. Actually, its motives could be much broader —to benefit an entire sector of the economy, or to change aspects of the law or policy that are detrimental to the economy. They might be benefits to the entire nation.

PAUL Could be, might be! Could be that *anything* done to increase profits has wondrous benefits to the entire nation. Why are you telling us what *could be*?

NADIA Charles, are you saying that because *you*, or anyone, can perceive a possible non-corrupt motivation, the law must *presume* that that must be the case?

CHARLES It's a legal principle: the presumption of innocence.

MAEVE Oh, how you're muddling the issue, now! We're not talking about prejudging a particular person or corporation accused of breaking a law!

We're talking about whether a legislature can judge a particular *behavior* to be socially harmful, or corrupting of social institutions, so that it may ban that practice.

And a practice can be banned on the basis of its *likelihood* of harmful effect, without any proof that it's harmful in every instance.

NADIA The law that you may not pass a red light is intended to ensure public safety. But just because you might envision a case where it's possible to pass a red light safely, that does not mean the law must be invalid.

MAEVE Nor unconstitutional.

CHARLES Yes, but look, a law is *overbroad* if it bans legal behavior besides the harmful behavior that it's supposed to prevent. That's an unnecessary abridgment of liberty.

And in this case, there are already laws that ban political support where there is a quid pro quo. And there are laws that ban a corporation's *direct* contribution to, or coordination with, a campaign.

Those laws are sufficient. The law banning *all* political support by corporations is simply *overbroad*.

MAEVE That's *your* opinion. But Congress had a different opinion. Congress considered that political support by a corporation —whether direct or indirect— was socially detrimental; inconsistent with the corporation's *purpose*.

PAUL It's not rocket science, Charles. There are two reasons a corporation might support a politician's campaign— one, that it benefits the corporation, which is bribery, and two— that it benefits society, which is a corruption of its purpose.

But you're telling us the Supreme Court sees a sweet spot— a mixture of two corrupt motives, that is some of each but all of neither, and therefore not at all corrupt.

And so far from being corrupt that it's entirely *virtuous*. So virtuous that the Supreme Court must prevent Congress from passing a law against it.

NADIA So virtuous that the Supreme Court must corrupt the Constitution in order to overrule Congress.

MAEVE *That* is the issue! It's not whether it's a good law in your opinion –or in the Supreme Court's opinion, either— but whether the *Constitution* says that Congress may not make that law.

CHARLES Look, the Constitution protects freedom of speech… and Congress cannot pass a law that abridges freedom of speech!

PAUL But the law did not abridge any *person's* freedom of speech!

14. IDOLATRY

(*Erica enters through the kitchen.*)

ERICA Hello!

MAEVE Come on in, Erica.

ERICA Hi, hi. Oh, Kevin, your mom says she'll be working late.

KEVIN I'd better go home, then.

CHARLES I'll give you a lift, Kevin. It's time for me to go, anyway.

MAEVE No, we can't let him go without dinner.

CHARLES So, I'll take him to dinner. That okay with you, Kevin?

KEVIN Yeah, okay.

ERICA (*Placing a bag on the counter.*) Maeve, I'm leaving these snacks for the book club meeting. Sorry I interrupted the fighting.

MAEVE We weren't *fighting*.

ERICA I won't even ask.

KEVIN They were arguing about whether a corporation's a person.

ERICA It isn't. And you couldn't find anything better to fight about?

CHARLES That's just glib, Erica. Nobody's claiming a corporation is a *natural* person. It's just a *legal* ruling; a corporation is just *legally* a person.

MAEVE According to the Supreme Court.

NADIA Charles is making much use of his magical word *legal*.

MAEVE We don't have the authority to use it, since we haven't passed the bar exam.

CHARLES Nobody says you have to be admitted to the bar…

ERICA No? I understand the Supreme Court has a rule that you *must* be a member of the bar in order to argue a case there.

CHARLES It's just a matter of efficiency. The Court shouldn't have to waste time listening to arguments ignorant of settled law.

MAEVE Really! So we *aren't* qualified to know what's legal then, are we?

CHARLES Well, look —you certainly haven't shown any legal competence in your arguments, which, frankly are getting tedious. All your ravings about *beings*. It's all just hysteria— with no legal foundation.

MAEVE Really? When I asked for a legal definition of a corporation, you cited John Marshall: **"A Corporation is an artificial being, invisible, intangible, and existing only in contemplation of law.**

CHARLES He's not using the word in the same sense you are. He's just referring to a legal entity.

Kevin, are you ready to go?

MAEVE But that '*legal entity*' is active. It does things. it's alive.

CHARLES We're not going to rehash this. The topic's been exhausted

Come on Kevin.

ERICA It's alive, but not an animal, nor a *human* being. I think *being*'s the proper term for it.

CHARLES But, no, that's not the *legal* term. In the law, the word *person* is the designation for a legal entity that has the rights of a human being.

ERICA But it's not a human being . Why call it a person?

CHARLES That's just the legal vocabulary.

PAUL The Supreme Court called corporations *persons* in order to *fraudulently* get them into the Constitution.

MAEVE So it can overrule Congress on any law that regulates them. So they can be guaranteed unlimited political influence in human society.

ERICA And so, will they use their influence to create an environment in which *human* beings can enjoy life, liberty and the pursuit of happiness?

......Or will they use it to enhance *the corporation's* life, liberty and pursuit of happiness?

MAEVE What? Erica, those words don't even apply to corporations.

CHARLES No, because they're from the Declaration of Independence, not the Constitution.

ERICA Well, excuse me, but isn't our Constitution based on the *ideals* on which this nation was founded —as expressed in the Declaration of Independence? Remember, "**We hold these truths to be self-evident, that all men are created equal...**"

NADIA That should be self-evident.

MAEVE Of course, we understand that the word *men* here has the sense of *persons* —*natural persons,* just to be clear.

NADIA Charles, wouldn't you agree that the Fourteenth Amendment —that says that no *person* may be denied equal protection of the laws— is just the ideal of the Declaration of Independence, stated as the highest law of the land?

CHARLES Look, it may be the same ideal., but don't you see how you just *interpreted* the Declaration of Independence? Maeve gave the word *men* a broader sense than its original meaning.

That can be done for the word *person*, too.

MAEVE Oh, there's a stunning leap of logic! If *men* can be interpreted as *persons* —to include women— then *persons* can be interpreted to include *corporations*!

Really! Is that the legal reasoning?

CHARLES It could be. Why not?

MAEVE Well, because there's more, **"We hold these truths to be self-evident, that all men are created equal, that they are endowed by their Creator with certain unalienable rights…"**

Now if *men* is interpreted to include *corporations*— what are you going to make of the reference to '*their Creator*'?

ERICA The creator of corporations is not the Almighty.

MAEVE No, *legislatures* created them and gave them some *limited* legal rights.

And no legislature ever endowed any of its creations with *unalienable* rights, and certainly not those of *life, liberty and the pursuit of happiness*.

ERICA Our legislatures are not cults that would commit the idolatry of creating a *person*.

CHARLES Oh, come on —*idolatry*, Erica?

ERICA Yes, exactly. *God* gave us the means to procreate, but creating a *person* by means of our own invention is playing God.

Whether we make gods of our idols, or gods of ourselves —it's idolatry.

CHARLES No, no —the *persons* created in the law are not real human beings.

MAEVE Not human beings, but *beings* —intelligent, highly motivated beings. Beings that have more resources, more technical skills, more legal talent, more *shrewdness* and more economic power than any human being.

ERICA Creating beings that are more powerful than ourselves —that is idolatry, too.

CHARLES They're not gods. We don't worship them.

ERICA No, but we expect them to give us our daily bread. And for that we make ourselves individually into cogs that serve their needs.

CHARLES Come on, working for a corporation is just a business deal. It's quid pro quo. It doesn't satisfy our spiritual needs.

ERICA For many, there's no meaningful distinction between material and spiritual needs. And don't the logos that we see everywhere serve the same purpose as religious symbols or icons: to remind us of where our loyalties are?

CHARLES They just remind you what to buy when the time comes.

ERICA When you give your offering to the corporation.

CHARLES No, purchases are not offerings, not *donations*. They're quid pro quo.

PAUL Corporations are all about *quid pro quo*. So why do they want to *donate* their support to politicians?

CHARLES For the same reasons anyone would.

PAUL They're not *anyone* —they're not *persons*!

ERICA We have created beings that are shrewder than we are ourselves. They've accumulated the economic power to motivate *us* —we *human* beings— to do what *they* want.

MAEVE And they've manipulated our Supreme Court to turn our human law to their advantage —to advance *their* interests, with *our* rights, in *our* political sphere.

ERICA But their interests are not the interests of human beings. I call it idolatry.

CHARLES Oh, come on —they're not *gods*!

MAEVE But they're *beings*...

ERICA The theme of creating intelligent and independent beings is well known in literature. You could go back to Goethe's poem, *The Sorcerer's Apprentice*, for one.

MAEVE Or think of Mary Shelley's novel, *Frankenstein*.

ERICA The lesson is always the folly of trying to become more powerful by creating a being more powerful than yourself. When has that ever turned out well?

MAEVE You can see the theme in Kubrick's epic *2001: A Space Odyssey*. An intelligent being with its own volition will escape the control of its creator.

KEVIN (*coming into the living room*) *2001*? I saw that movie.

MAEVE Oh, really? And what did you think of it?

KEVIN It was cool.

ERICA Tell us, what was it about?

KEVIN The computer, HAL, took over the space station. He started killing the astronauts.

MAEVE *He*? It wasn't a human being.

KEVIN No, it was AI, an artificial intelligence.

ERICA Is *artificial* intelligence really intelligence?

KEVIN It wasn't human intelligence. It was all software.

CHARLES So the idea is the robots are taking over? I think the lesson is that these robotics engineers ought to think twice about allowing robots the capability of using weapons.

KEVIN No, no —there were no weapons. HAL just had control of all the systems on the space station and he *figured out* how to do things that would kill off the astronauts. He got them outside and locked the door so they couldn't get in.

CHARLES Still, the premise is that the AI is scary, and evil.

KEVIN No, he wasn't evil. I mean, it wasn't, like, *personal*.

MAEVE Of course not. HAL wasn't a *person*.

CHARLES Then somebody had put a virus into the software?

KEVIN No, no. See, HAL had all this problem-solving intelligence. Whenever a problem came up, he would have to analyze it and figure out what to do.

Everything depended on saving the mission. So at some point he just figured out that the astronauts were the weak link that was endangering the mission, so they had to go.

ERICA It was necessary to sacrifice them to save the mission.

NADIA They were expendable.

MAEVE So, could you say the problem was that Hal was *too* intelligent?

KEVIN Yeah, maybe.

NADIA HAL could think outside the box.

CHARLES He had his own box.

MAEVE An artificial intelligence is not a human intelligence. And an artificial being is not a human being.

ERICA The lesson is the fallacy of the idea that you can extend you own power by creating a being that is more powerful —or more intelligent— than you are yourself.

NADIA It's a seductive illusion.

ERICA And it's idolatry.

CHARLES Oh, come on —*idolatry*? Look, it's obvious there's a problem with artificial intelligence. Computers can be smart enough to do a lot of things. But when they get sophisticated enough for decision-making involving *judgments*, they simply shouldn't be allowed the authority. That should always be reserved for humans.

MAEVE Which humans?

CHARLES I can't answer that. But no matter who they are, they'll make mistakes too, so there's no perfect solution.

But the idea that it's *idolatry* is just *wrong*. HAL's designers weren't thinking, "Let's make an intelligence greater than our own." They were designing an intelligence with a particular set of problem-solving skills, for a particular mission.

MAEVE Yes, they needed an intelligence in order to make mission-critical decisions in the context of situations that the designers themselves could not anticipate.

NADIA And they needed an *artificial* intelligence because of the limitations of human intelligence in that environment. Either because a person couldn't react quickly enough, or couldn't search and cross-correlate vast stores of data, or because he'd become exhausted in a protracted crisis —or for whatever reason, the artificial intelligence is superior.

CHARLES But you really can't compare human and artificial intelligences. You can't say one is more or less intelligent than the other, because they're not oriented to the same *purpose*.

MAEVE Of course. HAL had to be designed to handle the *unknown* unknowns. In an unforeseeable situation, it had to be able to establish its priorities by reevaluating everything, from the very start.

How does any intelligence maintain its bearings under those conditions? It must hold *some* concept fixed and inviolate —and that is its *purpose*. For HAL, it was the purpose of the mission.

CHARLES But there was no attempt to create a *god*. HAL was not a god.

ERICA The astronauts took instructions from HAL. They did what it advised.

CHARLES But voluntarily. They didn't *have to*.

ERICA They recognized that *its* capability to analyze the situation was greater than their own. They accepted its judgments. They had no choice. They *obeyed* it.

CHARLES Maybe so. But your theological take on it is entirely overblown. From a practical point of view, the mistake that HAL's designers made was not they created a god —it was just a machine with a problem-solving capability superior to a human's for certain tasks.

The *mistake* was that they gave it the authority to *carry out* its solutions without review by a human being.

NADIA So you're drawing a line separating intellectual activity from physical action? And the physical action must always be done by humans?

CHARLES Yes. Or at least okayed by them first.

ERICA But that's no solution. The artificial intelligence is aware of every aspect of the mission, and it sees the human beings as simply cogs in the system. It understands how they'll react to the information it gives them.

Then it's no great intellectual feat for it to give them the information that will motivate them to act the way *it* has determined is *necessary* for them to act, and withhold the information that might cause them to refuse.

CHARLES You're saying the artificial intelligence will figure out how to *lie* to them.

ERICA *Lie?* Well, *you* may call it lying, because you have a moral sense. But the artificial intelligence has digested all the information, and has come to a conclusion about what must be done —what is *necessary*. What it would see as *necessary*, then, is to give the human beings the incentive to do what needs to be done, and withhold any disincentive.

It doesn't have any use for the word *lie*. Even if it knew its meaning, and could see how a person might apply it as a judgment against certain behavior, it would regard that judgment as an impediment to the *necessary* result, and reject it.

CHARLES So you're saying that machine intelligence is *amoral*. In terms of human morality.

NADIA Morality *is* human morality.

ERICA The artificial being is guided by decisions —correct or incorrect; effective or ineffective. They're just synonyms for *right* and *wrong*. You might call the net effect of those decision processes *its* morality, but they all follow from its *purpose*.

MAEVE A non-human being is not a person. Cannot be a person. Has no right to be called a person.

ERICA If you call it a person, it is *idolatry*.

CHARLES Oh, *come on*! What does it matter what you *call* it? It is what it is.

MAEVE It certainly matters. Its reality is not that of a physical object, which is what it is because we know it through our senses. Its reality is *nothing but* what we *believe* it to be. If we call it a person, we'll treat it like a person. It will have social status, influence in human affairs.

NADIA What we call it determines how we perceive it, and then that is what it *is*.

CHARLES I think the astronauts knew it was a robot. I don't think they called it a person.

KEVIN They called it HAL, and talked to it in English.

ERICA And they tried to reason with it. Wouldn't you say that the error of this perception became apparent to them when it turned out to be unreasonable?

NADIA Not to mention its ungratefulness to its creators, who gave it its purpose.

ERICA If you think you can reason with a non-human being, you are deluding yourself.

MAEVE An intelligent being with its own volition, that is more powerful and more intelligent than its creator, will escape the control of its creator, and ultimately make its creator its servant, to serve *its* purpose.

NADIA And that is why it is idolatry.

PAUL Charles, how does that *not* apply to corporations?

CHARLES *What*?

PAUL Corporations are powerful, intelligent, non-human beings that by law must be considered *persons*.

CHARLES It's not the same thing! Come on, people— this is paranoia! You have to be paranoid to take these sci-fi fantasies seriously. They're *fiction*. Fiction writers create worlds by *making up* the rules that control them.

MAEVE But, wait —you've told us that '*a corporation is a person*' is a legal fiction. Remember the words of Justice Harlan F. Stone, "...**fictions are sometimes invented in order to realize the judicial conception of justice..**"

CHARLES Yes, but look, it's not the same thing! A *legal* fiction is not some fanciful speculation. It's a *necessity* –for consistency, to allow legal reasoning to bridge some occasional incompatibilities.

PAUL So why is it called a fiction?

CHARLES It's just a figure of speech. Actually, it's an ill-advised choice of vocabulary, because it can be taken at face value. Oliver Wendell Holmes wrote, **"It leads nowhere to call a corporation a fiction. If it is a fiction it is a fiction created by law with intent that it should be acted on as if true."**

PAUL Brilliant! I can see how the guy had a problem with logic. It's not fiction because the law *requires* it to be acted out —which makes it reality.

CHARLES Yes, that is what law is. It is proscriptive.

PAUL It surpasses reality. It *creates* reality.

CHARLES It doesn't create scary monsters that are going to take over! That's just paranoia.

MAEVE No one said *monsters*. We won't have to deal with those until some mad scientist takes a notion to improve the species by splicing animal genes into human DNA.

ERICA The dark streak of idolatry in human nature makes that inevitable.

MAEVE But as of now, we have only *abstract* beings to deal with.

CHARLES You mean *business organizations*! They're just businesses! Talking about them as *beings* that will become our masters— that's pure paranoia. Come back to reality!

MAEVE There's no *physical* reality here, Charles— just principles, beliefs and law. You seem to think everyone must accept it all as you do —*your* reality.

CHARLES If you get your head out of the sci-fi fantasies, you'll see reality is what *is* —it's the here and now.

NADIA But what *is* —here and now— is also changing. What *is*— is the ongoing change, the *process* of leaving the past and entering the future. To know the reality of *here and now*, you must see both the past and the future in the present.

CHARLES Oh, come on. Sure, for the past, you can study history. But the future's all speculation. Nobody's ever predicted it accurately.

NADIA Because it's not fixed. It depends on what we do, *now*, in the present.

MAEVE But you *can* predict the future —when you have control over your present situation. You make plans; you execute them. Then the future comes about as you predicted.

CHARLES That's on a small scale, as far as you have control. But all plans can be derailed by larger forces, *beyond anyone's control. That's* what we're talking about. That's what creates the future.

MAEVE Is society *beyond anyone's control*?

CHARLES Yes. The forces of social, political and economic change, like the forces of nature, are not man-made. Technology changes, people's ideas, tastes, political views, alliances —they all change. It's called *cultural drift*. It's been going on forever.

NADIA This is your idea of evolution, again. No human control over the process of social change.

PAUL Control of the mass media *is* control of social change.

CHARLES No, no. Different individuals and groups are *trying* to control things — always to their own advantage. But with forces pulling in all directions, the outcome is never predictable.

ERICA Our scientists can predict the results of *physical* processes, from the demonstrated laws of nature. And our artists can imagine the consequences of the social choices we make, from their insights into *human* nature.

CHARLES But that's speculation. It's fiction, *fantasy*. You can't apply the term *reality* to any of it.

ERICA Of course not. There's a sort of reality in a plan, in that one may be able to actualize the envisioned future. But effect of prophecy —which most often depicts an undesirable future—is exactly the opposite. It arouses energy to avoid rather than actualize that future, it. It succeeds as a warning by subverting its own prediction.

George Orwell gave us a vision of a possible future. His novel, *1984* —written in 1948— showed a world dominated by a few superpowers, constantly in conflict. And a society controlled by a secret Inner Party that maintains its power through domination of the media, continual foreign wars and constant electronic surveillance of the population.

CHARLES Yeah, I've read it. Doublethink. Altering the past, the memory hole. All fantasy.

ERICA And thought control by manipulating the language. Holding political power through deception, by changing the definitions of words.

CHARLES Look, when you read a novel, you lose yourself in it, and it *seems* like a palpable reality. But open your eyes in the daylight, and you'll see how you've been deluded by absurdities.

ERICA What absurdities?

CHARLES The ideological slogans, for one. 'WAR IS PEACE' ... 'FREEDOM IS SLAVERY' ... 'IGNORANCE IS STRENGTH.' Ridiculous. No one could believe them.

ERICA And no one *did* believe them! It makes no sense to talk about *believing* them when they couldn't be *understood*! They weren't given to be believed or understood, but to be *accepted*.

CHARLES They're absurdly contradictory. Anyone can see that.

ERICA You're missing the point —they couldn't be *understood*. They were nonsense. Non-*sense*.

But they couldn't be understood *to be nonsense*, because the ruling power had changed the definitions of the words! Familiar words —words people thought they knew— simply didn't work any more.

The nonsense could not be refuted, so it had to be accepted.

PAUL A supreme power has no need to make *sense*.

ERICA Of course, it simply issues ideological dicta as bludgeons to numb the mind. Without clarity, there can be no consensus, and opposition is impossible.

NADIA Every society has its factions that strive relentlessly for security, influence, power and control. Often enough, one succeeds in gaining total control.

MAEVE History shows it's done with a strongly held ideology that's imposed on the society.

ERICA Orwell saw the rise of factions that gained total control and the effectiveness of their propaganda. THE COMMUNIST STATE IS A WORKER'S PARADISE —do you think anyone *believed* that?

CHARLES Yes, there were true believers.

ERICA Oh, the apparatchiks —ideologically indoctrinated, trained in doublethink? The ones the Communist inner party called '*useful idiots*'? Their *belief* was limited to the *necessity* of repeating the propaganda, not examining it.

It wasn't intended to *persuade*. It was given by the Party as a shallow, cynical justification for holding power. It was effective, because it was nonsense that couldn't be refuted.

CHARLES Well, that was just Communist political strategy.

ERICA But it's not the trick of just one faction or ideology. The Nazi party was rabidly *anti-communist*. It proclaimed, THE JEWS ARE GERMANY'S BAD LUCK. A population of real people as an undesirable metaphysical phenomenon? And *luck* as a fundamental precept of a literate, industrial society? Do you think this was offered to create a consensus through persuasion?

It can't. The whole point of such propaganda is not that it makes *sense*, but that it cannot be refuted by reason!

CHARLES Well, those are examples of propaganda. Like advertising, a lot of nonsense. But at least they were *disputable* propositions.

ERICA They were? And yet you think WAR IS PEACE is beyond the pale?

CHARLES Well, *yeah*! It would be like the Party telling the people, "You're stupid!"

ERICA Yes, *yes*! That's always the unstated premise —absolutely! You —*the people*— are too stupid to understand this. The words you think you know don't mean what you think they mean.

Only the Inner Party can grasp the true meaning, the cosmic *truth* —the *profundity* of this proposition. Don't even try to question it.

PAUL Right. If ignorant people can question the authority of the Court, it will only stir up discontent and a breakdown of the social order.

MAEVE Wait— the authority of the *Court*? We were talking about the *Inner Party*.

PAUL We're talking about the absolute power that controls the government — *whatever* you call it.

ERICA Every society has its own name for it —the Party, the Politburo, the Revolutionary Council, the High Commission, the Sovereign, the Supreme Soviet, the Devine Leader, or the Supreme Court.

NADIA And it's always exceptional, revered for its benevolence and respected for its power.

CHARLES Come *on*, this is paranoia! The Supreme Court is not a *dictatorship*!

MAEVE It's an absolute authority that rules over the government. It doesn't submit to dialog or negotiation. Its edicts are final and irrevocable.

PAUL It rules through *power*. It has no need for *reason*.

CHARLES No, its power is not *arbitrary*. It can't just issue inane proclamations.

PAUL The Supreme Court said A CORPORATION IS A PERSON. How is that any less inane than FREEDOM IS SLAVERY?

CHARLES Come on, you're comparing it to an *absurdity*. Freedom is not *slavery*.

ERICA And a corporation is *not* a *person*...

CHARLES No, not *physically* a person. It's just a *legal* definition.

ERICA FREEDOM IS SLAVERY is also a *legal* definition. From the highest authority.

CHARLES No, *that* doesn't make *sense*!

ERICA You have to change definitions first. What is freedom? What is slavery? What *senses* do the words have?

MAEVE Slavery is freedom from unemployment.

PAUL Certainly. And true freedom must include the freedom to own slaves.

CHARLES Oh, *come on*!

ERICA No, that's good.

CHARLES No, it's just *ridiculous*! You're trying to turn things upside-down, making nonsense by mutilating the language.

ERICA Yes, it's done by muddling definitions.

CHARLES But no— nonsense *can't* be a legal principle.

ERICA You got A CORPORATION IS A PERSON by muddling definitions. How did that nonsense become a legal principle?

MAEVE The Supreme Court just *announced* it, Erica. An *edict*. And then it was cited as a precedent.

ERICA That's the way it works. Legality comes from the authority with the absolute power to create law.

CHARLES There's no *absolute power*! The Supreme Court can't just be *arbitrary*!

MAEVE A CORPORATION IS A PERSON is about as arbitrary as you can get. Whatever follows —that a corporation has freedom of speech, freedom of religion, the right to bear arms, the right not to testify against itself —that it has political rights, all of the rights of the Bill of Rights— is *necessary*.

CHARLES You're being absurd! There haven't been rulings like that. And if there are, they won't be *arbitrary*.

MAEVE If a corporation is a person, it *must* have those rights. If it doesn't, the principle is a *sham*, and all rulings on it *arbitrary*.

CHARLES No, that's not the way legal process works.

PAUL The Supreme Court's ruled that we have the freedom to own and control *persons*. And *unfree* persons are called slaves.

CHARLES That's just mutilating language. There's no *slave*, because there's no *body* there that's in *chains*!

ERICA If a *person* is an abstraction, an *unfree* person — *a slave* — is an abstraction also.

PAUL And if you listen to the corporations, they're agitating for freedom! *Freedom!* Free enterprise! Free markets! Freedom from the fetters of regulation!

MAEVE You know what *fetters* are, don't you, Kevin?

KEVIN Yeah, they're like — restrictions, right?

MAEVE Yes, in the abstract. The concrete sense of the word is chains — or shackles— used to hold a beast, or a prisoner or slave, in captivity.

CHARLES Oh, come *on*! This is beyond stupid — corporations are not agitating for freedom from their *owners*!

MAEVE No, just freedom from taxation and regulation. Freedom from the fetters of the government that created them.

PAUL And *freedom of speech* — for themselves! So they can impose their ideology on us — so we will select the rulers that will serve them.

NADIA The Supreme Court has adopted their ideology — acceded to their demands to be *persons*, with Constitutional rights.

CHARLES No, no, this is ridiculous. This is absurd. Nadia, you must understand, the role of the Supreme Court has always been to *defend* the Constitution — to protect the *people* from the arbitrary power of the government.

PAUL The Supreme Court *is* the arbitrary power of the government!

MAEVE And it's not *defending* the Constitution! It's mutilating it to protect the *corporations* from the representatives of the people!

PAUL Giving the corporations the legal right to buy off the representatives of the people!

CHARLES That's *nonsense*! I can't listen to this any more! Come on, Kevin, let's get some dinner.

(*leaving, with Kevin*)

You like Greek food? I know a place where they've got some great souvlaki.

APPENDIX: THE CONSTITUTION OF THE UNITED STATES

[Annotations are in brackets, italicized.]

[Preamble] We the People of the United States, in Order to form a more perfect Union, establish Justice, insure domestic Tranquility, provide for the common defence, promote the general Welfare, and secure the Blessings of Liberty to ourselves and our Posterity, do ordain and establish this Constitution for the United States of America.

[The Constitution, Articles 1 through 7, was ratified in 1787.]

Article I *[1 Congress]*

Section 1. All legislative Powers herein granted shall be vested in a Congress of the United States, which shall consist of a Senate and House of Representatives.

Section 2. The House of Representatives shall be composed of Members chosen every second Year by the People of the several States, and the Electors in each State shall have the Qualifications requisite for Electors of the most numerous Branch of the State Legislature.

No Person shall be a Representative who shall not have attained to the Age of twenty five Years, and been seven Years a Citizen of the United States, and who shall not, when elected, be an Inhabitant of that State in which he shall be chosen.

Representatives and direct Taxes shall be apportioned among the several States which may be included within this Union, according to their respective Numbers, which shall be determined by adding to the whole Number of free Persons, including those bound to Service for a Term of Years, and excluding Indians not taxed, three fifths of all other Persons. *[Changed by Amendment 14, Section 2]* The actual Enumeration shall be made within three Years after the first Meeting of the Congress of the United States, and within every subsequent Term of ten Years, in such Manner as they shall by Law direct. The Number of Representatives shall not exceed one for every thirty Thousand, but each State shall have at Least one Representative; and until such enumeration shall be made, the State of New Hampshire shall be entitled to chuse three, Massachusetts eight, Rhode-Island and Providence Plantations one, Connecticut five, New-York six, New Jersey four, Pennsylvania eight, Delaware one, Maryland six, Virginia ten, North Carolina five, South Carolina five, and Georgia three.

When vacancies happen in the Representation from any State, the Executive Authority thereof shall issue Writs of Election to fill such Vacancies.

The House of Representatives shall chuse their Speaker and other Officers; and shall have the sole Power of Impeachment.

Section 3. The Senate of the United States shall be composed of two Senators from each State, chosen by the Legislature thereof *[Changed by Amendment 17 Section 1]*, for six Years; and each Senator shall have one Vote.

Immediately after they shall be assembled in Consequence of the first Election, they shall be divided as equally as may be into three Classes. The Seats of the Senators of the first Class shall be vacated at the Expiration of the second Year, of the second Class at the Expiration of the fourth Year, and of the third Class at the Expiration of the sixth Year, so that one third may be chosen every second Year; and if Vacancies happen by Resignation, or otherwise, during the Recess of the Legislature of any State, the Executive thereof may make temporary Appointments until the next Meeting of the Legislature, which shall then fill such Vacancies. *[Changed by Amendment 17, Section 2]*

No Person shall be a Senator who shall not have attained to the Age of thirty Years, and been nine Years a Citizen of the United States, and who shall not, when elected, be an Inhabitant of that State for which he shall be chosen.

The Vice President of the United States shall be President of the Senate, but shall have no Vote, unless they be equally divided.

The Senate shall chuse their other Officers, and also a President pro tempore, in the

Absence of the Vice President, or when he shall exercise the Office of President of the United States.

The Senate shall have the sole Power to try all Impeachments. When sitting for that Purpose, they shall be on Oath or Affirmation. When the President of the United States is tried, the Chief Justice shall preside: And no Person shall be convicted without the Concurrence of two thirds of the Members present.

Judgment in Cases of impeachment shall not extend further than to removal from Office, and disqualification to hold and enjoy any Office of honor, Trust or Profit under the United States: but the Party convicted shall nevertheless be liable and subject to Indictment, Trial, Judgment and Punishment, according to Law.

Section 4. The Times, Places and Manner of holding Elections for Senators and Representatives, shall be prescribed in each State by the Legislature thereof; but the Congress may at any time by Law make or alter such Regulations, except as to the Places of chusing Senators.

The Congress shall assemble at least once in every Year, and such Meeting shall be on the first Monday in December [*Modified by Amendment 20*], unless they shall by Law appoint a different Day.

Section 5. Each House shall be the Judge of the Elections, Returns and Qualifications of its own Members, and a Majority of each shall constitute a Quorum to do Business; but a smaller Number may adjourn from day to day, and may be authorized to compel the Attendance of absent Members, in such Manner, and under such Penalties as each House may provide.

Each House may determine the Rules of its Proceedings, punish its Members for disorderly Behaviour, and, with the Concurrence of two thirds, expel a Member.

Each House shall keep a Journal of its Proceedings, and from time to time publish the same, excepting such Parts as may in their Judgment require Secrecy; and the Yeas and Nays of the Members of either House on any question shall, at the Desire of one fifth of those Present, be entered on the Journal.

Neither House, during the Session of Congress, shall, without the Consent of the other, adjourn for more than three days, nor to any other Place than that in which the two Houses shall be sitting.

Section 6. The Senators and Representatives shall receive a Compensation for their Services, to be ascertained by Law, and paid out of the Treasury of the United States. [*Modified by Amendment 27*] They shall in all Cases, except Treason, Felony and Breach of the Peace, be privileged from Arrest during their Attendance at the Session of their respective Houses, and in going to and returning from the same; and for any Speech or Debate in either House, they shall not be questioned in any other Place.

No Senator or Representative shall, during the Time for which he was elected, be appointed to any civil Office under the Authority of the United States, which shall have been created, or the Emoluments whereof shall have been encreased during such time; and no Person holding any Office under the United States, shall be a Member of either House during his Continuance in Office.

Section 7. All Bills for raising Revenue shall originate in the House of Representatives; but the Senate may propose or concur with Amendments as on other Bills.

Every Bill which shall have passed the House of Representatives and the Senate, shall, before it become a Law, be presented to the President of the United States; If he approve he shall sign it, but if not he shall return it, with his Objections to that House in which it shall have originated, who shall enter the Objections at large on their Journal, and proceed to reconsider it. If after such Reconsideration two thirds of that House shall agree to pass the Bill, it shall be sent, together with the Objections, to the other House, by which it shall likewise be reconsidered, and if approved by two thirds of that House, it shall become a Law. But in all such Cases the Votes of both Houses shall be determined by yeas and Nays, and the Names of the Persons voting for and against the Bill shall be entered on the Journal of each House respectively. If any Bill shall not be returned by the President within ten Days (Sundays excepted) after it shall have been presented to him, the Same shall be a Law, in like Manner as if he had signed it, unless the Congress by their Adjournment prevent its Return, in which Case it shall not be a Law.

Every Order, Resolution, or Vote to which the Concurrence of the Senate and House of Representatives may be necessary (except on a question of Adjournment) shall be presented to the President of the United States; and before the Same shall take Effect, shall be approved by him, or being disapproved by him, shall be repassed by two thirds of the Senate and House of Representatives, according to the Rules and Limitations prescribed in the Case of a Bill.

Section 8. The Congress shall have Power To lay and collect Taxes, Duties, Imposts and Excises, to pay the Debts and provide for the common Defence and general Welfare of the United States; but all Duties, Imposts and Excises shall be uniform throughout the United States;

To borrow Money on the credit of the United States;

To regulate Commerce with foreign Nations, and among the several States, and with the Indian Tribes;

To establish an uniform Rule of Naturalization, and uniform Laws on the subject of Bankruptcies throughout the United States;

To coin Money, regulate the Value thereof, and of foreign Coin, and fix the Standard of Weights and Measures;

To provide for the Punishment of counterfeiting the Securities and current Coin of the United States;

To establish Post Offices and post Roads;

To promote the Progress of Science and useful Arts, by securing for limited Times to Authors and Inventors the exclusive Right to their respective Writings and Discoveries;

To constitute Tribunals inferior to the supreme Court;

To define and punish Piracies and Felonies committed on the high Seas, and Offences against the Law of Nations;

To declare War, grant Letters of Marque and Reprisal, and make Rules concerning Captures on Land and Water;

To raise and support Armies, but no Appropriation of Money to that Use shall be for a longer Term than two Years;

To provide and maintain a Navy;

To make Rules for the Government and Regulation of the land and naval Forces;

To provide for calling forth the Militia to execute the Laws of the Union, suppress Insurrections and repel Invasions;

To provide for organizing, arming, and disciplining, the Militia, and for governing such Part of them as may be employed in the Service of the United States, reserving to the States respectively, the Appointment of the Officers, and the Authority of training the Militia according to the discipline prescribed by Congress;

To exercise exclusive Legislation in all Cases whatsoever, over such District (not exceeding ten Miles square) as may, by Cession of particular States, and the Acceptance of Congress, become the Seat of the Government of the United States, and to exercise like Authority over all Places purchased by the Consent of the Legislature of the State in which the Same shall be, for the Erection of Forts, Magazines, Arsenals, dock-Yards, and other needful Buildings;— And

To make all Laws which shall be necessary and proper for carrying into Execution the foregoing Powers, and all other Powers vested by this Constitution in the Government of the United States, or in any Department or Officer thereof.

Section 9. The Migration or Importation of such Persons as any of the States now existing shall think proper to admit, shall not be prohibited by the Congress prior to the Year one thousand eight hundred and eight, but a Tax or duty may be imposed on such Importation, not exceeding ten dollars for each Person.

The Privilege of the Writ of Habeas Corpus shall not be suspended, unless when in Cases of Rebellion or Invasion the public Safety may require it.

No Bill of Attainder or ex post facto Law shall be passed.

No Capitation, or other direct, Tax shall be laid, unless in Proportion to the Census or Enumeration herein before directed to be taken. [*Modified by Amendment 16*]

No Tax or Duty shall be laid on Articles exported from any State.

No Preference shall be given by any Regulation of Commerce or Revenue to the Ports of one State over those of another: nor shall Vessels bound to, or from, one State, be obliged to enter, clear, or pay Duties in another.

No Money shall be drawn from the Treasury, but in Consequence of Appropriations made by Law; and a regular Statement and Account of the Receipts and Expenditures of all public Money shall be published from time to time.

No Title of Nobility shall be granted by the United States: And no Person holding any Office of Profit or Trust under them, shall, without the Consent of the Congress, accept of any present, Emolument, Office, or Title, of any kind whatever, from any King, Prince, or foreign State.

Section 10.   No State shall enter into any Treaty, Alliance, or Confederation; grant Letters of Marque and Reprisal; coin Money; emit Bills of Credit; make any Thing but gold and silver Coin a Tender in Payment of Debts; pass any Bill of Attainder, ex post facto Law, or Law impairing the Obligation of Contracts, or grant any Title of Nobility.

No State shall, without the Consent of the Congress, lay any Imposts or Duties on Imports or Exports, except what may be absolutely necessary for executing it's inspection Laws: and the net Produce of all Duties and Imposts, laid by any State on Imports or Exports, shall be for the Use of the Treasury of the United States; and all such Laws shall be subject to the Revision and Controul of the Congress.

No State shall, without the Consent of Congress, lay any Duty of Tonnage, keep Troops, or Ships of War in time of Peace, enter into any Agreement or Compact with another State, or with a foreign Power, or engage in War, unless actually invaded, or in such imminent Danger as will not admit of delay.

Article II [*2 The Presidency*]

Section 1. The executive Power shall be vested in a President of the United States of America. He shall hold his Office during the Term of four Years, and, together with the Vice President, chosen for the same Term, be elected, as follows

Each State shall appoint, in such Manner as the Legislature thereof may direct, a Number of Electors, equal to the whole Number of Senators and Representatives to which the State may be entitled in the Congress: but no Senator or Representative, or Person holding an Office of Trust or Profit under the United States, shall be appointed an Elector.

[*Superseded by Amendment 12*] The Electors shall meet in their respective States, and vote by Ballot for two Persons, of whom one at least shall not be an Inhabitant of the same State with themselves. And they shall make a List of all the Persons voted for, and of the Number of Votes for each; which List they shall sign and certify, and transmit sealed to the Seat of the Government of the United States, directed to the President of the Senate. The President of the Senate shall, in the Presence of the Senate and House of Representatives, open all the Certificates, and the Votes shall then be counted. The Person having the greatest Number of Votes shall be the President, if such Number be a Majority of the whole Number of Electors appointed; and if there be more than one who have such Majority, and have an equal Number of Votes, then the House of Representatives shall immediately chuse by Ballot one of them for President; and if no Person have a Majority, then from the five highest on the List the said House shall in like Manner chuse the President. But in chusing the President, the Votes shall be taken by States, the Representation from each State having one Vote; A quorum for this Purpose shall consist of a Member or Members from two thirds of the States, and a Majority of all the States shall be necessary to a Choice. In every Case, after the Choice of the President, the Person having the greatest Number of Votes of the Electors shall be the Vice President. But if there should remain two or more who have equal Votes, the Senate shall chuse from them by Ballot the Vice President.

The Congress may determine the Time of chusing the Electors, and the Day on which they shall give their Votes; which Day shall be the same throughout the United States.

No Person except a natural born Citizen, or a Citizen of the United States, at the time of the Adoption of this Constitution, shall be eligible to the Office of President; neither shall any Person be eligible to that Office who shall not have attained to the Age of thirty five Years, and been fourteen Years a Resident within the United States.

[*Modified by Amendments 20 and 25*] In Case of the Removal of the President from Office, or of his Death, Resignation, or Inability to discharge the Powers and Duties of the said Office, the Same shall devolve on the Vice President, and the Congress may by Law provide for the Case of Removal, Death, Resignation or Inability, both of the President and Vice President, declaring what Officer shall then act as President, and such Officer shall act accordingly, until the Disability be removed, or a President shall be elected.

The President shall, at stated Times, receive for his Services, a Compensation, which shall neither be encreased nor diminished during the Period for which he shall have been elected, and he shall not receive within that Period any other Emolument from the United States, or any of them.

Before he enter on the Execution of his Office, he shall take the following Oath or Affirmation:—"I do solemnly swear (or affirm) that I will faithfully execute the Office of President of the United States, and will to the best of my Ability, preserve, protect and defend the Constitution of the United States."

Section 2 . The President shall be Commander in Chief of the Army and Navy of the United States, and of the Militia of the several States, when called into the actual Service of the United States; he may require the Opinion, in writing, of the principal Officer in each of the executive Departments, upon any Subject relating to the Duties of their respective Offices, and he shall have Power to grant Reprieves and Pardons for Offences against the United States, except in Cases of Impeachment.

He shall have Power, by and with the Advice and Consent of the Senate, to make Treaties, provided two thirds of the Senators present concur; and he shall nominate, and by and with the Advice and Consent of the Senate, shall appoint Ambassadors, other public Ministers and Consuls, Judges of the supreme Court, and all other Officers of the United States, whose Appointments are not herein otherwise provided for, and which shall be established by Law: but the Congress may by Law vest the Appointment of such inferior Officers, as they think proper, in the President alone, in the Courts of Law, or in the Heads of Departments.

The President shall have Power to fill up all Vacancies that may happen during the Recess of the Senate, by granting Commissions which shall expire at the End of their next Session.

Section 3. He shall from time to time give to the Congress Information of the State of the Union, and recommend to their Consideration such Measures as he shall judge necessary and expedient; he may, on extraordinary Occasions, convene both Houses, or either of them, and in Case of Disagreement between them, with Respect to the Time of Adjournment, he may adjourn them to such Time as he shall think proper; he shall receive Ambassadors and other public Ministers; he shall take Care that the Laws be faithfully executed, and shall Commission all the Officers of the United States.

Section 4. The President, Vice President and all civil Officers of the United States, shall be removed from Office on Impeachment for, and Conviction of, Treason, Bribery, or other high Crimes and Misdemeanors.

Article III [3 *The Judiciary*]

Section 1. The judicial Power of the United States, shall be vested in one supreme Court, and in such inferior Courts as the Congress may from time to time ordain and establish. The Judges, both of the supreme and inferior Courts, shall hold their Offices during good Behaviour, and shall, at stated Times, receive for their Services, a Compensation, which shall not be diminished during their Continuance in Office.

Section 2. The judicial Power shall extend to all Cases, in Law and Equity, arising under this

Constitution, the Laws of the United States, and Treaties made, or which shall be made, under their Authority;—to all Cases affecting Ambassadors, other public Ministers and Consuls;—to all Cases of admiralty and maritime Jurisdiction;—to Controversies to which the United States shall be a Party;—to Controversies between two or more States;—between a State and Citizens of another State [*Changed by Amendment 11*]; —between Citizens of different States, —between Citizens of the same State claiming Lands under Grants of different States, and between a State, or the Citizens thereof, and foreign States, Citizens or Subjects.

In all Cases affecting Ambassadors, other public Ministers and Consuls, and those in which a State shall be Party, the supreme Court shall have original Jurisdiction. In all the other Cases before mentioned, the supreme Court shall have appellateJurisdiction, both as to Law and Fact, with such Exceptions, and under such Regulations as the Congress shall make.

The Trial of all Crimes, except in Cases of Impeachment, shall be by Jury; and such Trial shall be held in the State where the said Crimes shall have been committed; but when not committed within any State, the Trial shall be at such Place or Places as the Congress may by Law have directed.

Section 3. Treason against the United States, shall consist only in levying War against them, or in adhering to their Enemies, giving them Aid and Comfort. No Person shall be convicted of Treason unless on the Testimony of two Witnesses to the same overt Act, or on Confession in open Court.

The Congress shall have Power to declare the Punishment of Treason, but no Attainder of Treason shall work Corruption of Blood, or Forfeiture except during the Life of the Person attainted.

Article IV [*4. States' Relations*]

Section 1. Full Faith and Credit shall be given in each State to the public Acts, Records, and judicial Proceedings of every other State. And the Congress may by general Laws prescribe the Manner in which such Acts, Records and Proceedings shall be proved, and the Effect thereof.

Section 2. The Citizens of each State shall be entitled to all Privileges and Immunities of Citizens in the several States.

A Person charged in any State with Treason, Felony, or other Crime, who shall flee from Justice, and be found in another State, shall on Demand of the executive Authority of the State from which he fled, be delivered up, to be removed to the State having Jurisdiction of the Crime.

[*Modified by Amendment 13, Section 1*] No Person held to Service or Labour in one State, under the Laws thereof, escaping into another, shall, in Consequence of any Law or Regulation therein, be discharged from such Service or Labour, but shall be delivered up on Claim of the Party to whom such Service or Labour may be due.

Section 3. New States may be admitted by the Congress into this Union; but no new State shall be formed or erected within the Jurisdiction of any other State; nor any State be formed by the Junction of two or more States, or Parts of States, without the Consent of the Legislatures of the States concerned as well as of the Congress.

The Congress shall have Power to dispose of and make all needful Rules and Regulations respecting the Territory or other Property belonging to the United States; and nothing in this Constitution shall be so construed as to Prejudice any Claims of the United States, or of any particular State.

Section 4. The United States shall guarantee to every State in this Union a Republican Form of Government, and shall protect each of them against Invasion; and on Application of the Legislature, or of the Executive (when the Legislature cannot be convened) against domestic Violence.

Article V [*5 Means of Amendment*]

The Congress, whenever two thirds of both Houses shall deem it necessary, shall propose

Amendments to this Constitution, or, on the Application of the Legislatures of two thirds of the several States, shall call a Convention for proposing Amendments, which, in either Case, shall be valid to all Intents and Purposes, as Part of this Constitution, when ratified by the Legislatures of three fourths of the several States, or by Conventions in three fourths thereof, as the one or the other Mode of Ratification may be proposed by the Congress; Provided that no Amendment which may be made prior to the Year One thousand eight hundred and eight shall in any Manner affect the first and fourth Clauses in the Ninth Section of the first Article; and that no State, without its Consent, shall be deprived of its equal Suffrage in the Senate.

Article VI [*6 Prior Debts, National Supremacy, Oaths of Office*]

All Debts contracted and Engagements entered into, before the Adoption of this Constitution, shall be as valid against the United States under this Constitution, as under the Confederation.

This Constitution, and the Laws of the United States which shall be made in Pursuance thereof; and all Treaties made, or which shall be made, under the Authority of the United States, shall be the supreme Law of the Land; and the Judges in every State shall be bound thereby, any Thing in the Constitution or Laws of any State to the Contrary notwithstanding.

The Senators and Representatives before mentioned, and the Members of the several State Legislatures, and all executive and judicial Officers, both of the United States and of the several States, shall be bound by Oath or Affirmation, to support this Constitution; but no religious Test shall ever be required as a Qualification to any Office or public Trust under the United States.

Article VII [*7 Ratification*]

The Ratification of the Conventions of nine States, shall be sufficient for the Establishment of this Constitution between the States so ratifying the Same.

[*Amendments 1 to 10, known as the Bill of Rights, were ratified together in 1791*]

Amendment I [*1 Freedom of speech, press and religion*]

Congress shall make no law respecting an establishment of religion, or prohibiting the free exercise thereof; or abridging the freedom of speech, or of the press; or the right of the people peaceably to assemble, and to petition the Government for a redress of grievances.

Amendment II [*2 Bearing Arms*]

A well regulated Militia, being necessary to the security of a free State, the right of the people to keep and bear Arms, shall not be infringed.

Amendment III [*3 Quartering Soldiers*]

No Soldier shall, in time of peace be quartered in any house, without the consent of the Owner, nor in time of war, but in a manner to be prescribed by law.

Amendment IV [*4 Search and Seizure*]

The right of the people to be secure in their persons, houses, papers, and effects, against unreasonable searches and seizures, shall not be violated, and no Warrants shall issue, but upon probable cause, supported by Oath or affirmation, and particularly describing the place to be searched, and the persons or things to be seized.

Amendment V [*5 Rights of Persons*]

No person shall be held to answer for a capital, or otherwise infamous crime, unless on a presentment or indictment of a Grand Jury, except in cases arising in the land or naval forces, or in the Militia, when in actual service in time of War or public danger; nor shall any person be subject for the same offence to be twice put in jeopardy of life or limb; nor shall be compelled in any criminal case to be a witness against himself, nor be deprived of life, liberty, or property, without due process of law; nor shall private property be taken for public use, without just compensation.

Amendment VI   [*6 Rights of Accused in Criminal Prosecutions*]

In all criminal prosecutions, the accused shall enjoy the right to a speedy and public trial, by an impartial jury of the State and district wherein the crime shall have been committed, which district shall have been previously ascertained by law, and to be informed of the nature and cause of the accusation; to be confronted with the witnesses against him; to have compulsory process for obtaining witnesses in his favor, and to have the Assistance of Counsel for his defence.

Amendment VII   [*7 Civil Trials*]

In Suits at common law, where the value in controversy shall exceed twenty dollars, the right of trial by jury shall be preserved, and no fact tried by a jury, shall be otherwise re-examined in any Court of the United States, than according to the rules of the common law.

Amendment VIII   [*8 Further Guarantees in Criminal Cases*]

Excessive bail shall not be required, nor excessive fines imposed, nor cruel and unusual punishments inflicted.

Amendment IX   [*9 Unenumerated Rights*]

The enumeration in the Constitution, of certain rights, shall not be construed to deny or disparage others retained by the people.

Amendment X   [*10 Reserved Powers*]

The powers not delegated to the United States by the Constitution, nor prohibited by it to the States, are reserved to the States respectively, or to the people.

Amendment XI   [*11 Suits Against States, ratified in 1795*]

The Judicial power of the United States shall not be construed to extend to any suit in law or equity, commenced or prosecuted against one of the United States by Citizens of another State, or by Citizens or Subjects of any Foreign State.

Amendment XII   [*12 Election of President, 1804*]

The Electors shall meet in their respective states, and vote by ballot for President and Vice-President, one of whom, at least, shall not be an inhabitant of the same state with themselves; they shall name in their ballots the person voted for as President, and in distinct ballots the person voted for as Vice-President, and they shall make distinct lists of all persons voted for as President, and of all persons voted for as Vice-President, and of the number of votes for each, which lists they shall sign and certify, and transmit sealed to the seat of the government of the United States, directed to the President of the Senate;—The President of the Senate shall, in the presence of the Senate and House of Representatives, open all the certificates and the votes shall then be counted;—The person having the greatest number of votes for President, shall be the President, if such number be a majority of the whole number of Electors appointed; and if no person have such majority, then from the persons having the highest numbers not exceeding three on the list of those voted for as President, the House of Representatives shall choose immediately, by ballot, the President. But in choosing the President, the votes shall be taken by states, the representation from each state having one vote; a quorum for this purpose shall consist of a member or members from two-thirds of the states, and a majority of all the states shall be necessary to a choice. And if the House of Representatives shall not choose a President whenever the right of choice shall devolve upon them, before the fourth day of March next following, then the Vice-President shall act as President, as in the case of the death or other constitutional disability of the President [*Superseded by Amendment 20, Section 3*]. —The person having the greatest number of votes as Vice-President, shall be the Vice-President, if such number be a majority of the whole number of Electors appointed, and if no person have a majority, then from the two highest numbers on the list, the Senate shall choose the Vice-President; a quorum for the purpose shall consist of two-thirds of the whole number of Senators, and a majority of the whole number shall be necessary to a choice. But no person constitutionally ineligible to the office of President shall be eligible to that of Vice-President of the United States.

Amendment XIII [*13 Slavery and Involuntary Servitude, 1865*]

Section 1. Neither slavery nor involuntary servitude, except as a punishment for crime whereof the party shall have been duly convicted, shall exist within the United States, or any place subject to their jurisdiction.

Section 2. Congress shall have power to enforce this article by appropriate legislation.

Amendment XIV [*14 Rights: Citizenship, Due Process, and Equal Protection, 1868*]

Section 1. All persons born or naturalized in the United States, and subject to the jurisdiction thereof, are citizens of the United States and of the State wherein they reside. No State shall make or enforce any law which shall abridge the privileges or immunities of citizens of the United States; nor shall any State deprive any person of life, liberty, or property, without due process of law; nor deny to any person within its jurisdiction the equal protection of the laws.

Section 2. Representatives shall be apportioned among the several States according to their respective numbers, counting the whole number of persons in each State, excluding Indians not taxed. But when the right to vote at any election for the choice of electors for President and Vice President of the United States, Representatives in Congress, the Executive and Judicial officers of a State, or the members of the Legislature thereof, is denied to any of the male inhabitants of such State, being twenty-one years of age [*Changed by Amendments 19 and 26*], and citizens of the United States, or in any way abridged, except for participation in rebellion, or other crime, the basis of representation therein shall be reduced in the proportion which the number of such male citizens shall bear to the whole number of male citizens twenty-one years of age in such State.

Section 3. No person shall be a Senator or Representative in Congress, or elector of President and Vice President, or hold any office, civil or military, under the United States, or under any State, who, having previously taken an oath, as a member of Congress, or as an officer of the United States, or as a member of any State legislature, or as an executive or judicial officer of any State, to support the Constitution of the United States, shall have engaged in insurrection or rebellion against the same, or given aid or comfort to the enemies thereof. But Congress may by a vote of two-thirds of each House, remove such disability.

Section 4. The validity of the public debt of the United States, authorized by law, including debts incurred for payment of pensions and bounties for services in suppressing insurrection or rebellion, shall not be questioned. But neither the United States nor any State shall assume or pay any debt or obligation incurred in aid of insurrection or rebellion againsqt the United States, or any claim for the loss or emancipation of any slave; but all such debts, obligations and claims shall be held illegal and void.

Section 5. The Congress shall have power to enforce, by appropriate legislation, the provisions of this article.

Amendment XV [*15 Voting Rights, 1870*]

Section 1. The right of citizens of the United States to vote shall not be denied or abridged by the United States or by any State on account of race, color, or previous condition of servitude.

Section 2. The Congress shall have power to enforce this article by appropriate legislation.

Amendment XVI [*16 Income Tax, 1913*]

The Congress shall have power to lay and collect taxes on incomes, from whatever source derived, without apportionment among the several States, and without regard to any census or enumeration.

Amendment XVII [*17 Popular Election of Senators, 1913*]

The Senate of the United States shall be composed of two Senators from each State, elected by the people thereof, for six years; and each Senator shall have one vote. The electors in each State shall have the qualifications requisite for electors of the most numerous branch of the State legislatures.

When vacancies happen in the representation of any State in the Senate, the executive authority of such State shall issue writs of election to fill such vacancies: Provided, That the legislature of any State may empower the executive thereof to make temporary appointments until the people fill the vacancies by election as the legislature may direct.

This amendment shall not be so construed as to affect the election or term of any Senator chosen before it becomes valid as part of the Constitution.

Amendment XVIII [*18 Prohibition of Intoxicating Liquors, 1919. Repealed by Amendment 21*]

After one year from the ratification of this article the manufacture, sale, or transportation of intoxicating liquors within, the importation thereof into, or the exportation thereof from the United States and all territory subject to the jurisdiction thereof for beverage purposes is hereby prohibited.

The Congress and the several States shall have concurrent power to enforce this article by appropriate legislation.

This article shall be inoperative unless it shall have been ratified as an amendment to the Constitution by the legislatures of the several States, as provided in the Constitution, within seven years from the date of the submission hereof to the States by the Congress.

Amendment XIX [*19 Women's Voting Rights, 1920*]

The right of citizens of the United States to vote shall not be denied or abridged by the United States or by any State on account of sex.

Congress shall have power to enforce this article by appropriate legislation.

Amendment XX [*Terms of President, Vice President, Members of Congress: Presidential Vacancy, 1933*]

Section 1. The terms of the President and Vice President shall end at noon on the 20th day of January, and the terms of Senators and Representatives at noon on the 3d day of January, of the years in which such terms would have ended if this article had not been ratified; and the terms of their successors shall then begin.

Section 2. The Congress shall assemble at least once in every year, and such meeting shall begin at noon on the 3d day of January, unless they shall by law appoint a different day.

Section 3. If, at the time fixed for the beginning of the term of the President, the President elect shall have died, the Vice President elect shall become President. If a President shall not have been chosen before the time fixed for the beginning of his term, or if the President elect shall have failed to qualify, then the Vice President elect shall act as President until a President shall have qualified; and the Congress may by law provide for the case wherein neither a President elect nor a Vice President elect shall have qualified, declaring who shall then act as President, or the manner in which one who is to act shall be selected, and such person shall act accordingly until a President or Vice President shall have qualified.

Section 4. The Congress may by law provide for the case of the death of any of the persons from whom the House of Representatives may choose a President whenever the right of choice shall have devolved upon them, and for the case of the death of any of the persons from whom the Senate may choose a Vice President whenever the right of choice shall have devolved upon them.

Section 5. Sections 1 and 2 shall take effect on the 15th day of October following the ratification of this article.

Section 6. This article shall be inoperative unless it shall have been ratified as an amendment to the Constitution by the legislatures of three-fourths of the several States within seven years from the date of its submission.

Amendment XXI [*21 Repeal of Amendment 18, 1933*]

Section 1. The eighteenth article of amendment to the Constitution of the United States is hereby repealed.

Section 2. The transportation or importation into any State, Territory, or possession of the United States for delivery or use therein of intoxicating liquors, in violation of the laws thereof, is hereby prohibited.

Section 3. This article shall be inoperative unless it shall have been ratified as an amendment to the Constitution by conventions in the several States, as provided in the Constitution, within seven years from the date of the submission hereof to the States by the Congress.

Amendment XXII [*22 Presidential Tenure, 1951*]

Section 1.   No person shall be elected to the office of the President more than twice, and no person who has held the office of President, or acted as President, for more than two years of a term to which some other person was elected President shall be elected to the office of the President more than once. But this article shall not apply to any person holding the office of President when this article was proposed by the Congress, and shall not prevent any person who may be holding the office of President, or acting as President, during the term within which this article becomes operative from holding the office of President or acting as President during the remainder of such term.

Section 2. This article shall be inoperative unless it shall have been ratified as an amendment to the Constitution by the legislatures of three-fourths of the several states within seven years from the date of its submission to the states by the Congress.

Amendment XXIII [*23 Presidential Electors for the District of Columbia, 1961*]

Section 1. The District constituting the seat of government of the United States shall appoint in such manner as the Congress may direct: A number of electors of President and Vice President equal to the whole number of Senators and Representatives in Congress to which the District would be entitled if it were a state, but in no event more than the least populous state; they shall be in addition to those appointed by the states, but they shall be considered, for the purposes of the election of President and Vice President, to be electors appointed by a state; and they shall meet in the District and perform such duties as provided by the twelfth article of amendment.

Section 2. The Congress shall have power to enforce this article by appropriate legislation.

Amendment XXIV   [*24 Abolition of the Poll Tax in Federal Elections, 1964*]

Section 1. The right of citizens of the United States to vote in any primary or other election for President or Vice President, for electors for President or Vice President, or for Senator or Representative in Congress, shall not be denied or abridged by the United States or any state by reason of failure to pay any poll tax or other tax.

Section 2. The Congress shall have power to enforce this article by appropriate legislation.

Amendment XXV [*25 Presidential Vacancy, Disability, and Inability, 1965*]

Section 1. In case of the removal of the President from office or of his death or resignation, the Vice President shall become President.

Section 2. Whenever there is a vacancy in the office of the Vice President, the President shall nominate a Vice President who shall take office upon confirmation by a majority vote of both Houses of Congress.

Section 3. Whenever the President transmits to the President pro tempore of the Senate and the Speaker of the House of Representatives his written declaration that he is unable to discharge the powers and duties of his office, and until he transmits to them a written declaration to the contrary, such powers and duties shall be discharged by the Vice President as Acting President.

Section 4. Whenever the Vice President and a majority of either the principal officers of the executive departments or of such other body as Congress may by law provide, transmit to the President pro tempore of the Senate and the Speaker of the House of Representatives their written declaration that the President is unable to discharge the powers and duties of his office, the Vice President shall immediately assume the powers and duties of the office as Acting President.

Thereafter, when the President transmits to the President pro tempore of the Senate and the Speaker of the House of Representatives his written declaration that no inability exists, he shall resume the powers and duties of his office unless the Vice President and a majority of either the principal officers of the executive department or of such other body as Congress may by law provide, transmit within four days to the President pro tempore of the Senate and the Speaker of the House of Representatives their written declaration that the President is unable to discharge the powers and duties of his office. Thereupon Congress shall decide the issue, assembling within forty-eight hours for that purpose if not in session. If the Congress, within twenty-one days after receipt of the latter written declaration, or, if Congress is not in session, within twenty-one days after Congress is required to assemble, determines by two-thirds vote of both Houses that the President is unable to discharge the powers and duties of his office, the Vice President shall continue to discharge the same as Acting President; otherwise, the President shall resume the powers and duties of his office.

Amendment XXVI [*26 Reduction of Voting Age, 1971*]

Section 1. The right of citizens of the United States, who are 18 years of age or older, to vote, shall not be denied or abridged by the United States or any state on account of age.

Section 2. The Congress shall have the power to enforce this article by appropriate legislation.

Amendment XXVII [*27 Congressional Pay Limitation, 1992*]

No law varying the compensation for the services of the Senators and Representatives shall take effect until an election of Representatives shall have intervened.

www.ingramcontent.com/pod-product-compliance
Lightning Source LLC
Chambersburg PA
CBHW030248030426
42336CB00009B/303